SCHOOL DESEGREGATION IN THE NORTH

VICTOR JONES, *Advisory Editor*

Professor of Political Science and
Research Political Scientist,
University of California, Berkeley

SCHOOL DESEGREGATION IN THE NORTH

The Challenge and the Experience

EDITED BY

T. BENTLEY EDWARDS
University of California, Berkeley

AND

FREDERICK M. WIRT
Denison University

CHANDLER PUBLISHING COMPANY
124 SPEAR STREET, SAN FRANCISCO, CALIFORNIA 94105

Science Research Associates, Inc., 259 East Erie Street, Chicago, Illinois 60611
Distributors   A Subsidiary of IBM

CONTENTS

III. *THE EDUCATIONAL CHALLENGE*   153

IV. *THE GREATER NEW YORK EXPERIENCE*   173

V. *SOME LESSONS FOR POLICYMAKERS*   297

NOTES   331

·················· PREFACE ··

Both inspiration and prototype for the present volume is the doctoral dissertation of Edward B. Fort, now Superintendent of Schools, Inkster, Michigan. Professor Victor Jones, Advisory Editor in Political Science to Chandler Publishing Company, suggested that a collection of similar material would be valuable for practitioners and students in education, political science, and other fields, as they seek understanding of the problems challenging those who want educational equality for minority groups—particularly the Negroes—in the United States.

The case studies of response to the challenge of *de facto* segregation concern ten communities, four close to New York City and the others in California. The Eastern communities include New York City, the suburb of Manhasset on Long Island, and the neighboring communities of Englewood and Teaneck in New Jersey. The California communities include Sacramento, Berkeley, Riverside, San Bernardino, Mill Valley, and Sausalito.

Three articles have been added to the case studies in the hope that they will increase the usefulness of the book. Together the first two chapters establish an interdisciplinary basis for understanding, providing first a model of political decision making, and second a summary of the social and psychological consequences of various ways of grouping children for instructional purposes. The third analytical selection is the well-known article by Alan B. Wilson establishing the relationship between segregation and the aspirations of high school boys. Except for this article, all the materials are published here for the first time.

We should like to thank all those who have helped to produce this book: our colleague Victor Jones, who suggested it; the contributors, both those who finished early and had to wait and those who rallied to provide the needed balance; and Mrs. Gertrude Funkhouser, secretary to the Curriculum Division of the Department of Education at Berkeley. Dr. Webster has emphasized the value of the latter's assistance in the foreword to his recently published book.*

Here it is, then, another blow at the wall of prejudice separating Americans. May that wall soon come tumbling down.

T. BENTLEY EDWARDS
FREDERICK M. WIRT

Berkeley
December, 1967

---

* Staten W. Webster (ed.), *The Disadvantaged Learner* (San Francisco: Chandler Publishing Company, 1966).

SCHOOL DESEGREGATION IN THE NORTH

part I

The Social and Ethical Challenge

1 POLICY OUTCOMES OF DESEGREGATION CASES: A FRAMEWORK FOR ANALYSIS

FREDERICK M. WIRT

Professor of Political Science, Denison University

When the present volume was being prepared, Dr. Wirt served as Visiting Professor of Political Science at the University of California, Berkeley, on leave from Denison University, Granville, Ohio. He has published on questions relating American values and civil rights and has served as a consultant in these matters. Case studies of difficulties encountered in providing desegregated schooling for Negroes have made it possible for him to apply the analytical techniques of political science to the understanding of educational arrangements.

Professor Wirt provides a model for political decision making which can be used to understand the policy outcomes of the activities described in the case studies.

1. All political decision making in the United States operates within an environment of broad cultural values including
   a. belief in the legitimacy of majority decisions with the right of minorities to some protection,

3

  b. desire for free and open education for all,
  c. ambivalence toward race differences,
  d. attachments to equality and liberty which conflict at some points.
2. Operating within the framework of general values is a multiplicity of interest groups pursuing more narrow values, such as money, ownership of property, privileged status, tax benefits, or superior education. Interest in a particular problem as well as the power to follow the interest varies widely among the citizenry.
3. Political decision making is pursued within an institutional and legal framework which provides federal, state, and local government with taboos, positive authorizations, and permissive limits.
4. Although many men can be garbed with the same official cloak of authority, they hold different values and behave differently. Despite the existence of role perceptions in the popular mind, the influence of a given official, such as the school superintendent, upon the decision-making process can vary from one incumbent to another.

....

Education for their children has always occupied a special place in the hearts of Americans. Probably in no other country has so much been done to assure education for so many children. However, the policy did not spring full-blown at the founding of the Republic, but has instead developed over time, first slowly and then in this century precipitately and massively. Free public education spread with the increasing enfranchisement of voters, as voters who could not afford private schools for their children used their political power to establish and fund free education. In this process minimal goals were continually escalated, from grammar or elementary school education a century ago to a high-school education as the desired objective in the first part of this century. And in our own time we have seen this objective expanded to a widespread desire for some education at the college level.

While there has been a general belief that politics and education should not mix—thus the common practice of ostensibly nonpartisan school boards—the truth is that in a special sense our public education has always been embroiled in politics. Politics, even if not the politics of the cut and thrust of political party battle, has operated to shape the form and direction of educational policy. By "politics" we mean the struggle of private groups to further their values by enlisting the support of government. Political parties frequently serve as devices for mobilizing group support and for integrating the organs of government so as to translate private group objectives into public policy. Yet in educational policy, parties have traditionally not served these functions, whence comes the popular notion of the separation of education and politics.

But the strife of political parties is but one aspect of the broader meaning of politics, which is a struggle to marshal governmental power in legislatures, administrative agencies, executive offices, and, indeed, even the cloistered calm of courts. All these branches of government are public forums in which decisions are made affecting differentially the values of private groups.

From such a perspective it is possible to see that elections to school boards, these boards' decisions, and referenda on school issues constitute a sub-area of politics. As we shall see later in this chapter, public institutions, private groups, and public officials interact within a given social environment to produce an outcome that comprises public policy on education. In this general perspective of political science, the public decision-making process affecting education is linked in special ways to other decision-making policy processes. In these terms, then, politics and education not only do mix, but necessarily must mix.

A special phase of this interrelationship between politics and education has become highly visible in the last decade in the problem of school integration. For most of this period, attention has been dramatically and sensationally focused upon the confrontation of national and state governments in the South, where through time the full armament of the federal government has been brought to bear to eliminate segregation patterns based upon race. This form of segregation, imbedded in law and reinforced by local traditions and public officials, has faced ever greater attack from the courts and from Congress and the President. *De jure* segregation is very slowly yielding to this attack, despite such last-ditch defense efforts as those by the Wallaces of Alabama.

But another form of school segregation, less publicized and hence less visible, has also been coming under attack during this period—the northern form of school segregation which rests upon the increasing geographic separation of white and Negroes in metropolitan areas. It has arisen as one of the consequences of the transformation of the urban scene since World War II. Great numbers of Negroes have moved to the inner cities of the North while equally great numbers of whites have moved out to the suburbs, thereby creating in many urban areas a bull's-eye pattern of residence, with a Negro inner core and a white outer ring. As a consequence, as one moves from the center to the outside the proportion of nonwhites drops off, not in a gradual pattern but in a line that looks like the path of someone falling off a cliff. The result, of course, has been to leave behind inner-city schools that are overwhelmingly segregated—not by law but as a consequence of the facts of urban change—a phenomenon accordingly labeled *de facto* segregation.

Parents of children in these schools have not everywhere been happy with this situation. Increasingly in the past decade they have become more outspoken in their objections and better organized to do something about it. Despite the publicity given to an occasional disturbance over such segregation, little systematic information has been gathered on what has occurred in particular instances. It is certain that northern cities will increasingly be the scene of protest against *de facto* segregation. It is important, then, to examine the available evidence of what has occurred in order to raise if not to answer some queries about this special mixture of politics and education. Under what conditions does *de facto* segregation become so intolerable that political protest is mounted? What groups get involved on opposing sides and what justifications do they offer for their views? What strategies do they employ to further their ends? What roles are open to the professional educators and the elected educators, both ingredients and influences in the matrix of opposing forces? In our many-tiered government, at what level does the conflict get eventually settled? What form does the policy outcome take, after all the hue and cry are done? What effect does it have upon education? And what does all of this tell us about the relationships between our public education system and the political environment in which it is imbedded?

The case reports in this book have been drawn together to show something about the relationship between these two facts of social life. Each report was written by a close participant or observer in the case. As a collection, these pieces offer a wide array of sources of information—ordinances and statutes, minutes of the proceedings of public bodies, newspaper stories, interviews with important actors, collections of socio-economic data, and attitude surveys. The locales of the cases range in size from small suburbs to the largest city in America, just as the participants range from persons low on the status scale to state governors and judges.

But the task in this and the concluding chapter is to grasp the similarities, as well as the dissimilarities, which exist in these cases. To do so, it is important that the reader understand in detail the framework of analysis applied here and in the concluding chapter. What "model" of political behavior can be constructed beforehand which will encompass the variety of these cases? If such a model can be sufficiently explicit, it will enable the reader to look for like elements in different cases. It will also enable the author to draw together material which may verify suspected uniformities. Without some such organizing model, each case is nothing more than a discrete anecdote, interesting in itself but providing little illumination of the general pattern. While the model which will be offered in this chapter has been made very complex and sophisticated in analyses elsewhere, it will be kept to its minimum components here so that readers who are not political scientists can understand what we are about.[1]

THE MODEL FOR POLITICAL DECISION MAKING

The term "model" refers to a conceptual framework designed to explain the interrelationship among a number of factors involved in a given event or process. A model has only abstract reality; it is a theoretical statement used to explain or interpret components of reality. As Bloomberg and his colleagues have stated, "A theoretic model is a mythical universe in which only events that interest us occur. Moreover, all of them can be explained because this universe is composed of only those variables and relationships which fit into propositions about such events."[2] The special utility of a model is that it enables us to examine and compare events or processes which at first glance may seem dissimilar, and to construct and test expectations (hypotheses) which the model generates.

The model of political decision making here offered, and as diagrammed in the figure on page 8, shows public policies as the outcome of the interplay among (1) broad cultural values, (2) the specific values of interest groups with different resources and opposing objectives, (3) a legal-institutional framework for making authoritative decisions, and (4) public officials who with their resources must ulti-

MODEL OF PROCESS OF POLITICAL DECISION MAKING

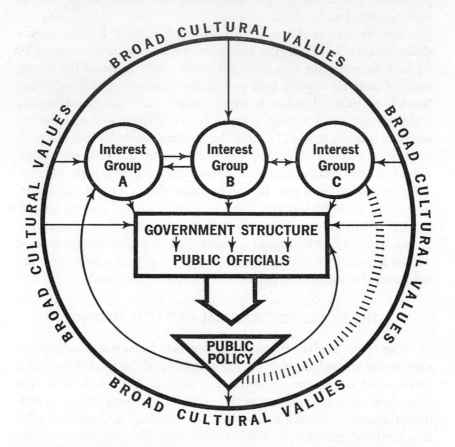

mately make and administer the policies. Each component of this decision-making system requires elaboration for the sake of clarity. But in examining each we must not lose sight of the fact that each operates in relationship to the others.

Broad Cultural Values

All decision making operates within an environment of broad cultural values. Different policy outcomes can be expected from culture to culture because, among other reasons, these broader values differ; such differences help to account for the different outcomes of policy in, say, the United States and the USSR.

One such set of values relates to how public decisions are to be made. In the United States one finds belief in the legitimacy of majority decisions and in the right of minorities to have some protection against the majority and to appeal to it to change its mind. Although we take these general values for granted, American history is filled with the conflict between majority and minority in determining how far each may go in pursuing its will. This conflict is paired with conflicting impulses toward variety and conformity, pluralism and homogeneity. Those groups which emphasize the essentially pluralistic nature of our society seek to carve out small realms in which they are free to express, in belief and action, their differences from those who push toward a sameness in belief and behavior. Thus beliefs in variety and in sameness mirror at the social level the conflict between majority and minority principles found at the political level.

Implicit in these sets of conflicts is the belief in popular sovereignty. Majority rule is thought to be the only feasible way of manifesting the popular will, and that will is the only one accorded ultimate legitimacy. Two aspects of the relationship between popular sovereignty and majority will may be found in two more narrow but still general cultural values—free and open education for all and ambivalence toward race differences. Each of these narrower values offers an insight into different aspects of the operations of the basic principles. Free and open education, so widely accepted as a cultural value because it so widely met a prevalent cultural need, became a commandment. Few have challenged its essential worth, as through at least a century the belief in free and open education has been widely reinforced by implementing legislation. Here, there were no majority will and minority will, for consensus reigned.

But in the beliefs about race the two wills did not coincide, giving rise to the dichotomy between belief and practice which Myrdal correctly labeled "the American dilemma." On the one hand, there was the widespread belief that all Americans should share in and pursue the advantages of a free society; any one man's claim to fairness in this sharing and pursuing was pretty much equal to another man's. On the other hand, attachment to principles of equality and liberty has been uncertain at best, because throughout our history, even to this day, what a majority of Americans say they believe about these principles is not borne out in practice.[3] That whole policy area that we term civil liberties demonstrates a historical pattern of minorities claiming legitimacy for their interpretations of what to believe or how to act against the majority's claim to exclusive legitimacy for its interpretations. In one respect this is a clash between majority and minority over the meaning of liberty. But in another respect it is a clash between the majority's devotion to equality (at least for itself) and the minority's attachment to liberty, suggesting that the widespread cultural values of equality and liberty at some points are contradictory and antagonistic. Thus the majority may assert its liberty to deny equality to a minority.

Interest-Group Values

Operating within the framework of these general values we see a multiplicity of interest groups pursuing more narrow values. While interest-group activity has invidious overtones in the popular mind, that activity is of long standing in American history and, it may be argued, is inextricably involved with our democratic system. Our constitutional forefathers were well aware of the fact that there were many interests within the total polity and that these would compete with one another in seeking the sanction of governmental power. James Madison, writing in *Federalist Paper 10*, suggested that one could cure the evils of factional controversy by either removing its causes or controlling its effects. The first method would require restrictions on liberty, a cure worse than the disease. Thus it was necessary to control the effects of faction. But factional disputes, with supporting interest groups, were "sown in the nature of man," because men differ about their interests. In Madison's words,

But the most common and durable source of factions has been the various and unequal distribution of property. Those who hold and those who are without property have ever formed distinct interests in society. Those who are creditors, and those who are debtors, fall under a like discrimination. A landed interest, a manufacturing interest, a mercantile interest, a moneyed interest, with many lesser interests, grow up of necessity in civilized nations, and divide them into two different classes, actuated by different sentiments and views. The regulation of these various and interfering interests forms the principal task of modern legislation and involves the spirit of party and faction in the necessary and ordinary operations of government.

Thus a second major component of the conceptual framework for understanding "the necessary and ordinary operations" of decision making in the American system is the existence of a widespread set of interest groups. Such groups vary in about as many ways as one can devise. Clearly, their motives and values are manifold, going far beyond the catalogue which Madison provides. Certainly, too, the resources utilized by each are highly varied and differentially available, if by resource one means size, money, leadership ability, time, energy, and status—anything which may convince others, including lawmakers. Groups' strategies will vary also, even though all are alike in seeking to mobilize the optimum combination of resources which will enable them to protect or promote their interests. Finally, variety appears in the policies which constitute the outcome of the total process. Such policies may be regarded as rewards or payoffs if successfully achieved. Typically these involve the defeat or issuance of a bill, administrative order, or judicial decision granting or denying such specific items as a franchise, subsidy, tax benefit, tariff, urban-renewal program, or school-busing decision.

If the foregoing seemed to complicate the combinations of forces which operate in the decision-making process so much that no systematic statement is possible, maybe it would help to simplify somewhat the interest-group characteristics by use of the schema advanced by Bloomberg and Sunshine.[4] We might say that all interest groups on any given issue could be classified on the basis of having or not having power and interest in the subject. Some have both power and interest, some have neither, and some have more of one than of the other. It is reasonable to expect that we will hear more from those having both power and interest than from those having neither. Those who have power but no interest in the subject matter do have a "decision-making potential"; if they become concerned they could bring their power to bear and thus affect the final outcome. Those who lack power but have an interest also have a potential, for they may gather power by mobilizing those with no interest but high power.

In any decision area, how the population is distributed among these four types of groups will have an important effect upon the outcome. Those with high power and high interest, for example, could agree on a policy alternative, thus making for very little controversy in the public arena. But if groups significant for both power and interest were split on alternatives, we could reasonably expect a high degree of controversy in the arena—and different sets of strategies from those in the first case. For example, under the second condition, we may see much more effort directed toward mobilizing those who have high power but no interest. Whatever the case, it should be possible with this kind of schema to determine exactly how decision making at one place and time differs from the process elsewhere, and to generate some expectations about the conditions under which certain strategies are employed and certain policy outcomes result.

The Legal-Institutional Framework

Implicit in the first two components, broad cultural and narrow group values, is a third component of the model, namely, the institutional and legal framework within which political decision making is pursued. We may conceive of this in two terms, first the formal structure and process of government, and second the legal or constitutional principles which govern the first. This formal framework is important in providing taboos (it is bad form to shoot the school board that vetoes a program you desire), positive authorizations (the school board does have the power to veto), and permissive limits (the school board may not choose to veto the program).

Another consideration for understanding the politics of decision making is that formal institutions and processes suggest, and frequently dictate, courses of action by contending interest groups and public officials. A group claiming a school board action is unconstitutional cannot march promptly to the U.S. Supreme Court, but must start with local courts and climb up the appellate ladder. Action directed to a city council when it lacks jurisdiction over education is an exercise in futility. Thus formal arrangements not only attract contending groups but can shape the nature and direction of the struggle.

Federalism is the most significant formal, institutional factor to be considered in this book. One aspect is the constitutional requirement (although the Constitution itself is remarkably vague on the topic) that national and state governments have separate jurisdictions in which their authorities operate independently of the other, as well as some areas in which they operate concurrently. The reader should reject any picture of two watertight compartments, because the power relationships between the two levels of government have become incredibly interlinked today, sometimes reinforcing and sometimes opposing one another—a development of such complexity that this chapter can only touch upon it. What is important for present purposes is to understand two elements of this formal arrangement. First, under some conditions the national and state governments will differ over the exact nature of the policy to be pursued, each having what it regards as a legitimate claim to determine the outcome. Second, the permissive elements of the principle of federalism mean that an extraordinary variety of governmental forms and policies exist within the 50 states.

Another institutional factor of great importance is that in the American system power is never exercised at any level completely free of check from some other form of power. This check and balance schema, with its underlying pervasive fear of the exercise of power (our secular notion of original sin), means that in political decision making there may be many steps before an ultimate decision is reached, because there are many channels of appeal for those disgruntled by original decisions. Decision making therefore can be seen as a flow, in which combinations of groups interact at successive stages in an effort to determine the final outcome. This formal characteristic of government, though it contributes to constant bickering and protracted deliberation, has the effect intended by the Founding Fathers. It forestalls quick decisions that might be arbitrary ones, trampling upon the rights and interests of both majority and minority.

The Public Officials

Besides the cultural-value environment, the interest groups, and the institutional framework, the role of public officials is important in the conceptual scheme. While technically these officials may be regarded as a part of the government structure described above, such a perception would be unrealistic. Although many persons can be garbed with the same official cloak of authority, they are nevertheless men and women who differ in their moral and value outlooks. The result is that the same authority may be variously applied. The focus here is upon the figures who make the authoritative decisions (that is, those decisions which bear the imprint of the state and its legitimacy). School board members, councilmen and mayors, state governors, various administrators, and the incumbents of positions in the national branches of government—these are the official actors who singly or in combination form an important component in decision making.

An official may be seen operating in a matrix of claims put upon his authority. One set of claims comprises the actions and words of interest groups who want the official to do or not do something—what

is often loosely termed "pressure." Another set of claims reflects the
authority and discretion he is supposed to exercise. Whatever his
wishes, or those of others, he cannot do what the laws say he may not
do. The notion of checks and balances has very real meaning for any
public official, both because he wishes to do only that which he is
authorized to do and also because if he does otherwise, he lays himself
open to charges of abuse of discretion (if not worse) instigated by
some group which has suffered from his abuse.

Yet another claim upon the official arises from his own set of
values. As noted above, two men with the same authority and in the
same set of pressure-group conditions may arrive at different decisions
as to policy. Not even the judges of courts of this land escape the claim
of personal value, as recent studies of judicial voting behavior have
demonstrated, or as has been demonstrated from our earliest history in
the texts of judicial decisions, especially dissents. Certainly one part of
this set of personal claims would be a man's ambitions, for his decisions may have effects which carry surprisingly far into the future, and
may destroy or elevate him.[5]

A final set of claims which operate upon the public actor consists
of the expectations of others, alive and dead, as to how he should
perform. Recent research in political science, borrowing heavily from
social psychology, has focused upon the way in which "role" operates
to teach and reinforce expected behavior. Just as the child is taught
the role of being a boy or a girl, so public officials learn through very
informal means what their conduct should and should not be.[6] School
board members differ in their notions of their representative role; some
think their task is to give the people everything they desire (even
though some popular desires could hurt educational quality), whereas
others think their task is to provide the best possible education even if
the public objects. Some school superintendents perceive their role to
be that of a leader of the board in policy innovation, while others
believe they should only follow the board. Thus, differential role
perceptions can create differential behaviors in the decision-making
process.

All this makes clear that any effort at viewing the public official as
some kind of automaton, whose behavior is simply the resultant of the
combinations of external forces operating upon him, is misguided. He
is no phonograph reproducing with high fidelity a popular impression.
What he will do is a result of what he may, should, and must do. What

he wishes is not totally irrelevant to the outcome. What a man may do but should not, he often will do because of his preferences. Also, the personality of the actor becomes an important component because of the way he may interact with other public actors to affect the outcome. Some officials are wise in forming combinations which augment power and achieve objectives, while others simply never learn how that game is played.

THE POLICY OUTCOMES

The Model Combined

From this matrix of cultural environment, institution, groups, and officials emerge policy outcomes, the final component in this conceptual framework. Precise knowledge of the input factors can enable us to predict with some degree of success what the outcomes will be. Or we may reason backward, analyzing the outcomes in terms of who won and who lost, and thus learn something about the broad cultural values, strong and weak interest groups, and public officials in the matrix. There is no certainty that the outcome, once arrived at, is final. A policy that has laboriously worked its way through this matrix is thereupon administered, but the process of administration can affect the political environment by stimulating further deliberation and decision making—a feedback effect whereby officials and the electorate learn how efficient and effective the actual policy is. Or, in larger terms, policy outcomes may be analyzed in terms of their effects upon the total social and political system, even to the point that these systems are altered or sustained as a consequence.

The diagram on page 8 shows the flow of factors involved in the decision-making process. All components operate within the influence of broad cultural values, some of which, such as equality and liberty, may be opposed. Interest groups draw upon these broader values for justification of their specific interests. Some groups, such as A and B in the diagram, may have complementary interests reflecting similar broad values, and hence may work together. Others, such as B and C, may have opposing interests reflecting opposing broad values, and hence are in conflict. All impinge upon a formal structure of government and its officials, who in turn are bounded by some broad values. From this interaction of private groups and formal government, mediated by the role of the official, comes a public policy. Such policy has further effects, upon the milieu of broad values which it explicates, upon the interest group whose values it enhances (A) or blocks (C), and upon government and the officials who administer it.

Such a diagram cannot encompass all of the reality. It does not picture the ongoing nature of the process, not showing that what happens here at Time 1 influences the policy outcome at Time 2. The diagram, furthermore, does not illustrate the proportion of the total public involved, which for one issue can be small (and this is characteristic) but for another can be large. It does not show how many levels of government or sets of officials enter into the outcome, nor that the combination varies with issue and with time. But it does illustrate the major set of components which come into play whenever public policy is made. While different combinations of values, government, officials, and outcomes operate from issue to issue, the general components and general process remain constant. Like all such models, this one serves to structure one's thinking on the broad outlines of reality.

Diversity

It is important to remember that the outcomes of American policy making have been both undoctrinaire and highly diverse. We have never been a very doctrinaire people when it comes to the question of what government should do. With a casual disregard for over-all design that has shocked European observers, we have from the earliest days experimented in both the forms and policies of our government. We have been confronted with an ever-increasing variety, quantity, and quality of social problems as the nation moved from an agrarian to a mature industrial economy. In the process, we have given little thought to questions of consistency and relevance concerning what some like to term "basic national values"; we have worked out answers to these problems in a mood which could best be characterized as "Let's see if this works." Given the variety of this nation—in resources, origins, and values—it is not surprising that the end products of public policy making demonstrate a variety bewildering to the native as well as to the foreigner.

Forms of governing vary with the level of government involved and with the locale; not even the names of the forms remain consistent, for county and parish can be the same, while the "town" in New England and "town" in the Midwest are quite different things. What government does in one state or community with wide popular sup-

port is regarded as the mark of the beast in other places. The origin
and incidence of revenue are patchwork affairs across the nation, just
as the volume and objects of expenditures are equally variegated. In
some sections a problem is just beginning to be recognized as a
problem, which elsewhere has long since been structured and funded
in established programs. In driving from city to city as well as from
state to state, one crosses not merely jurisdictional lines; he crosses
through border stations of policy outcomes. Some are quite invisible,
but some are as visible as the abrupt change in the smoothness of the
road, in the cleanliness of the streets, and in the expanse and beauty of
the school house. Not for us has been the French school system,
wherein an official at Paris can say precisely what part of a course is
being taught at that hour in every school in France. For Americans the
very thought is unthinkable.

Such variety is an important indicator of significant underlying
characteristics of the American society. It is a mark of the heterogeneity of the people and their resources and of the constitutional
principle of federalism, which encourages diversity. Contemporary
critics of Americans who see only those things in which they are alike
fail to see that the diversity in governmental forms and policy reflects
an underlying diversity in the people themselves. Americans and their
communities differ in their needs, preferences, and resources, with
consequent diversity in their policy outcomes. Community needs vary
with size, for example; hamlets have little need for an assistant superintendent on school segregation problems. The resources of our communities are equally various, depending upon the presence of large
industry or high income; the little hamlet could not afford that special-
ist if it needed him. Furthermore, what one community regards as
important another may not, so that the psychological factor of preference helps account for diversity; the people of a hamlet may just not
want that assistant superintendent. Thus the permutations and combinations engendered by the variables of needs, resources, and preferences underlie the extraordinary diversity of local policy.

This diversity, however, would not be possible had there not
existed the constitutional principle which permitted and encouraged
it. The desire for local control as the appropriate means for working
out local problems was a guiding factor in the compromises which
produced the Constitution. The development of federalism from a
simple to a complex arrangement has been fully explored elsewhere

and is not the concern of this book. What is important is the understanding that the federal principle fitted well a multifaceted people
wanting to find their own, and different, answers to local problems—
with a resulting variety of local policy which seems to defy any effort at
systematic analysis.

Yet this variety of policy based upon our decentralized system is
matched by a countertrend of national policy centralization. This
nationalizing effect stems from the impact of major social events—
notably wars and depressions—upon many interest groups. Local institutions often were unable to meet these groups' demands for aid in
meeting social crises, and so the groups turned to state or to national
government to achieve what was denied them locally. Sometimes the
result was national-state cooperation in handling a social problem, and
sometimes it was national dominance. The building of national programs for roads, social welfare, and regulation of the economy are
well-known examples of this nationalizing process.[7]

The most dramatic illustration of the nationalizing process has
been in civil rights. Local protection of their rights to an equal
education was found futile by the Negroes, so they turned to the
federal courts. When success here brought only limited results at the
local level, they besieged Congress for a national law while dramatically publicizing their case with local demonstrations against the
inequities they challenged. The subsequent Civil Rights Act of 1964
brought to bear all organs of the national government on the problem.
Although the results are not yet clear, the framework of national
power is now available as it never had been before.

The Decision Process in Northern School Desegregation

This book presents the policy area of northern school desegregation, to which will be applied in the final chapter some systematic
analysis relying upon the model of political decision making given
here. Case studies have their limits, as well as their uses, in social
research. The usual problem of the case study is the difficulty of
generalizing from the singular experience. But here we have a series of
case studies on a common problem that should enable us to arrive at
some generalizations. Such generalizations should enable us to answer
certain kinds of questions. What are the significant broad cultural
values which are operating in these cases? How do the interest groups
of parents (both white and Negro), administrators, teachers, business-

men, and others employ resources and strategies to forward their interests? What are the significant institutional frameworks which are brought to bear here, and how do they shape the outcome? What is the role of the public official within the matrix of claims upon his authority—and what are his limits? What is the meaning of the outcomes achieved, in terms of who won and who lost, and in terms of the effect of these outcomes upon the community and its school policies?

There may be another set of generalizations possible here which would answer questions of more practical significance to those presently caught up in this controversy. Under what conditions is desegregation accomplished easily or with difficulty? What kind of political situation leads to an outcome of significant desegregation or of no action? Is there a critical factor in the set of components involved in decision making which can operate as a key to facilitate desegregation or to block it? And, finally, can these cases and the accompanying analysis make possible predictions about the kinds of policy outcomes to be expected under different sets of social and political conditions?

In some respects these questions may seem presumptuous, for they assume that in the complexity arising from different sets of conditions it is possible to discern uniformities of behavior which encourage prediction. For those who believe in the infinite variety of man or those who believe it is not possible to see political complexity as anything other than a "buzzing, booming confusion," talk about uniformities and prediction *is* presumptuous. But those who have labored to produce the case reports that follow offer their studies in the belief that there is something to be learned about this policy area from what has taken place in their locales. And the editors believe that *not* to search for uniformity and its consequent prediction leaves us prey to Santayana's aphorism that if we learn nothing from history we are doomed to repeat its errors.

Public education, like all professions, has been a cooperative effort, in which much is learned from the experience of others, enabling far-flung men and women to perform prediction, although they might not call it that. It is to the profession of teachers and school administrators and to the policy makers under whom they work that this book is dedicated. The editors' hope is that they will find in these pages some insight to enable them in the midst of this current controversy better to perform the work to which they are dedicated.

2 | EXCELLENCE AND OPPORTUNITY

T. BENTLEY EDWARDS
Professor of Education, University of California, Berkeley

Dr. Edwards is Professor of Education at the University of California. He is a former Canadian and for a long time taught high school science in Vancouver, British Columbia. For brief periods he was a chemistry instructor at St. Mary's College and Chico State College. He has been at Berkeley since 1953. His major research interest is in the attitudes of children and youth as related to success in school.

Schools perform a sorting function as well as a teaching function. Performance of one function sometimes interferes with performance of the other. For example, the sorting goes on at all educational levels and works toward homogeneity among those who remain. But if each is to be equally well taught, differences in style and outlook must be nurtured. Hence teaching should result in greater diversity. Tests used to evaluate teaching and learning are also used to sort the children. In elementary and high school and increasingly in college the tests used emphasize common learnings, so that pupil performance can be readily compared. The prestige of these tests directs the attention of teacher and pupils to the end that educational excellence is seen as mastery over a set body of subject matter. In the following chapter, attention is drawn to two consequences of this interaction between the two functions of the school, both of them to the disadvantage of the children of the poor. First the children are segregated according to their ability to manage oral and written communication, and then increasingly abstract and complex oral and written language is used to teach them new ideas.

As the ranks of the students are thinned, mass devices for sorting can be less frequently used and diversity necessarily is fostered. But by this time, usually at the college level, children from the lower classes have been all but eliminated.

Many topics are introduced into this chapter, but all of them can be related to the inflexibility of present educational procedures. Children from the lower classes, and this includes a disproportionately large number of Negroes, suffer most from this inflexibility. Children from better homes are helped by being taught to use complex language. They are also taught to put up with what goes on in the classroom in order to be rewarded later. Hence certain classes and certain schools get more and more lower-class children.

Responding to pressure from minority groups for equality of educational opportunity, larger units of government are insisting upon desegregated schools and paying for compensatory education.

Reference was made in the opening chapter to the widely held American view that free public education should be open, that there should be equality of educational opportunity. Against this was posited an ambivalence toward race differences whereby the civil liberties of the Negro have been abridged. In the clash of group interests, especially over the distribution of property, the highly visible Negro minority has been at a disadvantage. As a result, a higher percentage of Negroes is found in the lower socio-economic classes than in the population generally.

To the American belief in free public education and ambivalence toward race, a third idea must be added. It is the belief that excellence demands segregation. A substantial number of parents and teachers think that, applied to the schools, this means that attempts to teach children who learn slowly in the same school with those who learn fast must inevitably slow down the learning rate of the faster children. Rate of learning standard school material is closely related to socio-economic status. As a result school segregation means segregation by class, and because Negroes are overrepresented in the lower classes it means, to a greater or lesser extent, segregation by race.

The interplay of these three ideas or concepts, equality of educational opportunity, ambivalence toward race, and segregation for excellence, will be used in presenting some additional information and understanding needed to comprehend the educational dispositions that result, or are likely to result, from the policy decisions described in the case studies that follow.

Status of Negro Education

As part of a recent survey by the U.S. Office of Education of nearly one million U.S. children, a variety of test scores was collected on pupil achievement and motivation. According to the report, "achievement shows the accomplishments of the school to date; motivation shows the interest it has created for further achievements."[1]

Tests given in grades 1, 3, 6, 9, and 12 covered reading and mathematics ability. In the two final grades, tests in five areas of general information were also given. Standardized test scores are reported. For the twelfth grade, "the order of the racial and ethnic groups is nearly the same on all tests. Following the whites in order are Orientals, Indians, Mexican-Americans, Puerto Ricans, and Negroes."[2] Evidently the schools are not equally successful with all ethnic groups.

It must be emphasized that this order represents the test results in the twelfth grade. One possible explanation of the changes of this order by the time the students reach twelfth grade may be that the high school differentially selects from the various ethnic groups. That is to say, the Negroes of modest achievement may be more likely to remain in school than the less able of, for example, the Puerto Ricans and American Indians.

Social-Class Influence

Neither are the schools equally successful with all social classes. Since the pioneering Harvard lectures of Allison Davis, and the work of the Hollingsheads in "Elmtown," numerous studies have clarified understanding of the relationship of school success to occupation of the father, or to some equally valid indicator of socio-economic status of the child's family.

"Reading, writing, calculation, and analysis of information are becoming basic requirements for independence, productive work, political participation, and wise consumption."[3]

The major pathway to social mobility in this country continues to lie through an educational program that leads to a skilled vocation. But here, as in all other countries of the world, children are selected for advanced educational opportunities according to their success in the early years of schooling, and the measures of success used all correlate highly with the socio-economic status of the parents. Equality of educational opportunity must surely mean that the schools must find ways of improving the chances for success of the children of ethnic minorities and of the poor.[4] As U.S. Commissioner of Education Harold Howe puts it: "Some youngsters—those born and raised in the inner city ghetto, for instance—require much more than an 'average' education just to give them an average start in life."

Separating Race and Class Influences

If the schools are to be successful in devising better than average education for those born in the inner-city ghetto, the influence upon learning of class and racial discrimination must be untangled.

Many Negro children in northern cities attend schools in which more than half the children are Negroes. In the first grade, 72 percent do so; in the 12th grade, 35 percent.[5]

The Coleman report states that when socio-economic status is controlled, differences among schools account for only a small fraction of differences in pupil achievement. However, the report goes on to say that the achievement of minority pupils depends more on the schools they attend than does the achievement of majority pupils.[6]

Wilson, seeking to separate the influence of class and race, makes a similar finding. He concludes from his analysis of data collected in Richmond, California, that, "while the racial composition of a school has a negligible effect, often, on the achievement of both Negro and white students, the social class composition has a much more pronounced effect on the achievement of Negroes than on whites."[7]

The explanation usually given for this finding is that in some way the school itself has a greater effect upon Negro than upon white children. That is to say, Negroes obtain a greater advantage than do whites from attending a higher-status school, and a greater disadvantage than do whites from attending a lower-status school.

Another explanation is possible. Negro children may be sorted more rigorously because of racial discrimination. Consider, for example, a group of Negro children whose parents have achieved a modest degree of social success. If the group were white, many of them would be living in districts which entitled them to attend higher-status schools. Because of the clash of special interests in the society, only the ablest and most aggressive of the Negro group will be able to move out of the lower-status neighborhood. The children of these families will also be more likely to succeed in school than will the children of those families that are left behind. Hence they will demonstrate, in predominantly white schools, a higher degree of achievement than will those left behind in the Negro schools.

The Negro Revolt

If the alternative explanation just provided for the differing influence of the schools upon Negroes and whites is even partly sufficient to account for the findings, the mounting frustrations of the Negro leaders can be understood. The clash of special interests is exceptionally hard upon them.

The year 1963 has been called the year of the Negro Revolt. In that year, organizations began the extensive use of non-violent demonstrations. "Sit-ins," "stand-ins," "pray-ins," and marches by citizens carrying only placards drew the attention of thoughtful Americans everywhere to the injustices perpetrated in both northern and southern states against American Negroes. When pictures appeared on television and in news magazines of various authority-wielders using force to prevent and disperse "passive resistance," the sympathy of many Americans was aroused. For the first time in more than a hundred years, amelioration of the plight of the Negro was accelerated beyond that of a snail's pace.

To the time of his death on November 22, 1963, President Kennedy provided powerful leadership for desegregation. Since that time, President Johnson has persuaded Congress to vote law after law in what he himself has called the "War on Poverty."

Before a consideration of various combinations of compensatory and desegregated schooling that various proponents have suggested, bases for grouping school children will be examined. These can be viewed in the light of the "Statement on Race" of a distinguished committee of scientists assembled by the United Nations Educational, Scientific and Cultural Organization (UNESCO), which says, "Available scientific knowledge provides no basis for believing that the groups of mankind differ in their innate capacity for intellectual and emotional development."[8]

EXCELLENCE AND SEGREGATION

At the center of any argument for the partial separation of one segment of society from another is the generalization, usually unstated, that excellence demands segregation. To live in a "choice" residential section of the town it is necessary to have "choice" neighbors. To keep the water in the local swimming pool clean and free from infection it is necessary to allow it to be used only by people who are clean and free from infection. Selection of neighbors, or of people generally, is difficult. In fact, making any choice is difficult and so most people seek relief in the adoption of a "rule of thumb." Avoidance of the difficulties of selection of people is accomplished by the adoption of stereotypes. Without the inclination, or perhaps the time, to make a careful examination, the chooser asks of himself, "How does he talk?" "What does he look like?" "How do I feel when I am with this person?" "What does he do?"

The assumption that excellence demands segregation can be considered as it relates to a number of social activities—health control and public education among them.

Application of the assumption to matters of health seems to be straightforward. But the need to isolate people with infectious diseases is much less insistent than it once was. The attention of the medical profession is directed toward mass immunization, as well as toward the care of individual sufferers, and strict attention is paid to matters of public health. The fearsome days when the plague wiped out cities, or the leper was forced to sound his bell, lie in the past. When non-infectious illnesses such as heart ailments and duodenal ulcers are concerned, the treatment may require changes in working and eating habits. To produce such changes, different tastes must be induced, so the treatment becomes educational as well as medicinal.

In the case of education the argument for segregation tends to be self-fulfilling. The social stratification which goes with educational segregation will, to some extent, be transmitted from one generation to another. Those with the most education will, generally speaking, gain social advantages which can, to some extent, be passed along from father to son. These advantages are likely to include a home in a desirable neighborhood, good clothes, regular meals, participation in the discussion of complex ideas, and ways of speaking and behaving that facilitate social interaction. Along with functional advantages such as those, the culturally advantaged child acquires non-functional and superficial characteristics of speech, manner, and appearance that render him easily recognizable to his fellows. On the basis of these superficial characteristics he is given access first to education, then to money and position. He clearly is not a "slob."

The most obvious superficial characteristic of a man is the color of his skin. Because, only a century ago, the black man was a slave, the assumption is still made by some people that he is unlikely to contribute to social excellence and so must be segregated. Such segregation, denying as it does equal opportunity for education, money, and position to the American Negro, because he is a Negro, is seen by many people, black and white, as a denial of the Negro's civil rights. But many of those with money and position retain a strong emotional attachment to the argument that excellence demands segregation and refuse to reexamine their bases for rank-ordering people with respect to an assumed potential for excellence. They see only the possibility of contamination of those social advantages which they and their fathers before them have acquired. This application of the argument for segregation brings the concept of property rights into headlong conflict with the concept of civil rights, and American society is faced with its "dilemma."[9] The spores of discord carried by slavery lay hidden for years, but in 1963 the current Negro Revolt burst forth.[10] No completely satisfactory resolution of the dilemma has yet been proposed, but a number of softening influences are apparent.

So far no one seems willing to abandon completely, in educational procedures, the idea that excellence requires segregation, although methods of deploying adolescents for secondary education indicate movement away from segregation. Today the idea of "equal education for all" is advanced as more consonant with American social purposes.

Most American youth attend comprehensive high schools. These provide instruction in college-preparatory subjects, courses for general citizenship education, and programs leading directly toward employment.[11] Typically college preparation consists of taking courses in foreign languages, mathematics, science, English, and history. In the first three of these subjects, segregation is achieved by making the demands of the introductory course such that fewer than half the students are able to continue. In fact, where a third course is offered, only half of those who have completed the second course are likely to enroll. In a typical high school of 1500 students, there will probably be but one class of fewer than thirty students in each of the top courses of foreign languages, mathematics, and science. Success in the beginning courses of these subjects correlates highly with the social position of the family.[12]

Courses in English and history are compulsory, so nearly all students continue to enroll in these subjects until they leave school. Some schools frankly practice ability grouping, which means that students are separated according to I.Q., reading achievement scores, teacher recommendations, or a combination of these. Teachers generally argue that teaching is more efficient with ability grouping,[13] though the research evidence is indecisive.[14] Once more, the academic stratifications produced are influenced, more or less, by the social stratifications in the community.[15] In a few schools, students are grouped unselectively for English and history. High-quality instruction should be possible in such heterogeneous groupings, but because high school teachers are seldom prepared to teach mixed groups, students are seldom motivated to achieve excellence, and the standards of instruction falter.

The preceding discussion of segregation in American high schools fits most closely the programs of high schools located in towns with a single high school. In the larger cities, with a number of high schools, each entire high school is most likely to follow the pattern of residential segregation.

In higher education in America segregation as a pathway to excellence is considered to be normal practice. Any attempt to throw open the doors of such institutions as Harvard or the University of California would meet resistance. Segregation of the best students, presumably in the interest of achieving excellence, is built formally into the plan for higher education in California.[16] In states where the state university is required to accept at least all of those who have been able to graduate from high school, the drop-out rate in the lower division is enormous.

The Question of the "Gifted"

The problem of selection is difficult. Which children are the genuinely "gifted"? Which children should be provided with the best nurturance that society has to offer? If the response is that in American society all should be nurtured with equal assiduity, then the concept of selection can be logically applied and children can first be carefully tested and then assigned to procedures that are equally good but different from each other. However, the answer given in America today, judging by the way in which educational advantages are provided, is either that the "slow learner" should be given the best educational opportunity, or that the best facilities should be reserved for the "gifted." By and large, the average child, and this means most of American children, is given a most unimaginative treatment. Furthermore, a few people are beginning to raise questions about methods used to select "gifted" children. Some are concerned with creativity;[17] others consider motivation of paramount importance.[18]

Despite Turner's contention that society in the United States of America[19] practices contest mobility, that it is a social system in which the pathway to success is left open indefinitely, entrance to college is determined for most children in American elementary schools at least by the end of the third grade.[20] Elementary school practices are still largely dominated by schemes of instruction that fit the concept of the intelligence quotient (I.Q.). This is an elaborate rationalization for the widespread belief that capacity for intellectual learning is relatively fixed and distributed in the population according to the Gaussian curve of probability. According to this scheme, which fits closely with present practice, the I.Q. of most children varies from 50 to 150. There are isolated examples that lie without these limits, and the mean I.Q. is 100. The mathematical formula prophesies success in college for a certain proportion and failure to learn to read for another proportion.

Many will argue that the I.Q. concept of scholastic aptitude is realistic and that a concept ascribing almost unlimited potential to the great majority of human beings is sentimental. However, the success of gifted teachers with unpromising pupils[21] should lead to the suspicion that man's intellectual capabilities are still largely uncharted, let alone untapped. It is one thing to be convinced that no human being will ever run a mile in three minutes; but it is quite another thing to be convinced that the summit of man's intellectual achievement is anywhere in sight. It is far worse to be convinced that a fourth of mankind must trail so far behind as to be incapable of dignified living.

The built-in concept of unusual success for some, and corresponding failure for others, makes the acquisition of education a highly competitive race. The opposing idea is that children from poor homes, of whom a disproportionately large number are Negroes, are at a disadvantage and that the existence of cultural handicaps does not accord with the belief in "fair play" Americans have inherited from Anglo-Saxon founding fathers.

An entirely different view of the variations found among children is possible, namely, that different children have different potentials and that they must be taught different things in different ways. But there seems little likelihood that such a view will become popular in educational institutions, as it would demand the dethronement of the standard disciplines. Hence, for the foreseeable future, the amelioration of the evils produced by segregation in the pursuit of excellence will continue to derive largely from compensatory education. As experiments are conducted, and educators learn slowly and painfully how to compensate the child for his limited endowments, they will also learn to discriminate genuine indicators of learning potential from those which are spurious. It is most likely that education will continue to be regarded as a race or a competition in which certain prizes are to be sought, but it is also likely that children will not continue to be hobbled by the discrimination and consequent discouragement that presently accompany irrelevant characteristics. The child from a poor home will not be put in a slow class because his appearance or manners color the teacher's estimates of his educational potential.

An entirely distinct development is possible—the discarding of the assumption that segregation in education is needed for the production of excellence. A few brave pioneers are recorded in the history of pedagogy,[22] but nowhere has segregation been abandoned in more than one school, and rarely in more than a single classroom. The reason it has not is that pedagogy is largely an unexplained art. Teachers can be taught their subjects, and to some extent they can be taught how to maintain discipline in the classroom, but whatever they acquire of the art of teaching what they know to others, they must pick up for themselves and adapt to their own personalities.[23] Hence the teaching of children, the treatment they receive from their elders, will continue to receive far less emphasis than the selection of children who learn easily certain standard kinds of information and ways of thinking.

The favorite pedagogical belief of most eminent university professors, that people learn by being talked at, is true only for those who have been carefully selected for this exotic treatment. And even these chosen ones sometimes rebel at the treatment![24] To learn from a typical university course, the student must somewhere have acquired the necessary motivation. This motivation can be of two kinds. The student can have acquired a taste for learning or he can have learned to want something for which the learning is a prerequisite. The best students are thought to possess the former, which is sometimes referred to as intrinsic motivation. Both kinds of motivation are acquired, and they must be acquired, of course, from those who have them. The evidence to date indicates that intragenerational influences greatly exceed intergenerational influences, especially among children from poor homes.[25]

Besides acquiring a taste for learning, children must learn to manipulate the symbols by which learning is communicated. Again, children from poor homes learn their language chiefly from each other rather than from parents or other adults. Unless they have opportunities for prolonged association with children who have learned to talk about complex abstractions, children from poor homes can never expect to acquire the needed language and symbolic skills.

Learning symbolism and acquiring motivation can probably be augmented by various schemes of compensatory education. Evidence is available that achievement in science and mathematics is more accessible to children from poor homes than is achievement in language and history.[26] Apparently many children are introduced to the symbolism of science and mathematics in school, whereas the language facility of children entering kindergarten shows extensive variation. Hence compensatory education might, with profit, concentrate on the development of skill in science and mathematics to begin with,[27] although success in school will sooner or later require skill in reading and writing.

But the most hopeful sign for children from poor homes is the increasing demand for desegregated schooling. The Supreme Court decision of May 1954 states very clearly that the idea of "separate but equal" is untenable with respect to schools. But nowhere in the text of this decision is the idea that excellence demands segregation explicitly abandoned. Failure to come to terms with the segregation idea reflects the contest throughout the educational history of the United States of America between the views of Jefferson and of Jackson. Jackson took the position that Jack was as good as his master; Jefferson's view was essentially aristocratic. The Jeffersonian view has recently been cleverly lampooned by Michael Young.[28]

At the present juncture, Jacksonian views are being pushed by one segment of society, and Jeffersonian views by another. The accepted compromise seems to be one set of schools but with segregated classes, and with special efforts to help the handicapped children make up for their deficiencies.

Remedies for Segregated Schools

A number of ways to restore class and racial balance in the schools have been suggested. Immediate improvement of slum schools has also been suggested under the name "compensatory education." Both these methods are being tried, as the case studies that follow show. Details of the methods will be summarized.

The obvious method of restoring racial balance to schools in segregated parts of the city is to bus children back and forth until a predetermined mix is obtained. This method has been tried and is still being used. It is not popular with anyone. Mothers complain when their small children must travel long distances; children complain when they are driven past their old school to go to a new one; and taxpayers object to the additional expense.

A less obvious, but important, first step is a clear declaration of policy by the school board. According to a report issued by the Commission on School Integration of the National Association of Intergroup Relations Officials in 1963, only two states, New York and California, have adopted formal statements of policy on school segregation; a number of city boards of education have followed suit.[29]

If those in control of urban schools are not to ignore the racial imbalance in the schools they operate, they need to make an ethnic census. Such counts are now being urged by several Negro organizations, although they are still opposed to records being kept of the race of an individual child.[30] Hence, the ethnic census is usually compiled from observations by the teacher and not from the more reliable basis of individual records, a fact which underlines the relationship between the special problems of the Negro and his high visibility.

The case studies that follow will document the use of citizen groups to study the problem of Negro schools in northern and western cities. The study commission, with the ethnic census and the declaration of policy, constitutes general attacks on *de facto* segregation. There are a number of more specific methods.

Specific Desegregation Methods

Various devices may be employed by a school board to reduce racial segregation in addition to, or sometimes in lieu of, extensive busing. These include site selection, zoning, the Princeton Plan, open enrollment, closing down a school, special schools, feeder-pattern control, modified plant use, and educational parks. The most widely used devices are illustrated in the next few pages with diagrams from a pamphlet of the U.S. Commission on Civil Rights called "Schools Can Be Desegregated."*

The educational park is a large area in the city where a number of schools are located. It is almost like a college or university campus in its appearance. The obvious handicap is that nearly all children must be transported, some of them for long distances. A less obvious handicap is the isolation of the children from the community, and even from the group activities of their own parents. Educational parks are being planned or considered by three cities studied in this book—Berkeley and Sausalito, California, and New York City—as well as Albuquerque; East Orange, New Jersey; Philadelphia; Pittsburgh; and St. Paul.

Various rezoning devices, using existing buildings, have been used in many communities. The simplest plan is to close a racially imbalanced school and assign its pupils to other schools. School closing was the technique used in Manhasset, New York, and was part of the plans adopted by Englewood and Teaneck, New Jersey—among the communities studied in this book—and also has been used in Evanston, Illinois; Syracuse and White Plains, New York; and Xenia,

---

* CCR Clearinghouse Publication No. 8, June 1967, obtainable from Office of Staff Director, U.S. Commission on Civil Rights, Washington, D.C. 20425.

NEW YORK EDUCATION PARK PLAN

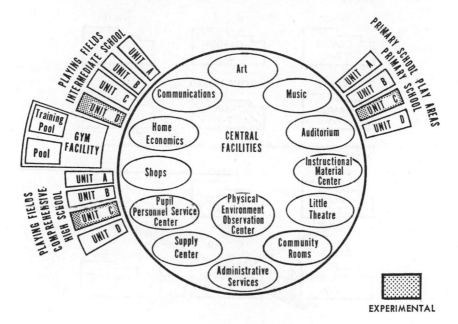

EXPERIMENTAL

PLAN FOR NEW YORK'S NEW EDUCATION PARK
PROVIDES FOR PRIMARY SCHOOLS FOR 2,800
PUPILS, INTERMEDIATE SCHOOLS FOR 3,600, AND
A COMPREHENSIVE HIGH SCHOOL FOR 4,000.
STUDENTS WILL BE GROUPED IN UNITS OF 700
EACH IN THE PRIMARY SCHOOLS, 900 IN THE
INTERMEDIATE SCHOOLS, AND 1,000 IN THE HIGH
SCHOOL. THE CENTRAL UNIT WILL OFFER COMMON
FACILITIES FOR ALL SCHOOLS IN THE COMPLEX.*

* DIAGRAM ADAPTED FROM SATURDAY REVIEW,
NOVEMBER, 1966 AT 93.

Ohio. An alternative to school closing is the formation of an education complex by utilizing schools functionally within a consolidated attendance zone. Plans for education complexes in New York City are discussed in this book, and also are being considered in Rochester.

The Princeton Plan (or "pairing") ties two elementary schools together. The years of schooling for a given child are split between the two schools. He may go to one school for three or four years and then change to the other one, or he may shift back and forth annually. The plan is limited to mixing the populations of two adjacent schools. Originated in Princeton, New Jersey, pairing of schools is one of the

SCHOOL CLOSING

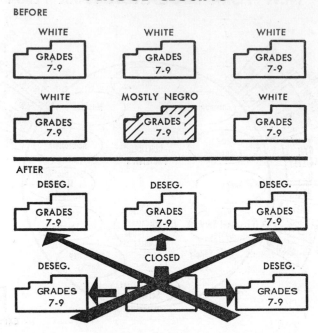

many plans used in New York City and has been under consideration in two other cities studied in this book, Sausalito and Riverside, California. Pairing also is used in Coatesville, Pennsylvania, and Greenburgh, New York.

A number of cities have converted a racially imbalanced school into a central school teaching a single grade (or two or three grades) to children from the entire city or a large part of it. Central schools have been used in three school districts examined in this book: Berkeley, Englewood, and Teaneck. Schools offering special curricula —both regular full-time schools catering to talented children and supplementary part-time schools offering enrichment programs to all children—have been established in New York City, as described in this book, and in Cleveland, Mount Vernon (a New York suburb), Los Angeles, and Philadelphia. Such schools are called "magnet" because they are intended to attract children on a voluntary basis.

Compensatory Education

Federal and state funds have been directed through such legislation as the Elementary and Secondary Education Act of 1965 toward

EDUCATION COMPLEXES

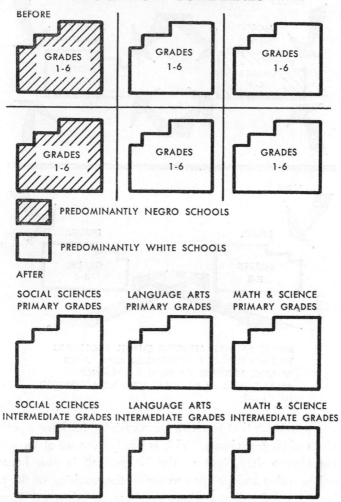

BEFORE

GRADES 1-6

GRADES 1-6

GRADES 1-6

GRADES 1-6

GRADES 1-6

GRADES 1-6

PREDOMINANTLY NEGRO SCHOOLS

PREDOMINANTLY WHITE SCHOOLS

AFTER

SOCIAL SCIENCES
PRIMARY GRADES

LANGUAGE ARTS
PRIMARY GRADES

MATH & SCIENCE
PRIMARY GRADES

SOCIAL SCIENCES
INTERMEDIATE GRADES

LANGUAGE ARTS
INTERMEDIATE GRADES

MATH & SCIENCE
INTERMEDIATE GRADES

bolstering educational provisions in schools for the poor. For each child from a family whose income is below a specified level, the school board can request $250 to provide special education services. The city of Oakland, California, for example, was assigned two and a half million dollars to pay for additional teachers of reading during the spring semester of 1966. Shapiro claims that by placing more adults in the classroom with children from underprivileged homes, he has been able to raise achievement generally in a dramatic fashion.[31]

One of the unanticipated consequences of the publicity given to

PAIRING

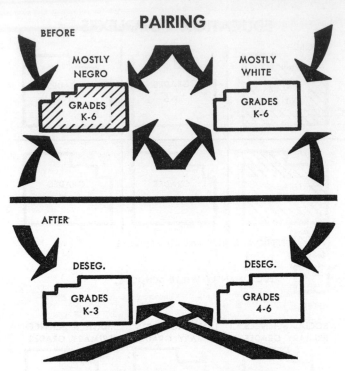

BEFORE PAIRING, STUDENTS ENROLL ACCORDING
TO EACH SCHOOL'S ATTENDANCE AREA. AFTER
PAIRING, STUDENTS OF BOTH ATTENDANCE
AREAS ENROLL IN THE TWO SCHOOLS ACCORDING
TO GRADE.

the war on poverty is that teachers are remaining for longer periods on the faculties of Negro schools.[32] This is partly because of the attention paid generally to the plight of the Negro, but is also because of additional attention and prestige awarded the teaching of the poor in the universities and colleges where teachers are educated. Ironically, the methods suggested for improving the education of the underprivileged include a number of devices suggested and tested under the auspices of the movement called Progressive Education.[33] Critics who struck blindly at American education during the decade 1950–60, and belittled an educational philosophy that is essentially humane, directed the attention of those school people whom they were able to influence away from the special difficulties of the poor. The hazards of unenlightened criticism, no matter the extent to which responsible criticism may be needed, is now distressingly apparent.[34]

CENTRAL SCHOOLS

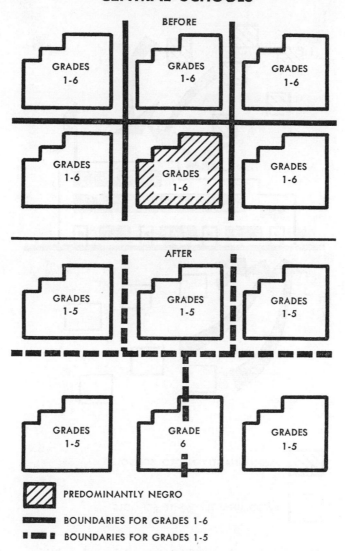

BEFORE

GRADES 1-6 | GRADES 1-6 | GRADES 1-6

GRADES 1-6 | GRADES 1-6 | GRADES 1-6

AFTER

GRADES 1-5 | GRADES 1-5 | GRADES 1-5

GRADES 1-5 | GRADE 6 | GRADES 1-5

PREDOMINANTLY NEGRO

BOUNDARIES FOR GRADES 1-6

BOUNDARIES FOR GRADES 1-5

Merely placing children from deprived environments next to children from homes where ideas abound cannot by itself bring about equality of educational opportunity. Changes in patterns of school attendance have brought close together children of the middle and lower classes. Unless each class is carefully prepared for the encounter, stereotypes are likely to develop which are well-nigh ineradicable

MAGNET SCHOOLS

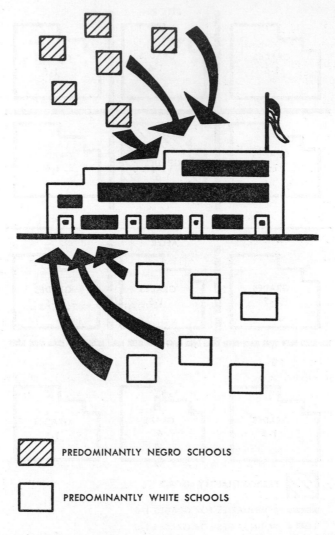

▨ PREDOMINANTLY NEGRO SCHOOLS

☐ PREDOMINANTLY WHITE SCHOOLS

and more harmful than those which form when the children are kept apart in separate schools. The middle-class children, even those taught at home to be gentle and considerate, are likely to find their new friends difficult to understand, often at odds with the teacher, and in the possession of habits of speech and dress that hinder intimacy. The lower-class children see their fresh classmates as affected, almost too good to be true, and unusually desirous of pleasing the teacher.

Though they share the same classroom, lines of demarcation will still be there.[35]

With the utmost care the children must be prepared for each other and the children who are disadvantaged provided with extra opportunities. New educational practices such as programed instruction, flexible scheduling, and team teaching can be expected to provide numerous opportunities for individualized instruction. Such additional ideas as the introduction of more adults into the classroom must be considered in order to compensate these children for the opportunities they may have missed in their family life. Such individualization need place no hobble on the growth of the middle-class child when each is to be served according to his needs.

It may be that children from good homes must be held back while they wait for the slower children to catch up. If teachers in freshly integrated schools persist in using only present methods, this trend toward mediocrity is almost inevitable. The fear that their own children will be neglected is the motive that drives many middle- and upper-class parents to put their children in private schools. Placing slow children in separate classes means that, because of past discrimination, Negro children will crowd the slower sections and scarcely invade the faster sections. Educational equality seems no more likely than in segregated schools.

Difficulties encountered in school work by the children of the poor derive almost entirely from their small vocabularies and inability to make use of complex language. They have no words with which to relate any but the simplest of experiences, and when the teacher talks to them in any but the simplest of terms, they cannot understand. So long as the children of the poor remain segregated, they have no opportunity to increase greatly their vocabularies. Without the cognitive development that accompanies a growing vocabulary there can be no growth in motivation or interest. Even when a certain proportion of the children in a poor school are successful to the extent that they can demonstrate academic superiority over their fellow students, such success leads to disillusionment when competition with graduates of better schools is encountered on the job or in applications for advanced education. The poor communication that derives from a limited vocabulary is made even worse by a specialized accent and a tendency to use ordinary words in special ways. These two tendencies are inevitable when groups of people are segregated, and they account for the variety of dialects in which a number of modern languages may be expressed.[36]

For every modern language there is a standardized version that must be used in commercial and political discourse. Habitual use of the argot of the streets not only excludes the speaker from the commercial and political communication needed if comfort and a sense of well-being are to be arranged, it also restricts his social communicants to those who understand his speech and do not find it irritating.[37]

Compensatory education may be interpreted to mean the improvement of schooling in lower-class districts, including better buildings, specially trained teachers, and more suitable curricula. It may mean more expensive shops in which to pursue the more concrete interests of the children in every classroom; an assistant principal to check attendance; specialists in retardation and in remedial work; psychologists, nurses, and welfare workers; summer schools, field trips, and pre-opening programs; and a vigorous program of counseling and placement.

Federal Funds for Education

A full program of compensatory education is costly and, up to now, has been largely considered to be beyond the means of local communities. The use of federal funds for education has therefore been suggested. In recent years there has been a growing conviction that expenditures for education constitute a sound investment and that inequalities in educational opportunity in certain communities should be erased, so far as possible, with money assigned by the federal government.

Full realization of the economic value of education lies in the future, but in recent decades there has been decreasing reference to education as a privilege to be earned by the individual himself or provided by his parents, and increasing reference to education as a valuable national commodity.[38] The former concept treats education as precious in the sense that there is a limited supply. What is precious is the energy of communication. The cost of the energy required must be compared with the increased production of educated workers. In a world of automated industry, the energy required is apt to be slight in comparison with the increased output so that education becomes sound investment.

Harbison and Myers have found the extent of secondary education in a country to be the best index with which to predict the gross national product. Choice of secondary education rather than elementary or higher education may reflect the selective function of secondary education in most countries rather than the absolute worth of its content. The exact propaedeutic function of each of the secondary subjects, that is, the necessity in a program of instruction for, say, mathematics in the tenth grade, is yet to be determined. But a high school education is the only pathway to many vocations, certainly to the better-paying vocations, so that secondary education is ascribed the status of a bottleneck. Even the achieved status of high school education comes more easily in those countries where only a few youth are selected for college preparation. Because the purpose of a strictly college-preparatory school is easy to define, its output can be easily measured—how many graduates can get into the good colleges. In addition, graduates of the college-preparatory school are far more likely to be successful in the larger society and their nostalgic praise of the old school taken as a reliable measure of intrinsic worth. When the unsuccessful have gone to the same school, its reputation may gleam less brightly.

In the United States education is legally controlled by each of the sovereign states. The U.S. Office of Education in the Department of Health, Education, and Welfare has no assigned place in the educational hierarchy. Federal funds directed to education for general purposes and without assignment to a specific category of spending are therefore in the nature of outright gifts. Congressmen, mindful of their constituents, are reluctant to give up all control over the spending of assigned funds. Federal aid to education has therefore been categorical rather than general. The categories have included, over the years, agriculture and the mechanical arts, vocational education, educational research, aid to areas impacted with heavy concentrations of federal workers, education in science and mathematics, help for needy students, and most recently the special needs of the children of the poor.

Denied access to the established educational bureaucracy, the federal government has forged two weapons for the fight against ignorance: the contract, and the institute which selected teachers are paid to attend. Congress has, through a variety of laws including the necessary money acts, placed these weapons in the hands of several departments of the executive branch including the Departments of Health, Education, and Welfare, Agriculture, the Interior, Commerce, and Labor. In addition, fresh commissions, boards, and agencies have been created to administer federal aid to education.

Paid teacher institutes were financed first through the National Science Foundation, and were aimed largely at improving curricula in science and mathematics. Selected teachers of mathematics and science came to colleges and universities at federal expense to learn of recent findings in their subject. Subtly at some institutes, and more blatantly at others, the new curricula were espoused. Teachers went home and eventually experienced the pleasure of using a textbook they themselves had helped to write, and a course they had helped to plan.[39] To a very great extent the new courses were aimed at the culturally privileged—the children of the middle and upper classes. If anything, they tended to widen the gulf between the upper and lower classes. Later institutes have directed attention to linguistics, the several social sciences—including economics—and the audio-lingual method of teaching foreign languages. These subjects, especially foreign languages, have thus been given a much wider appeal.[40]

Departments of the executive branch advertised the opportunities for research and development, and personnel in colleges, universities, state, county, and local offices of education devoted more and more of their time and energy to the writing of proposals. These proposals were assessed, usually in Washington, and contracts were negotiated between the federal government and the agency from which a successful proposal had emanated. The hand of the Congress, though light on the rein, is there, influencing the way the proposal is written, and the way the contract is carried out. PERT, Project Evaluation Review Technique, makes no bones about the step-by-step connection with the original proposal that is expected. The wave of interest in the education of the underprivileged can be traced to the passage of laws expressing Presidential and Congressional concern.

Educational Technology

Conceivably, the delicate balance between the need for compensatory education and the demand for desegregation may be upset drastically by changes in educational technology. The "methods" of departments of education, formerly so reviled by some of their colleagues in other university departments, have attracted powerful attention not only from enlightened faculty in many university departments but from private industrial and business corporations as well.[41]

For instance, Francis Keppel, formerly Dean of the Graduate School of Education, Harvard University, and afterwards U.S. Commissioner of Education, is now Chairman of the Board which directs combined efforts by General Electric and Time-Life, Incorporated, toward a vastly improved educational technology. Already, their initial task forces are scouring the country for significant ways to establish and operate newly designed educational systems. This is but one example of numerous collaborations between publishers and electronic or computer firms.

Basic to an educational technology is the establishment of a sequence of learning. Until recently, this sequence was worked out intuitively by committees of teachers, by textbook authors, and sometimes by lawmakers. Following the preliminary work of B. F. Skinner,[42] which in turn made use of a neglected scheme invented by Sidney L. Pressey,[43] programs of instruction were devised. Teaching machines were invented to present the instructional programs to students, and these machines met with limited success. Now the earlier machines have all but disappeared, largely because it was found possible to present the essential learning device, the program, on the pages of a textbook.

A major criticism leveled at Skinner's so-called linear programs is that these bore some children and fail to teach others. Crowder[44] suggested branched programming, in which the learner is directed along one of a variety of sequences depending upon his early responses. But in any program the degree of flexibility is far from that which can be exercised by a wise and experienced teacher; the feedback from the pupil is limited; and the child never experiences the delight of formulating his own questions.

Modern computers are flexible. Their patience is well-nigh inexhaustible, and they can perform mental gymnastics based on a prodigious accumulation of stored data. Furthermore, the child can stimulate the computer in a variety of ways so as to call forth a seemingly limitless variety of computer responses. In fact, stimulus-response psychology is far better able to predict computer response than human response. Computer-based instruction has already proven highly successful.[45] Where instruction is computer-based, segregation loses some of its advantages in the race for excellence.

CONCLUSION

In this chapter, additional conceptual tools have been provided for the analysis of the case studies that follow. The first chapter outlined a model for decision making in a community, with particular reference to education. Starting from a generally accepted set of social values, the belief in free public education and the ambivalence toward race were seen as most pertinent to desegregation. The clash of special interests, the influence of law, the role of individuals and groups, and the competition for scarce resources provided additional principles used to construct the model.

The present chapter has summarized certain ideas and information needed to facilitate a view of the current educational scene. Following a brief attempt to untangle the influences of race and social class upon the child's learning, the concept of segregation for excellence was explored at length. This extremely important idea renders intelligible the use of federal funds and modified educational technology to prepare children born into the lower social classes for entry into desegregated schools. Although this tidy scheme can be expected to aid in the understanding of the case studies that follow, it does not mean that such a rational procedure has been followed in each of the described communities.

The educational procedures take place within the framework of decisions made by the community. However, the school system does interact with the community in a variety of ways. It is an open system and maintains its vigor to the extent that it leads, modifies, explains, and even, on occasion, shows a measure of defiance.

FURTHER SUGGESTED READINGS

The readings suggested here are in addition to those cited in the chapters and listed at the back of the book under *Notes*.

Anderson, Robert H., *Teaching in a World of Change*, N.Y.: Harcourt, Brace, and World, Inc., 1965.

Berger, Bennett M., *Working Class Suburb*, Berkeley and Los Angeles: University of California Press, 1960.

Bloom, Benjamin S., Allison Davis, and Robert Hess, *Compensatory*

Education for Cultural Deprivation, N.Y.: Holt, Rinehart, and Winston, Inc., 1965.

Clark, Burton, *Educating the Expert Society,* San Francisco: Chandler Publishing Company, 1962.

Clark, Kenneth B., *Dark Ghetto,* N.Y.: Harper and Row, 1965.

Dahl, John A., Marvin Laser, Robert S. Cathcart, and Fred H. Marcus, *Student, School, and Society,* San Francisco: Chandler Publishing Company, 1964.

Davis, Allison, *The Disadvantaged Child: A Program for Action,* Trenton, N.J.: New Jersey Education Association, 1964.

Dentler, Robert A., *et al.,* "The Educational Complex Study Project," *Integrated Education,* Vol. III, No. 3, June–July, 1965.

Eddy, Elizabeth M., *Walk the White Line,* Garden City, N.Y.: Anchor Books, Doubleday & Company, Inc., 1967.

Fuchs, Estelle, *Pickets at the Gates,* N.Y.: The Free Press, 1966.

Glazer, Nathan, and Daniel P. Moynihan, *Beyond the Melting Pot,* Cambridge: The Massachusetts Institute of Technology Press, 1963.

Halsey, A. H. (ed.), "Social Class and Linguistic Development: A Theory of Social Learning," *Education, Economy and Society,* N.Y.: Macmillan (Free Press of Glencoe), 1961.

Harrington, Michael, *The Other America,* Baltimore: Penguin Books, 1962.

Havighurst, Robert J., *Education in Metropolitan Areas,* Boston: Allyn and Bacon, Inc., 1966.

Hickerson, Nathaniel, *Education for Alienation,* Englewood Cliffs, N.J.: Prentice-Hall, Inc., 1966.

Holbrook, David, *English for the Rejected,* London and N.Y.: Cambridge University Press, 1964.

Humphrey, Hubert, *School Desegregation: Documents and Commentaries,* N.Y.: Thomas Y. Crowell, 1964.

Jackson, Brian, and Dennis Marsden, *Education and the Working Class,* London: Routledge and Kegan Paul, 1962.

Lewis, Oscar, *The Children of Sanchez,* N.Y.: Random House, 1961.

Lipton, Aaron, "Classroom Grouping and Integration," *Integrated Education,* Vol. II, No. 1, Feb.–March, 1964.

Mauch, James, "Education Park," *The American School Board Journal,* Vol. CL, No. 3, March, 1965.

Passow, A. Harry (ed.), *Education in Depressed Areas,* N.Y.: Bureau of Publications, Teachers College, Columbia University, 1963.

Pettigrew, Thomas F., *Profile of the Negro-American,* Princeton, N.J.: D. Van Nostrand Company, 1964.

Sexton, Patricia Cayo, *The American School: A Sociological Inquiry,* Englewood Cliffs, N.J.: Prentice-Hall, Inc., 1967.

————, *Education and Income: Inequalities in Our Public Schools,* N.Y.: The Viking Press, 1961.

————, *Spanish Harlem: Anatomy of Poverty,* N.Y.: Harper and Row, 1965.

Shuy, Roger (ed.), *Social Dialects and Language Learning,* Champaign, Ill.: National Council of the Teachers of English, 1965.

Silberman, Charles E., *Crisis in Black and White,* N.Y.: Vintage Books, 1964.

The Campus School, Syracuse, N.Y.: Campus Site Planning Center.

The White Plains Racial Balance Plan, White Plains, N.Y.: White Plains Public Schools, May 9, 1965.

part II

The

California Experience

3 | BERKELEY HIGH SCHOOLS INTEGRATE

DANIEL K. FREUDENTHAL
Coordinator of Research and Publications,
Berkeley Unified School District

Dr. Freudenthal is Coordinator of Research and Publications for the Berkeley Unified School District. He has served the district for nearly two decades and has, therefore, lived through the experiences he describes. His interest in the continuing problems of urban education remains both lively and sustained.

One of the most notorious efforts to circumvent the May, 1954, Supreme Court desegregation decision was the closing of the public schools in Prince Edward County, Virginia. Long after private schools were opened for white children, schools for Negro children were provided. The former superintendent of these latter schools, Neil V. Sullivan, is now Superintendent of Schools in Berkeley, California. The article that follows describes the adoption of an ingenious plan to desegregate the three junior high schools of Berkeley.

But the story is also a classic illustration of decision making in a community. Freudenthal's account may be focused by means of several

49

questions. What broad cultural values are operating? Are these peculiar to Berkeley, a college town, or are they representative of American towns? How do the various groups demonstrate their special interests—white and Negro parents, administrators, taxpayers, teachers, newspapers, businessmen? What are the institutional frameworks within which the decision making must occur? (All during the second war, a gaunt circular skeleton of steel stood beside the high school. It was the frame of a projected community theater big enough to seat thousands. It was finished and opened several years before the fight over the schools started, and provided an arena that could house all the warriors.) What was the role of the public officials? Superintendent Wennerberg certainly played a role different from that of his predecessors, and Superintendent Sullivan, in turn, was different again. What were the outcomes, and what was the effect upon the community?

It is too early to assess the result of sending all the ninth graders to the former Negro junior high school, and sending all the seventh and eighth graders to the other two, but the desegregation has been accomplished and the case study allows us to make some enlightened estimates. Under what conditions is desegregation accomplished easily, or with difficulty? What is the fit between the political situation and action, or inaction, on desegregation? What is the critical factor in a set of components? Is prediction possible?

Berkeley not only provides a safe and luxurious home for the chief campus of the state university; it also is a convenient social laboratory. The schools, the police force, the family, and all of Berkeley's institutions have been studied and re-studied. Social science rapidly reaches that point of uncertainty at which the scrutiny itself produces changes. This point was reached in Berkeley long before the desegregation moves began. The Berkeley story is colorful and interesting, but the special circumstances created by the presence of one of the world's best-known centers of learning should not be overlooked.

Otherwise the issue between those favoring retention of the neighborhood-school concept with an emphasis upon compensatory education and those in favor of desegregation seems reasonably typical. Perhaps the key sentence needed to understand the conflict between the proponents of neighborhood schools and those arguing for busing was offered by a professor of mathematics at one of the hearings: "It depends upon whose ox is being gored." Or can one afford a more idealistic view?

....

Racial segregation and discrimination are facts of life in Berkeley as in many communities and school systems, North and South. As

Hyman and Sheatsley pointed out in 1964, there is an increasing awareness throughout the land that racial discrimination in its various forms, from violent and virulent to soft and subtle, is indeed the chronic American dilemma.[1]

The facts are catching up with people everywhere. People in education are no exception even though many educators have preferred to disregard this major human problem of the century.[2,3]

Leaders in Berkeley, both lay and professional, were caught in the dilemma and recognized it earlier and less reluctantly than most. For six years, they had seen that there was *de facto* segregation in the schools and racial discrimination in the community, subtle in the form but segregation and discrimination nevertheless.

Between 1957–58 and 1963–64, measures were taken to improve the educational opportunities and facilities of all children. In the years immediately following, special programs were initiated for those children, primarily Negro, who had been neglected by the schools. Otherwise, they would remain second-class citizens of the community and the nation, as their parents and grandparents had been before them.

But during most of the period between 1957 and 1964, no direct action was taken to desegregate the Berkeley public schools. The historic United States Supreme Court decision of May 17, 1954, seemed not to apply.[4] However, by May, 1964, an educational leadership moved, under some pressure but without court litigation, to desegregate the junior high schools. (There was only one senior high school.) This desegregation was considered a prime condition for continued improvement in the education provided all children. It was undertaken also as an essential ingredient of that racial integration which in the long run would make Negroes and other minority groups a part of the educational mainstream of the schools and full participants in the economic, social, and cultural life of the community. The action to desegregate the junior high schools was received enthusiastically by an increasingly articulate and demanding citizenry of all races and social classes from every corner of the community. It was simultaneously met with a movement to recall the entire Board of Education—initiated by a polite, tightly organized group ostensibly in favor of "neighborhood schools" and of keeping everything "educational" in its place and everything "social" in its place. Underneath the facade of politeness and propriety lurked a fear and hostility reminiscent of the White Citizens' Councils of recent history and of the "know-nothingism" of the last century.

During the summer months of 1964, *recall* became the watchword of those Berkeley citizens who perhaps found desegregation in the South more palatable than a desegregation plan specific to their own city and involving their own children. Recall petitions were signed in sufficient quantity, and on October 6, a special election was held to vote on recalling and replacing the Board members who had concurred in the historic decision to desegregate.

The result was a resounding three-to-two victory for the incumbents, with solid support from every corner of the city. Here was a milestone for human relations in Berkeley, and a strong vote of confidence in the Board of Education and its professional advisors. One small community had given the practice of democracy a contemporary dimension. The price was courage of conviction, confidence, and organization by both educational leadership and supporting community. It was in an emerging tradition inaugurated in 1957.

A chronology of Berkeley's experience offers a significant lesson for educational leaders and their communities if it makes this single point: The fence is no longer a sitting place either appropriate or safe in educational or racial matters. Time is swiftly running out.

HISTORY AND CHANGE IN BERKELEY

Berkeley is a medium-sized and racially diverse city of 118,000.[5] Of a total of 15,700 in day-school enrollment, 8300 or 57 percent are white; 5800 or 37 percent are Negro. Most of the remaining 1300 or 6 percent are Oriental.[6,7]

This diversity is relatively new. A dramatic change in school enrollment reflected a change in the general population over the 25-year period from 1939–40 to 1963–64. During these years the total school enrollment was multiplied by about 1.4, while Negro school enrollment was multiplied by more than 12. The effect was to increase the ratio of Negro pupils from 4 percent to 37 percent of total enrollment. Table 1 tells the story.

The impact of war and cold war, with consequent job opportunity, had changed the population of Berkeley. The influx of immigrants, mostly Negro and often from the South, was part of the great national migration set off by World War II.

Berkeley is and has been a city of light industry and service trades, a bedroom city for San Francisco and a haven for retired

TABLE 1. GAINS IN NEGRO ENROLLMENT, BERKELEY
PUBLIC SCHOOLS, 1939 TO 1964

| | | Negro Enrollment | |
Year*	Total School Enrollment	No.	% of Total Enrollment
1939–40	11,013	471	4
1945–46	11,473	1,140	10
1947–48	11,476	1,466	13
1955–56	14,708	3,428	23
1958–59	15,375	4,420	29
1960–61	15,761	5,049	32
1963–64	15,690	5,805	37

* Enrollment figures taken as a visual tally by teachers in classrooms, reported March, 1964.

people, with one of the lowest ratios of school-age population to total population in the state. At the same time, it is and has been a university town, with a student population comprising 24 percent of the total population. The University of California has poured large payrolls and consumer demand into the city's economy but has provided little if any tax support for the public schools. Concurrently, it has demanded nothing but the best, educationally.

Berkeley, its population well educated and high in income by average standards, has never been able to attract sufficient industry to provide an adequate local tax base. It has long been noted as a community with a hard core "no" vote on any issue of public improvement, particularly as related to the public schools. Standpat organizations, ostensibly watchdogs of public morality and purse in city and schools, have arisen to oppose major changes in the status quo from fluoridation to fair employment and fair housing, and from school-bond and tax proposals to new reading methods.

Up to about 1960, the schools and the community had gone their separate ways, mutually indifferent to changing times and changing needs. A conservative Board of Education and an equally conservative educational leadership saw only a small, seemingly changeless city.

However, Berkeley was changing drastically.[8,9] The almost homogeneous white community of 1939 was by 1964 one of the most racially diverse cities in the West. It was a relatively privileged community in education and income. Nevertheless, the white advantages and Negro disadvantages at every point of community life paralleled those found in many northern cities. The quiet villagelike Berkeley—conservative, complacent, self-sufficient economically and ingrown culturally—was gone in fact if not in the minds of many Berkeleyans. It had been replaced by a racially mixed Berkeley with all of its strengths and problems. In the process, Berkeley had reached a crossroads in many aspects of community life. The impact of change was upon her.

The community's response to change was reluctant and uneven.[10,11] Segregated housing patterns persisted. Employment discrimination receded with something less than "deliberate speed." Needed community resources for mental health and for other social services, for recreation, and for urban renewal were as poorly provided as in most cities throughout the country. The emphasis seemed to be directed more toward property, esthetic, and administrative concerns than toward human values and toward improvement and financial support of school programs and facilities. The still dominant conservative leadership in city and schools was unready to meet the increasing demands of a racial minority, demands supported by growing numbers of the Caucasian majority, for a voice in its own destiny and its rightful place in life's mainstream.

THE INITIATIVE BY THE NAACP

On January 7, 1958, the Berkeley branch of the National Association for the Advancement of Colored People addressed the Berkeley Board of Education.[12] It pointed to the problem of racial separateness in the schools of an interracial but segregated community and asked, "What can we do to help?"

The Reverend Roy Nichols, the NAACP spokesman, was later to be the first Negro member of the Berkeley Board of Education and its first Negro president.

A reluctant Board, counseled by a reluctant superintendent of schools and staff, scheduled a long series of preliminary meetings between NAACP representatives and carefully selected, cautious members of the school staff, to consider the advisability of appointing a citizens' advisory committee to study "certain" racial problems in the public schools.

There was no restraining the NAACP, and six months later, on

June 10, 1958, sixteen citizens were named to a Board advisory committee under the chairmanship of a universally respected Municipal
Court judge, Redmond J. Staats, Jr.[13,14] This interracial committee
gathered information, with the help of a newly appointed Superintendent of Schools, C. H. Wennerberg, and eight school principals,
and sought solutions to the problems.[15] Mr. Wennerberg took office on
July 1; soon after the committee began its work.

THE RECOMMENDATIONS OF THE CITIZENS' ADVISORY
COMMITTEE AND THEIR IMPLICATIONS

On October 19, 1959, 21 months after the original NAACP inquiry, the Citizens' Advisory Committee reported to the Board on
"Interracial Problems and Their Effect on Education in the Public
Schools of Berkeley, California." The recommendations looked to a
new employment and placement policy which would culminate in an
interracial staff, enhanced educational opportunities for all children,
improved counseling services (especially for minority-group children), a curriculum reflecting the facts of American interracial life,
massive improvement in interracial relations and intercultural education through in-service and community training programs, and the
building of two-way communications between school staff and all of
the parents. The still reluctant Board adopted the recommendations of
the Citizens' Committee on the persistent recommendation of Superintendent Wennerberg.

Even before the report was published, implementation of its
recommendations had begun. The chronology of implementation[16,17,18]
was impressive despite the more than passive resistance of too many
staff members. For example:

1. The new fair-employment policy increased the number of non-Caucasian employees in all professional classifications by 64 percent.
2. Counseling practices were gradually refocused from the pessimistic
   perspective of "limited job opportunities" for Negro students toward the long view of "incentive" opening the door toward college
   and the professions to formerly discouraged students.
3. An intergroup-education project, involving one-fifth of the staff
   and, increasingly, members of the community, brought intergroup
   education and interracial relations into the classroom. It contin-

uously sought to introduce the facts of America's multiracial society into the total curriculum.

4. Annual community workshops on critical community issues in human relations, jointly sponsored by the schools and the Council of Social Planning, helped to educate citizens to the need for finding solutions to interracial problems in both schools and city.

5. A school-sponsored community effort offered teachers in all schools the best daily help of university students and adult volunteers in accordance with teacher desire and under teacher supervision.

6. Education was enriched and remedied as needed for disinherited children.

7. Education, generally, and all of its supporting services were continuously upgraded within the stringent limitations of financial ability.

In short, equal educational opportunity was given a new dimension, namely, compensation for disadvantage by means of comprehensive improvement and innovation in all educational programs and services. In addition, a more liberal policy of employing Negroes was combined with general upgrading of salaries and working conditions. All of this was inaugurated and pushed forward despite community divisions and staff differences. For, during this time, a new community-minded Board of Education backed the superintendent; and he stood firm. The hard core of resistance remained in community and staff, but except at times of tax or bond elections it was relatively quiescent. *De facto* segregation had not yet been recognized in Berkeley.

THE "PRESENTATION" OF CORE

On May 1, 1962, the Congress of Racial Equality made its *Presentation to the Berkeley Board of Education.*[19] It congratulated the Board on its "giant accomplishments" in implementing the recommendations of 1958. But its document showed that a study of Berkeley public-school day enrollments indicated the existence of identifiable *de facto* segregated schools. Eight had a Caucasian enrollment of 94 percent or more and two enrolled 94 percent or more non-Caucasian students. This distribution, it said, was "equally detrimental to the health and education of all children." Offering no pat solutions, CORE proposed a cooperative school-community study to ascertain the facts and make recommendations.

In accepting the report on May 1, 1962, and turning it over to the superintendent for study and recommendation, the Board stated that there obviously were racially segregated schools in Berkeley, largely due to the residential pattern of the community, and that this was educationally undesirable for students and community.[20] It pointed out that these undesirable conditions had long been recognized by both the Berkeley schools and the State Board of Education. It expressed a willingness to seek solutions.

On September 19, 1962, the Board accepted the superintendent's strong recommendation to appoint a broadly representative citizens' committee to define and study *de facto* segregation in the Berkeley public schools and to recommend ways in which it might be ameliorated or eliminated.[21] Eventually 36 citizens were enlisted in this committee. In the Superintendent's view and the Board's view, this was no new venture but a reiteration of years of work to enrich and improve educational opportunities, a redoubling of an already significant effort to improve human relations and education in an interracial community.

THE HADSELL REPORT ON *DE FACTO* SEGREGATION

For more than a year, under the chairmanship of Dr. John Hadsell, a Berkeley minister, the committee to study *de facto* segregation searched for the facts. On November 19, 1963, it offered its report and recommendations to the Board of Education before an overflow audience of 1200 citizens.[22,23,24] Just before the Hadsell committee reported, Superintendent C. H. Wennerberg, the educational leader most responsible for Berkeley's pioneer role in finding solutions to interracial problems, resigned as of June 30, 1964, to continue advanced graduate study.[25]

The Hadsell committee began with the recommendations of its predecessor of 1958, urging an intensification of effort to obtain and maintain a superior and racially balanced staff with which to upgrade teaching, counseling, guidance, and remedial services. It placed special emphasis on summer-school expansion on a racially integrated basis to meet both the enrichment and remedial needs of all who wanted these extra opportunities. It urged a comprehensive compensatory-education program from prekindergarten through the adult years and involving every school and every community resource. It coun-

seled renewed emphasis on intergroup education for the entire staff. It
suggested a community-wide Human Relations Commission to coordinate efforts in the interrelated areas of education, employment, housing, social welfare, and recreation. It pressed for continued educational upgrading up and down the line.

The Hadsell committee saw a tendency toward segregation
within even integrated schools as a by-product of a rigid system of
ability grouping and tracking. It recommended specific remedies in
the seventh grade, whereby students from feeder elementary schools
would be placed primarily in accordance with the recommendations
of their sixth-grade teachers rather than their seventh-grade counselors. It suggested a four-band ability-grouping system in junior high
school to ease the transition between groups and to facilitate opportunity within each group on the basis of student performance.

The committee came squarely to grips with the twin problems of
school desegregation and racial integration when it proposed partial
relocation of both elementary- and junior-high-school boundaries sup-
plemented in each instance by voluntary and limited open enrollment.
For the committee realized that schools had been built and enrollment
boundaries drawn as neighborhoods developed. Available school plant
and traffic safety had been the chief considerations. There had been
no attempt to correct for racial housing patterns.

This first Berkeley proposal in the interest of school integration
represented only a bare minimum on which a large majority of the
committee could agree. Yet for the first time, compensatory education
and school desegregation were treated as inseparable ingredients of a
racial integration essential to lasting improvement in the educational
opportunities for all children.

The public meeting at which the Hadsell study committee on *de
facto* segregation reported took on the nature of a public hearing.
Questions were raised ostensibly to clarify the facts. There was general acceptance of compensatory education as long as it was treated as
something separate and apart from school desegregation. Again, as
during the earlier days in 1958 and during the almost successful 1962
campaign for a city fair-housing ordinance, the divided community
articulated its differences with a clear and ominous mutual hostility as
the issue was joined and action to desegregate seemed imminent. The
need for a second public hearing was clearly indicated.

The second public hearing[26,27] was held on January 22, 1964, before 2500 people. More than fifty speakers from community-minded organizations spoke in solid support of the Hadsell committee's recommendations. In opposition, Citizens United, a tax-protest group of long standing and its embryonic offspring, Parents Association for Neighborhood Schools, spearheaded resistance to any boundary change which might upset the "neighborhood school" or the traditional grading and tracking system. They also took particular umbrage against the committee's general proposal that the schools become "color-conscious." Parent-teacher associations divided in their support somewhat, but not entirely, along racial lines.

Even the committee's supporters agreed that the weak spot in the report was the provision for redistricting, which envisaged large-scale changes in district boundaries and massive administrative machinery without significant effect on school racial imbalance.

A NEW PLAN FOR JUNIOR-HIGH-SCHOOL DESEGREGATION

During the interim between the unveiling of the Hadsell committee's report in November and the second public hearing in January, Miss Marjorie Ramsey, a junior-high-school English teacher, proposed, with the help of interested citizens and colleagues, a junior-high-school reorganization plan.[28] Inspired by the Princeton plan, the Ramsey proposal would desegregate Berkeley's three junior high schools by requiring all children in grades seven and eight to attend two of the junior high schools. All children in grade nine would attend the third school, which then would become an integral administrative part of the present senior high school. Thereby the senior high school would be transformed into a four-year high school, located on two campuses. The result would be integrated secondary schools throughout Berkeley.

At Superintendent Wennerberg's strong suggestion, the Board turned the Hadsell committee's proposals and the Ramsey alternative over to him for general staff study and reaction, with a report and recommendations due within two months. The superintendent, in turn, appointed a committee of five to "consult with the staff."[29,30,31]

An intensive six-week study culminated in staff consensus, the superintendent's strong recommendation, and Board approval of a staff task-force implementation study of the educational and financial feasibility of (1) the Ramsey junior-high-school reorganization plan;

(2) the Hadsell committee's proposal for elementary-school desegregation and possible alternative plans; (3) the proposals for compensatory education; (4) all other committee proposals.[32-39]

On May 19, 1964, Superintendent Wennerberg presented the task-force report in a public Board meeting before several thousand Berkeley citizens. He recommended adoption of the major Hadsell committee recommendations except those concerned with redistricting. As an alternative to the committee's redistricting proposals, he recommended that the large and predominantly Negro schools henceforth would house grades four to six while the smaller and predominantly white schools would house grades kindergarten to three. Here was another application of the Princeton idea.

He recommended a two-step implementation of the junior-high-school reorganization plan, the first step effective in the fall of 1964, whereby the single integrated junior high school would remain intact; children in grades seven and eight living in the rest of Berkeley would attend what had been the predominantly white junior high school; students in grade nine would attend the campus of the high school located at what had been the predominantly Negro junior high school. He also recommended the adoption of the flexible four-track ability-grouping system in all junior high schools and the earmarking of $200,000 in the 1964–65 budget as a compensatory-education fund to be specifically allocated as comprehensive plans were developed.

The Board unanimously approved all but one of the superintendent's recommendations. It indefinitely tabled the elementary-school redistricting proposal on the ground of unfeasibility.

THE RECALL MOVEMENT AND ITS DEFEAT[40-43]

The unambiguous Board decision on the superintendent's recommendation meant that immediate steps would be taken to desegregate the junior high schools. (The vote was 4 to 0; one member had resigned before the moment of decision.)

The enthusiasm of supporting organizations and individuals was matched by sharp opposition from the Parents Association for Neighborhood Schools (PANS), which had been organizing during the weeks after the Citizens' Committee's first report. Almost immediately, with the full cooperation and encouragement of Berkeley's sole newspaper, this new civic organization launched an effort to recall the entire four-member Board of Education. Among its supporters were the Retired Teachers Association, some University of California professors, some tax protesters, some parents unhappy with their children's progress in school, and some proponents of liberal causes who evidently found integration in the South more comfortable than integration of their own children in their own home town. These standpatters of many persuasions pooled their resources in what seemed, in the eyes of the Board's supporters, to take on the dimensions of a "holy crusade."

Almost immediately, the Berkeley Friends of Better Schools (The Friends) emerged to support the whole program to upgrade the schools and the total effort to combat *de facto* segregation.[44,45,46] It had representation throughout the community, among all races and national groups. Its chairman was a renowned university professor, and its cochairman a housewife and NAACP leader who had served on both the Board of Education's Citizens' Committee to Study *De Facto* Segregation and the City Welfare Commission's Advisory Committee on Fair Housing.

The issue was joined in a hurry.[47-51] Petitions for recall were on the streets by early June, the aim being to achieve the required 9000 signatures in time to schedule an election during the summer vacation while supporters of the Board among parents, university students, and university faculty were out of town. This timing would insure victory by default. The mayor of Berkeley interceded with a plan to take an immediate and unofficial straw vote on the junior-high-school desegregation plan as a substitute for recall, suggesting that the Board abide by this straw vote. His plan was acceptable to no one but the "recallers."

PANS failed in its first objective.[52-55] Its solicitors did not obtain sufficient signatures for a recall election until late July. The Friends immediately challenged the legality of the attempted recall in the courts, on the constitutional ground that there was a conflict between the city charter and the state's government code provisions. On the strength of this protest, the City Council by close vote refused to set an election date, pending a court decision. When the California Court of Appeals held that PANS was within its legal rights, the City Council scheduled the special recall election for October 6, 1964. The angry Parents Association for Neighborhood Schools had been delayed two full months in its plans to throw the Board out of office. It was unsuccessful in catching the community by surprise and winning its point during the quiet summer months.

Things happened during the interim.[56] Reverend Roy Nichols, chairman of the Board, resigned to take a pulpit in New York City and was replaced. A second member resigned to accept appointment as a judge but was not replaced. Consequently, what had been a recall of all members had become a recall of the two remaining members of the original four-member Board which had made the controversial decision.

PANS ran its own candidates against the incumbents.[57,58] A lawyer and president of PANS, proponent of the "neighborhood school" and opponent of "social experimentation with our children," opposed the new president of the Board, Mrs. Carol R. Sibley, a long-time and widely respected civic leader. A recently retired school employee for 40 years, a long-time principal and champion of the predominantly white junior high school and a proponent of the discarded ability-grouping and tracking system, opposed Sherman J. Maisel, a professor of business administration at the University of California.

An intensive door-to-door campaign was carried on for several months. There was widespread newspaper, television, and radio coverage.[59,60,61] Berkeley had again become a battle ground between those who sought the future educationally and interracially and those who would stand pat, come what may, saw nothing wrong with separate education as long as it was equal, and who rejected "social experimentation" as something "foreign to our way of life."

On July 1, in the midst of the recall campaign, Dr. Neil V. Sullivan took office as superintendent of schools.[62-67] He was fresh from a pioneering experience as the picked head of the "Free Schools" of Prince Edward County, Virginia, which had made compensatory-education history in a hostile southern community. The new superintendent brought with him long experience in suburban New York and in New Hampshire communities. He immediately spelled out his aim to make Berkeley education "worthy of imitation." His presence in Berkeley was met with great enthusiasm by supporters of the Board of Education but with somewhat less enthusiasm by the opposition.

On October 6, 57 percent of the voters of Berkeley went to the polls, a good turnout for a special election. They voted three to two to retain the incumbents in office. This was a solid reiteration of confidence in the Board, the new superintendent who promised to consolidate the gains of desegregation, and the former superintendent who had opened the door to change.[68][72] A majority of the voters had set the direction of Berkeley public education toward racial integration through desegregation in combination with comprehensive compensatory education. The final goal was excellence in total education, worthy of wide emulation. This was the culmination of six years of controversy. There could be no going back to "separate but equal."

NOT THE END

The community remained divided on one of the critical educational and social issues of the time. Though power was shifting, neither the majority nor the educational leadership could afford to disregard the persistent minority. Integrationist Board members continued to hold office from 1964 through 1967 but only against strong opposition by the disappointed PANS group and its allies.

Again Berkeley is on the move, as this book goes to press, and must complete total desegregation of every elementary school and classroom by September, 1968. This was the unanimous Board commitment of April 18, 1967.

While a staff task group was beginning a leisurely, federally funded study of *Integrated Quality Education: A Study of Educational Parks and Other Alternatives for Urban Areas,* groups of citizens joined both the teachers' union and the educators' association to demand immediate, complete desegregation of all the schools within the framework of quality education. The demand was clear: that after a year of planning, and community, student, and staff interchange on the issues and needed programs, desegregation would be completed on the first day of school in September, 1968. Task groups have completed preliminary reports to which public and staff have responded critically.

Superintendent Sullivan has recommended a "preferred Berkeley Plan" reflecting various responses and suggestions. That plan involves four strips, running east and west across Berkeley. All K–3 children in each strip would be divided among the small previously segregated white schools in the hills and the desegregated foothill schools; while all children in grades 4–6 would attend a single, large, previously

segregated Negro school in southwest Berkeley. Half the elementary
school student body would be transported. Most of the younger Negro
children would be transported. Most of the older white children
would be transported. Here could be a matter of real concern to many
members of the Negro community on the ground of unequal treatment. In any case, "Civil Rights" issues may be receding before the
realities of "Black Power." Transportation of white children from their
"protected" neighborhoods also could pose a critical community issue.
Present quiet might well be a prelude to polarization and "storm."

This is the plan which was tabled by the Board of Education on
May 19, 1964. The debate may begin again where it was left off four
years earlier. A Board decision is scheduled for February, 1968. Berkeley could make history once more. Not the end but a new and more
human beginning is in sight.

4

NO NEED TO KNOCK:
THE GARFIELD JUNIOR
HIGH SCHOOL EXPERIENCE

FRANCIS TEMPLETON GALBRAITH

Assistant Professor of Secondary Education,
San Francisco State College

Dr. Galbraith, Assistant Professor of Education at San Francisco State College, took the Ed.D. degree from the Berkeley campus of the University of California in 1966. He taught English at Garfield Junior High School when it was a *de facto* segregated school, a school for middle- and upper-class residents of Berkeley, including more than a sprinkling of the children of professors. He taught in Italy for a year and returned to find the ninth graders gone from Garfield and the seventh and eighth graders about equally divided between whites and Negroes.

In the preceding article, steps leading to the decision to integrate Garfield Junior High have been described. Here, Professor Galbraith describes vividly the feelings of an earnest teacher confronted with the American dilemma. Before integration, Garfield was a good prep school, with all the advantages of the homogeneously first rate. But it was also self-satisfied, and its students grew up nearly ignorant of the "social dynamite" stockpiling in their town.

Academic learning at Garfield is not what it was. It may become so again as teachers and pupils gain experience. But opportunity to learn has, for a large section of the Berkeley population, greatly improved. Galbraith believes that the gain in educational opportunity cannot be held under local control. He sees white families much more free to move than the Negroes. He issues a call for regional and even state control so that the spreading pattern of white suburban schools and Negro city schools can be permanently disrupted.

．．．

After years of teaching in an all-white junior high school, I had taken a leave and spent a year abroad. Upon returning, I discovered that my school had been integrated. Two of the three junior high schools in Berkeley had for years enrolled a substantial number of Negro children. My school, Garfield, had very few. For years, circumstances, of which the most important was the housing pattern, had caused this segregation.[1] As there is only one high school, there was no imbalance there.

The decision to change the racial percentage at Garfield Junior High stemmed from deliberation by the community dating back to 1958–59, when the first study of *de facto* segregation was issued.[2] This was followed by another formal report in 1963.[3] The reports recommended that *de facto* segregation be ended in the schools and that certain steps, both in curricula and in counseling, be taken to help Negro students in their school work. The Board of Education acted in May, 1964, adopting a plan to accomplish these objectives in the junior high schools. Although a staff report recommended that all the schools be desegregated, the School Board deferred action on the elementary schools to the indefinite future.[4]

THE OLD SCHOOL

So much change is taking place, some of it rather unpleasant, that I tend to favor those people and those institutions which survive the onslaught of the modern world. So it was that I came to love the old Garfield, its quaint individuality, the stories of its old teachers and their eccentric or whimsical ways, the fixed Victorianism of its earliest principal, the conservatism of its last principal prior to his retirement in 1964.

The length of Garfield's existence, practically unchanged by modern standards, was roughly 56 years—from about 1908, when it was created as an intermediate school, to 1964. This is a long period by our accelerated sense of time, yet the length of existence is not the sole element which made me love our school; rather it was a combination of factors—perhaps the stubborn individuality of its institutions, the "advisory" in place of the "homeroom" of other schools, the forty-minute period when almost all other junior high schools had fifty to sixty minutes, the nine-period day, the professional character of its choral music, its superb band and orchestra, the group of veteran teachers, some whose tenure went back forty years, and the loyal graduates, bound by ties of class and education to the neighborhood of the north Berkeley Hills. Students were highly motivated, as we have come to say of the modern student; many came from homes of extraordinary cultural opportunity. The Hills of Berkeley have a happy concentration of well-educated people due to the proximity of the Berkeley campus of the University of California. Unusual students, a relatively stable faculty, and a succession of conservative principals produced an ordered and well-adapted curriculum. A stable social order and a highly educated group of parents fixed the character of the school. "The one fixed point in a changing age," to borrow Sherlock Holmes's description of his friend Dr. Watson, describes the old Garfield.

Fixed points or orders in an institution so close to community life are possible only in an unchanging world. But the world had changed and the school had to change. The bricks and mortar remained the same, the outward manifestations still unchanged, but in the fall of 1964 the students who thronged Garfield's halls brought a profound change, a new challenge—a fully integrated student body, to be taught and to learn to participate together so that they would be prepared to do so as adults.

THE NEW SCHOOL

The decision of the Berkeley Board of Education was almost unique. The Board did not wait for the *de facto* segregation problem to force them to act, but boldly took the initiative to end all racial imbalance in the secondary schools. To achieve this, one of the junior high schools became a part of the high school. All the ninth-grade students in the district were eventually to attend it. The other two junior highs were to have the seventh and eighth grades with attendance boundaries reflecting the racial balance of the community as a whole.[5] Measures were taken to avoid segregation of minority children within the school, and efforts were made to provide teachers with some knowledge of minority life and culture.[6]

There was little time between the Board decision in May, 1964, and the opening of school in September. Thus approximately half the staff and many of the counselors and administrators were new either to the school or to their jobs. Since the new "West Campus," formerly Burbank Junior High, had not been adapted to house all the ninth-grade students, one of the other junior high schools, Willard, had to remain a three-year school for an additional two years. This delay meant that Garfield had an additional burden of approximately 200 students.

These factors and the "new students," largely Negro children from the lower-income classes, made the halls more crowded and much noisier. My general impression was that there was much more clamor and that the behavior was poorer. There was more running and shouting both in the halls and to some extent in the classrooms.

Classroom organization had been drastically changed with the objective of lessening the isolation of the Negro children. Formerly, at Garfield, we had grouped the seventh and eighth grades in as many as sixteen classes by test scores and teachers' recommendations. Those at the high end of the scale were the so-called gifted groups designated "X." In the last years of the old school all students were called "X" if their I.Q. were above 130 and if their reading scores were advanced three grade levels. Students below the "X" groups were designated "Y" and arranged in a descending order, the level of highest ability being "Y^1," the next "Y^2," and so forth. This scheme was abolished by the Board, and four levels were substituted. As a concession to the old system, some honors classes were allowed for the so-called gifted children.[7]

In the new system I found myself with five classes—the eighth-grade English honors class, an eighth-grade English class at the first level, and three seventh-grade third-level classes. Both eighth-grade classes reminded me of former ones—middle-class youngsters with a high degree of motivation who read well, wrote well, and could discuss and understand issues, principles, and concepts with a high degree of sophistication. Problems of discipline, beyond a certain minimum necessary between a teacher and his students meeting for the first time, did not exist. Communication was easy and comfortable. The students arrived at class on time, accepted my leadership and standards, brought their books, and eagerly participated in all the class events: discussions, oral reports, written work, and language lessons. There were problems, of course, but of an order I had faced many times before and could solve on the basis of my former experiences.

A brief digression concerning the grouping process throws light on the problems I was to face in the seventh-grade third-level classes. When students were divided into four groups by achievement, I.Q. scores, and teachers' recommendations, the purpose was to insure a somewhat equitable distribution of Negro students in each class. In actuality, Negro students represented roughly 10 percent in my eighth-grade classes and nearly 50 percent in the seventh-grade classes. Tracking in my experience seems to distribute the Negro children more heavily on the lower end of the achievement scale.[8]

In my seventh-grade classes, I found that few of my expectations were fulfilled; there were problems of class management which took valuable time—tardiness, missing books, and undone homework. There was in each class a brief, dramatic struggle against my imposition of general rules—rules against making loud noises, against eating in class, against interrupting speakers. This was an important struggle for me because it was a new one. I had never before faced defiance from children in the classroom. Gross misbehaviors were quickly eliminated, and the struggle for mastery on my part became the struggle for a change in the basic behavior of the underprivileged children.

Day-to-day classroom activities continued to reveal to me other problems which helped to explain the initial reaction of the seventh graders. Spelling lessons illustrate this. It is my custom to use the state seventh-grade speller.[9] Each list of words is accompanied by a series of short exercises designed to illustrate the particular principles of spelling for the lesson and to fix the meanings of the words by using them in fill-in exercises. The students take a pre-test on Wednesday and a final test on Friday for a grade.

The first test I gave showed some mistakes which persisted throughout the semester. The poor students misspelled many simple words; their written lessons were not done; and they failed to identify correctly some simple words. Many spelling mistakes were failures to add endings. The word "worked" would be spelled "work," the word "taken" spelled "take," and so on. Some children could not supply simple definitions in either a matching exercise or a multiple-choice question. I came to recognize that the spoken language of these students lacked the inflected forms of some words and that many common words listed in the state speller were not in these students' vocabulary. This lack of vocabulary extended to reading, where there was difficulty with many words normal to the vocabulary of the middle-class students. In addition to having these problems of unfamiliarity, many of these children could not break words into syllables or pronounce them without my aid.

Several months of work with these students taught me a pattern which seems to be successful. They show a general reluctance to commit themselves to certain kinds of class work. If the work involves oral reading, answering simple questions, or doing simple grammar lessons, they participate willingly; but once the work becomes written and silent, they seem less happy. Then the obstacles are great, and they are restless. The more oral recitation, the more positive are their motivations; the more individual the work, that is, the more they must pursue the work by themselves without positive oral reinforcers, the more negative their motivations. But mere techniques will never overcome their reluctance. Once I began to understand them, the children improved enormously in their behavior.

STAFF REACTIONS

To those teachers who had taught in the school for many years, the decision to integrate was not a popular one. For a variety of reasons mainly prudential, they maintained a public silence, but privately some of them expressed their unhappiness among our group. The unhappiness was not an expression of racial prejudice, but of self-interest. After all, the comfortable middle-class atmosphere of the school they knew would be disrupted, and they would be forced to deal with problems that they would rather not face. At first they expected that the school would be transformed into a sort of slum school where violence and threats of violence were commonplace. A large part of the first reactions was simply fear of the unknown future.

When school had begun and been in progress a month or so, there was a change in staff attitudes, at least in the old staff. The dominant problem was discipline. Experienced teachers were still angry at the Board of Education's decision, but their immediate problems of integration came to dominate their conversations. They were concerned with the role of the administrators and the counselors in backing up the classroom teachers who were trying to impose order in the classroom. The anger of the teachers shifted—away from the rather shadowy group responsible for what they called the "betrayal" of the old school, toward the nonteaching staff now blamed for "poor planning and support of the teachers." This period of teacher-pupil relations might be called the period of initial adjustment, when middle-class teachers tried to find a way of operating from period to period with children who exhibited behavior that these teachers had never faced before. The classrooms became scenes of a grim struggle to find a new order.

The struggle of the teachers created a new feeling of solidarity and sense of purpose similar to a wartime alliance of nations. Differences of opinion and interest were suppressed in the face of the large and pressing tasks which faced us. There was a great deal of activity —one group of teachers formed, quite spontaneously, a discipline committee and presented a program at a faculty meeting which was instructive and helpful. Several teachers with extensive experiences in slum schools gave informal talks concerning ways of constructively dealing with common classroom problems. Meanwhile, the two school deans slowly brought the most disruptive children to task and there was a general improvement in behavior.

The improvement was limited, however, and teachers knew the old school was gone. The improvement was the result of several factors: the worst offenders were suspended; the lesser culprits were crowding the detention hall after school; most of the improvement came from the teachers who individually adjusted their methods to more reasonable ends. Thus the initial period of adjustment ended and a period of relative progress commenced.

SUCCESS AND FAILURE

As the aim of ending Garfield's nearly all-white student body was to lessen racial prejudice in the community and more particularly in the children, one might ask, "Has the effort succeeded?" Sometimes the answer is *yes* and sometimes *no,* depending on the aspect of the question one is thinking about. First, it was too early after one school year to give a final answer. Second, some progress was made just from the presence of Negro children in the same building and in the same classrooms as white children. Physical proximity affects racial stereotypes that depend on the isolation of the races. This effect works in both directions from one social and racial group to another—there is a socialization which produces a new social behavior and new attitudes.

New attitudes, however, grow slowly, and I could see a slow change in the composition of the student groups. Here and there in the cafeteria, in the halls, and in the classrooms, I observed the beginning of the end of color-consciousness. In the cafeteria, four girls eat lunch, a Negro seventh grader and three white friends. In the classroom, a Negro boy jokes with his new friend, a white child from the Berkeley Hills. There is no sudden reversal of behavior, but there is at least the opportunity for some changes—the first fruits of the Berkeley Board's policy.

There are also negative answers to the question. The Negro children on the whole are not as skilled as their counterparts.* If intelligence testing is a true measure, it is closely related to verbal behavior. This type of behavior is poorly developed among the poorer Negro children, at least by middle-class standards. But this is not generally known to the other racial groups. Do they look down at the Negro child's verbal behavior and find their stereotype reinforced? Here I must rely on my experiences both in the school and in the class culture in which I live. I believe that racial prejudice, like class prejudice or political biases, follows the lead of the parents. Where there is racial prejudice in the home, the children will find the behavior of the Negroes to be evidence of inferiority. I believe that most children are not concerned (at least consciously) about the problem at all.

But prejudice in such a highly sophisticated community as Berkeley is extremely subtle. Some parents are moving out of the city to the suburbs. Some have moved their children into private schools since the Ramsey plan was adopted. This movement is not publicized—I have neither seen nor heard of any public mention or comment about this movement. Whether the percentage of Negro children

---

* I believe that generally the Negro children in my classes improved in the first year. The differences in my third-level classes lessened with respect to classroom performance.

is rising, I have no personal knowledge. If it is, perhaps the tragedy of Manhattan Island and the South Side of Chicago is being duplicated in Berkeley.

Are the Berkeley schools to be all-Negro and so defeat the far-sighted policies of the school board? Perhaps the answer to this question lies in the irony of local control. For in the same manner that it erects obstacles against effective school administration, against adequate tax support and professional teacher organizations, local control makes local solutions to ending racial segregation difficult if not impossible. The Berkeley plan is inadequate because it affects only Berkeley—its dimensions are too narrow. The problem of integration and segregation is more than a local community problem; it is a regional and state problem.

In spite of its limitations, none of which is the fault of the community, the Ramsey plan has provided some valuable insights for one teacher. I have been educated in a way I find valuable both in a professional sense and in a personal sense. I discovered that educational differences are largely objective; they arise from cultural and economic factors. The Negro child must find in the schools the means to overcome the poverty of his home. I discovered also that teachers could respond in positive ways to challenges arising from a policy many of them resented, challenges which forced them into closer and more productive collaboration. I discovered that there is a possible self-limiting factor working against our efforts to integrate the Berkeley schools because one race has an option to move away while another does not. The integration of individual school districts is no permanent solution. Integration must be done over an entire area so that there is less opportunity to thwart local community action.

5 | BERKELEY EPILOGUE

THOMAS H. PARKER

Vice-Principal, Garfield Junior High School

Mr. Parker, Vice-Principal of Garfield Junior High, has carried much of the responsibility for implementing the policy changes described by Dr. Freudenthal and Dr. Galbraith. His epilogue brings events to the opening of the 1967–1968 school year.

Garfield Junior High had major problems—including high staff turn-over and considerable student misconduct—during the first three years after it was desegregated. But turn-over has ceased to be a problem; student conduct has improved; and experiments in heterogeneous grouping are going forward.

■■■■■■■■■■■■■■■■■■■■■■■■■■■■■■■■■■■■■■

After three years of desegregation our school is emerging as a working laboratory in education and human relations. During the course of these three years many significant changes have occurred, among them:

1. A drastic change in student-body racial composition (from 90% Caucasian, 4% Negro, and 6% Oriental to 52% Caucasian, 38% Negro, and 10% Oriental).
2. A change in administration.
3. A 30% increase and a 50% turn-over in staff.
4. A change from 17 ability tracks to 4 ability groups.

These changes have not occurred easily—the first year was especially difficult, but each of the following two years has seen a significant improvement. The most dramatic examples of this improvement are improved student conduct and reduced teacher turn-over. There are fewer thefts, fights, and other incidents of misconduct, and rarely is race a factor in such incidents. Staff turn-over has—for all practical purposes—been eliminated. In the summer of 1967 we are losing only four persons out of a staff of 92 teachers and counselors.

Two major problems, however, remain at our school:

1. Ability grouping for instruction—which results in almost totally Negro classes in the bottom ability groups.
2. Student misconduct—which handicaps the learning process.

Of course, these concerns are not unique to our school—they exist to a greater or lesser extent in many schools. However, there is enough concern about these matters to cause serious discussions among the faculty. We are attempting to develop realistic, experimental heterogeneous classes for 1967–1968 and to involve both students and teachers in the development of a constructive student "Code of Conduct."

The case before our school was summed up in our last faculty meeting by one of our veteran teachers: "When I came to our school thirteen years ago, there was no question about the fact that our school saw academic excellence as its dominant value goal. Now, however, after the past three years I am sure that there is another value which is—in my book today—even more important—I mean human values. We must have both—we must find out how to have both."

This statement, a direct quotation, indicates what to me is our school's greatest strength—dissatisfaction with itself. It is this feeling which has produced: (1) retreats and meetings for our students so they can discuss problems from their perspectives; (2) exciting debates among faculty members about the philosophy and purposes of education; (3) experiments in heterogeneous grouping—two classes this year—24 next year; (4) overwhelming faculty support for a proposal which adds ten minutes to the school day for next year and gives us a more flexible program.

Everything we try does not and will not always work—we know this. However, we also know we must be looking for something better, that we must proceed from a desegregated school to a truly integrated school. The challenge is what makes our school a good place to work.

6

DECISION MAKING IN THE SACRAMENTO De Facto SEGREGATION CRISIS

EDWARD B. FORT

Superintendent of Schools, Inkster, Michigan

Edward B. Fort, who holds the Doctor of Education degree from the Berkeley campus of the University of California, is Superintendent of the Inkster Public Schools, a suburban district fifteen miles west of Detroit. Formerly he was Curriculum Administrator, Division for Improvement of Instruction, Detroit Public Schools. He has served as lecturer in school administration at the University of Michigan. Immediately prior to taking his doctorate he was principal of an elementary school in California.

The facts presented here are based primarily upon those in his unpublished doctoral dissertation, which was the prototype of the present collection of readings, as it was the inspiration for their publication.

Dr. Fort's case study of Sacramento's confrontation with *de facto* segregation in its public schools documents the series of events following a fire of incendiary origin that destroyed almost completely the

Stanford Junior High School. These events culminated in the publication by the Board of Education of a report by a Citizens' Advisory Committee on Equal Educational Opportunity. The Committee consisted of ten Caucasians, two Negroes, one Chinese, one Japanese, and one Mexican-American. On the basis of an impressive array of factual information, and guided by the definition of a segregated school as one with forty percent or more of its students from ethnic minorities, the Committee made seven recommendations. The political activity that preceded the appointment of the special committee illustrates, in a number of ways, the usefulness of the theoretical model provided in the introductory chapter. The recommendations themselves can be examined to see whether, assuming they are all implemented, they can be expected to improve the educational opportunities of Negroes living in Sacramento.

Certainly American commitment to free public education is clearly discernible, especially in Committee Recommendations 5 and 6, although the very need to make the recommendations derives from ambiguous values about race. To some Americans the Negro is inferior. Hence, when he moves from the agricultural South to a northern industrial city, he will first settle in temporary housing, then move to the heavily populated and less desirable blocks of more permanent dwellings. Narrow special interest tends to keep him there. With his ascribed inferiority he must not be permitted to contaminate the more desirable, and expensive, residential districts. No matter which of the highly correlating determinants of social class are cited—occupation, income, or education of father—the Negro, because of his race, is at a disadvantage.

Dr. Fort provides us with numerous glimpses of the institutional and legal framework. Elected members of the School Board are key figures in the unfolding drama. State Senator Albert S. Rodda writes letters to illustrate the semi-detached concern of state government. The NAACP initiates action in the courts. The institutionalized character of the public school is itself seen to be a barrier to integration. Buildings and teachers sometimes prove difficult to move.

Key figures are identified as they play significant roles. In the district office Dr. Donald Hall is an official charged with specific responsibility for desegregation. In the State Department of Education, Dr. Wilson Riles is assigned a similar task. These and other officials behave to some extent in anticipated ways, but the touches that Dr. Fort provides of the character and personality of the men beneath the official cloaks are worth watching for.

Children may have set fire to the school, or the arsonists may have been adults. Either way, the attention of the community was directed forcibly to de facto segregation. The action, if deliberate, was extreme, and demonstrates ignorance of less violent political recourse. Later in Dr. Fort's description reference is made to groups that make it their responsibility to support civil liberties and fair-housing laws, such as the Sacramento Council of Democratic Clubs. By seeking aid from such organizations the Negro leaders can augment their own weak political power, provided their high interest in the need for reform is sufficiently contagious. The part played by the newspapers is worth careful consideration.

The Sacramento story is a useful illustration of the way in which community conflict that began with violence was directed toward a rational confrontation, making enlightened use of acceptable political behavior.

■■

THE INCEPTION OF THE DE FACTO SEGREGATION CRISIS

During the early morning hours of Saturday, August 17th, a fire of incendiary origin broke out in the Stanford Junior High School. One hundred and sixty firemen battled the fire for a period of several hours and at one point it appeared that they would be able to contain the blaze in the shop wing and the gymnasium. However, the flames spread to the main part of the building and, in a matter of a few hours the building was reduced to a shell. Except for the cafeteria and five portable classrooms, the plant was destroyed completely.—*Board of Education Minutes*[1]

The incendiary destruction of this school building in August, 1963, was the first in a series of events which led, eventually, to the city's direct confrontation with *de facto* segregation[2] in its public schools. These events came to a head in October of that same year, when the Superior Court of Sacramento ordered the school district to take whatever steps were necessary to desegregate its junior high schools.

The Stanford Junior High School was completely gutted by the fire. School Superintendent Lawson's immediate concern was for the housing needs of the Stanford students who had already been programed for the fall semester. Costs to the District would be a matter for later discussion, though the Stanford plant was insured on a replacement basis for $1,419,116—less 5.3 percent for noninsurable property.[3] Two days after the fire, when the Board of Education met in emergency session, the superintendent was to find that he could not concentrate on student-housing needs alone. The smoldering issue of school attendance boundaries in relation to residential housing patterns—that is, of the schools' responsibility for desegregation—would burst into flame.

SACRAMENTO'S POPULATION TRENDS AND THEIR EFFECT ON THE SCHOOLS

Population Growth 1950–1960

Prior to any consideration of these events as they unfolded, some understanding of population trends in the city of Sacramento is necessary. Sacramento, a city of 191,667 in 1960, is located approximately eighty miles northeast of San Francisco and is the capital of the state of California. The site is relatively flat. Sacramento has attracted a multiracial population because of its peculiar political significance, its mild climate, and its growing economy. Included in this heterogeneous complex are several large groups of ethnic minorities: Negroes, Chinese, Japanese, Mexican-Americans, and Filipinos. It becomes apparent that Sacramento has fewer Negroes per thousand population than some other larger western cities. Interestingly enough, however, United States census figures suggest that the Negro population in Sacramento is increasing at a faster rate than that of the city's Caucasian majority.

According to population research by sociologist Leonard Cain, of the city's total population of 137,572 in 1950, Caucasians comprised 92.2 percent and numbered 126,889; Negroes numbered 4538 for 3.3 percent of the total; other minorities—mainly Japanese, Chinese, and Filipino—totaled 6145 for 4.5 percent of the total.[4]

A special census in 1955 showed that the total Sacramento population had grown to 157,179—a 14.3 percent increase. This 1955 total included 6907 Negroes, a 52.2 percent numerical growth since 1950 and an increase from 3.3 percent to 4.4 percent of the total population. In addition, "other" minority races had grown some 47.5 percent during the five-year period to number 9066 persons or 5.8 percent of the total. In contrast, the Caucasian majority had increased only 11.3 percent during the five-year interim to comprise 89.8 percent of the 1955 total—2.4 percent less than the Caucasian ratio of 1950.

Sacramento experienced a 21.9 percent increase in population to 191,667 between 1955 and 1960. Much of this growth is attributable to the annexation of residential areas south of the city. The Negro population had grown to 6.3 percent of the total, "other" minorities (Chinese, Japanese, Filipino) to 6.4 percent of the total, and the Caucasian had decreased to 87.3 percent of the total population.

The Concurrent Growth in Segregated Housing

Related to this steady growth in the Negro (and other minorities) population is the increasingly segregated housing pattern which evolved during the years following World War II. These patterns of racial "containment" are significant, as far as the schools are concerned, because of the District's historical adherence to the "neighborhood-school" policy.

An examination of census-tract figures for the years 1950, 1955, and 1960 clearly shows the extent to which housing segregation in the city grew. (See map for census-tract areas, with distribution of Negroes.) During the 1950–1960 decade, the city's Negro population grew from 4538 to 12,103 for a gain of 7565 persons. According to Cain, approximately 3841 of this gain resulted from annexation (census tracts 33–48, 51–53, plus a large part of tract 32), the increase in 32 census tracts which comprised the city in 1950 being approximately 3824. Census tract 32 gained in Negro population almost exclusively through annexation rather than through "internal urban growth."

A consideration of the remaining 31 tracts shows the following:

1. Only ten of the thirty-one tracts increased their percentage of Negroes as much as the city as a whole, that is, by 3 percent or more in 1950–1960.

2. Pockets of Negro containment developed, the most obvious one being the Oak Park District. Composed of census tracts 18, 27, and 28, this area showed a net gain of 2832 Negroes from 1950 to 1960. This figure represents approximately 74 percent of the total (nonannexed) increase in the entire city for Negroes between 1950 and 1960.[5] Research by sociologists Leonard Cain and Wilson Record of Sacramento State College suggests that the advent of urban renewal in the late 1940's and early 1950's contributed substantially to the growth of lower-middle-class "Negro housing" in this Oak Park area.

3. A predominantly Negro suburban area grew within the city, namely, census-tract areas 32 and 48. In 1950 this area (called Glen Elder) was totally Caucasian. By 1960, 856 Negroes had moved

into tract 32 and comprised 11 percent of its population. The racial transition in tract number 48 was even greater; this section of Glen Elder showed a racial composition that was 78.3 percent Negro.

4. The extreme south-central tracts (47, 49, and 50) and northeastern tracts (30, 31, 29, 52, 17, 54, and 55) of the city, containing many of the recently constructed suburban subdivisions, were for all practical purposes Caucasian.

5. The Old West End, comprising those census tracts in the northwest and central portions of the city, remained, urban renewal notwithstanding, 10 to 35 percent Negro.

The 1960 census further suggests the extent to which housing segregation has expanded to the county of Sacramento. Examination of the statistics shows that census tracts 65, 66, and 67, with a total of 3907 Negroes,

comprise the bulk of this segment of the county outside of the Sacramento city limits. So intense is the concentration of Negro families in Del Paso Heights that almost 45 per cent of the Negroes in the entire Sacramento metropolitan community are accounted for in this northern sector. Tract number 65 exemplifies the extent of the segregation with its Negro concentration of 50.6 percent of the total of 4,790 residents. Hence they are unable to compete for middle class suburban housing. The existence of heavy concentrations of Negroes in Oak Park, the to-be-rebuilt West End, Glen Elder sub-division and Del Paso Heights (Sacramento County) exemplify the feasibility of this contention. For example, the 1960 census for tract number 28 in Oak Park reveals that 308 owner-occupied homes were market valued at less than $5,000. This area, as the reader recalls, is 42.7 per cent Negro with 1,712 out of 4,012 residents belonging to that racial group. In addition, 104 owner-occupied houses in the same tract were valued at between $10,000 and $14,000. None cost $25,000 or more and only four ranged in value from $20,000 to $24,900.[6]

The following factors contributed to segregated housing patterns, in Cain's view:

1. *The economic factor*—because many Negro Sacramentans remain economically weak.

2. *Racial polarization*—that is, a desire to be with one's own group.

3. *Restricted mobility*—the inability of so-called middle-class Negroes to move, to any noticeable extent, into Caucasian middle-income areas. The Sacramento Fair Housing Committee attributes this condition to racial discrimination on the part of real-estate agencies, lending institutions, and sellers of property.

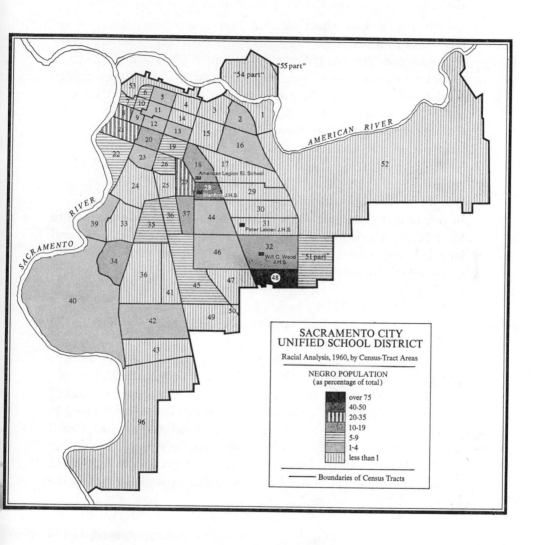

"55 part"

"54 part"

AMERICAN RIVER

53
6
5
4
3
2
1
10
9
11
14
8
12
13
15
16
21
20
19
22
23
26
18
17
52
24
25
27
American Legion El. School
28
Stanford J.H.S.
29
36
37
44
30
39
33
35
31
Peter Lassen J.H.S.
34
32
Will C. Wood
J.H.S.
51 part
36
46
48
41
45
47
50
40
42
49
43
96

RIVER

SACRAMENTO

SACRAMENTO CITY
UNIFIED SCHOOL DISTRICT

Racial Analysis, 1960, by Census-Tract Areas

NEGRO POPULATION
(as percentage of total)

over 75
40-50
20-35
10-19
5-9
1-4
less than 1

——— Boundaries of Census Tracts

THE SACRAMENTO CITY UNIFIED SCHOOL DISTRICT

The Geography of the District and Student Population Trends

For the 1963–64 school year, the Sacramento public schools comprised a unified school district with grades kindergarten through fourteen inclusive. The District was formed in 1936 as a unified school district when the high-school, elementary-school, and junior-college districts were unified under provisions of the state law pertaining to unification. At the time of this unification, the boundaries of the District approximated very closely the boundaries of the city of Sacramento.[7] (See map on p. 83 for school-district boundaries.)

Prior to 1958 there had been only one major addition to the land area of the original district.[8] This consisted of the officially annexed Oak Park District, mentioned earlier in the census-tract analyses. In July of that year seven elementary-school districts were annexed to the District. This addition nearly doubled the latter's land area and included large parcels of land—particularly to the south and northeast—suitable for subdivision development.

Finally, in July of 1959, the last major annexation to the District occurred when the Elder Creek school district was added. This area includes the "Negro suburb" mentioned earlier and is located in the south-central part of the District.

Statistical information indicates steady growth in the student population of the city's public schools. For example, student enrollment increased (grades kindergarten through fourteen) from 23,037 to 32,176 for the period 1952–1958. By 1959 this figure had jumped to 40,892 as a result of land annexations and birth-rate increases. Racial statistics are not available for the School District's population during the decade of the 1950's. However, it can be reasonably assumed that the ethnic composition of the District's students paralleled that of the total population of the city.[9]

By September, 1963, there were 54 K-6 schools in the District with a total enrollment of 27,424; 11 junior high schools containing 11,146 students; and 4 senior high schools with enrollments totaling 10,061 students. Excluding the Sacramento City College, the city's public schools contained 48,631 youngsters.[10] The significance of the fact that nearly 10 percent of the total was Negro and nearly 9 percent Oriental will be briefly explored later as a part of the analysis of the crisis itself.

The Board of Education and the Administration

The Sacramento City Unified School District is administered by an elected Board of seven members. Prior to November, 1960, five members—appointed by the City Council—served the School District. Following the 1960 election the seven policy makers included the following:

Attorney Milton Schwartz, whose legal views with respect to administrative planning after the fire which destroyed the Stanford Junior High School were a subject of community discussion.

Dr. Marie Babich, who retired after one three-year term.

Mrs. J. F. Didion, later elected vice president of the Board in January, 1963.

Mrs. Jewell Blucher, president of the Board at the time of the Stanford fire.

Attorney John Brown, later a supporter of the superintendent's initial postfire emergency plan.

Mrs. James Harvey, an incumbent for fifteen years.

Mrs. Carl Kuchman, whose views supporting the argument for immediate dispersal of the Stanford student body, after the fire, were a matter of discussion. Her views, incidentally, coincided with those of some community groups which would demand Board action on the matter of alleged *de facto* segregation.

A compulsory election, held one year later in a run-off for the three incumbents with the lowest previous winning votes, resulted in only one change. Mrs. Harvey was replaced by Mrs. Gladys Paulson, whose views would later prove to be supportive of those of the superintendent.[11]

These seven persons shared, rather intensively, in the decision making that evolved following the crisis precipitated by the fire of August 17, 1963.

The superintendent of schools in 1963, Dr. F. Melvyn Lawson, was and has remained the chief executive officer of the School District. Responsible to the superintendent are a deputy superintendent and four assistant superintendents in addition to a personnel director. The four assistant superintendents are responsible for the administration of elementary, junior high, and special schools; senior high schools; City College and adult education; business services; and research planning. The latter division, administered by Dr. Donald Hall, played a key role in the eventual District planning for securing means of eliminating the problem of racial imbalance in the junior high schools.[12] The aforementioned personnel make up the "cabinet" which advises the chief executive officer on all matters relative to the instructional, personnel, and business needs of the school system.

SCHOOL ATTENDANCE AREAS AND RACE

History

School attendance boundary areas were established to meet the growth of population in the District. As new residential areas were developed, schools were constructed to serve the residents of the area. Location of new schools and realignment of existing school attendance area boundaries have been primarily a matter of providing school facilities to a growing community, as rapidly and as conveniently located to the persons to be served as possible.[13]

As far as distance traveled is concerned, historically the District (since 1950) has agreed to a policy of "providing bus transportation for junior high school students traveling distances in excess of two miles enroute to the school (junior high)."[14]

According to Dr. Lawson, the superintendent, an unwritten policy followed by the District in establishing school attendance boundaries included a consideration of these factors prior to February 18, 1963: (1) pupil safety, (2) walking distance, (3) current and projected enrollments of schools affected by boundary-line changes, (4) continuity of pupil relationships, when possible—that is, assignment of students from groups of "feeder" elementary schools to the same junior high school and the use of the same procedure for students from junior to senior high schools, (5) availability of public transportation.[15]

On February 18, 1963, the Board formally adopted, as written policy, these five criteria. In addition, the Board adopted as a sixth criterion the *ethnic factor* "to be considered in conformity with the provisions of the California Administrative Code, Title 5, Chapter 1, Subchapter 8, Article 1.5, Section 2010."[16] This action was to have far-reaching implications. A critical point of inquiry later made by Superintendent Lawson concerned the matter of time. Was the student's racial background to be considered a factor with respect to existing boundaries? Or did the State Administrative Code apply to new boundaries only? This matter became an issue during the litigation proceedings of October, 1963.

Evidence later presented to the Sacramento Committee for Equal Educational Opportunity (Fall, 1964) substantiated the Superintendent's contention that these six criteria "were, in fact, used in establishing school attendance boundaries. There was no evidence of gerrymandering of boundaries for the specific creation of segregated schools or any other purpose."[17]

The Neighborhood-School Concept—Effect on Schools Racially

As previously indicated, patterns of segregated housing clusters have developed in Sacramento. The public schools have operated a neighborhood-school policy as related to school boundaries. The concurrent existence of housing segregation and neighborhood schools has had a pronounced effect upon the ethnic composition of the city's public schools. An examination of the map depicting Sacramento census tracts would suggest that youngsters attending schools in the northeast section of the city, in census tracts 1, 2, and 3, for example, are going to racially homogeneous schools almost totally Caucasian. The 1960 census indicates that this area contained only 99 Negro citizens or 2.2 percent of the total 13,646 persons residing there.

In contrast, census tracts 18, 27, and 28 are heavily Negro, with the latter two maintaining percentages of 20.8 and 42.7 respectively. This Oak Park area is, in fact, the neighborhood which was the feeder community for Stanford Junior High School, the institution that became the focal point for a community crisis concerned with alleged *de facto* racial segregation in the public schools. This school, because of its heavy concentration of Negroes in the feeder community, became in addition the overt example of the results of fortuitous housing patterns being coterminous with school attendance boundaries.

Research later conducted by the Sacramento Committee for Fair Housing as well as the Committee for Equal Educational Opportunity substantiates the contention that schools were racially segregated *de facto*. The Committee, in May of 1965, acknowledged in its report the fact that ethnic composition of Sacramento City schools reflected segregated housing patterns in the community. It went on to point out that in each of five schools—Argonaut, American Legion, Camellia, Donner, and Elder Creek—the Negro enrollment was more than 50 percent of the total student body. In addition, Washington School showed a Mexican-American enrollment in excess of 50 percent and Riverside School showed an Oriental registration greater than 50 percent. There were also seven other schools with a total minority enrollment greater than 50 percent. Thus, approximately 25 percent of the 53 elementary schools in the District had distinct ethnic imbalance.

The Committee concluded this particular section of the report by observing that "these schools are located within the residential areas of the District where minority groups are heavily concentrated. By contrast, there are six schools in which there are no Negro children enrolled."[18]

Stanford Junior High Attendance Area—Socio-Economic Analysis

Stanford Junior High School, focal point of Sacramento's 1963–1964 *de facto* segregation crisis, was located in the center of the District's junior-high-school attendance areas for that school year. Oak Park, consisting of census tract areas 18, 27, and 28, is the major "feeding area" for this once active attendance boundary. The earlier analysis of census-tract data suggests some indication of the racial concentration. Tract number 28, for example, was 42.7 percent Negro by 1960, with continuing growth evident.[19]

The school opened February 20, 1933, with its original buildings located on Tenth Avenue and Sacramento Boulevard. Some boundary changes, of a minor nature, were made from time to time. But, generally speaking, these lines—until the time of the fire—had been the subject of no major change.[20]

Based on an analysis of data secured from a random sample of the Stanford student body, these data on parent occupations are presented. Of those surveyed, 32 percent had fathers who would be listed as "unskilled" laborers; 36 percent of the fathers were "skilled"; 4 percent were professionally employed; 8 percent were in private business; 12 percent of the youngsters surveyed were "uncertain" about what, specifically, the father did.

Parental educational analysis showed that 64 percent of the mothers (in the sample) were high-school graduates. Only 56 percent of the fathers had diplomas. Both parent groups showed 4 percent with college degrees.

Data with respect to population mobility brought out that 36 percent of the families surveyed had never moved; 41 percent had moved ten or more times. In addition, the range of residential longevity at one location within the attendance area was from 1 year to 15 years. The mean was 7 years.[21]

THE BOARD MEETING—AUGUST 19, 1963

Initial Plans for a Displaced Student Body

Following a hurried round of administrative conferences with key personnel in the central-office staff on the day following the fire, Superintendent Lawson met with the Board of Education on the evening of August 19, 1963. He presented to the seven Board members three alternative approaches related to the immediate matter of housing the displaced Stanford student body. These approaches to the problem, based upon decisions made in executive conference, included the following:

A. House Stanford Junior High School's enrollment at the American Legion Elementary School and transport the American Legion pupils to neighboring elementary schools where the enrollment has been declining and there are available classrooms. *Advantages:* The American Legion Elementary School is in close proximity to the Stanford Junior High site and is well located to serve the Stanford attendance area. Moving the five portable classrooms now on the Stanford site to American Legion will make sufficient classrooms available. *Disadvantages:* To convert the American Legion plant so that an adequate junior-high-school program can be offered will cost a considerable amount of money and, in any case, cannot be accomplished by the opening day of school on September 10, 1963. Moreover, this plan will require the transportation of over 800 elementary pupils in the American Legion attendance area for a period of one and a half to two years. It will cost a great deal of money and will present problems to a great number of parents, especially those with younger children.

B. Use one of the other junior-high-school plants to house both its own enrollment and Stanford Junior High's enrollment on a double-session basis. *Advantages:* Complete junior-high-school facilities will be available to the Stanford pupils. *Disadvantages:* Since it will take one and a half to two years to reconstruct the Stanford plant, approximately 2000 to 2500 pupils will be placed on half-day sessions for this length of time. It undoubtedly will be necessary to transport the entire enrollment or a major portion of it, depending upon the junior high school chosen. This transportation will use money from the undistributed reserve which will be needed for textbooks and other educational supplies required in the operation of Stanford Junior High School.

C. Move portable classrooms and place them on the rear of the Stanford site. *Advantages:* By moving at least thirty-five portable classrooms to the Stanford Junior High site, an adequate junior high school can be provided without the need of expending a substantial amount of the limited undistributed reserve for pupil transportation. *Disadvantages:* It will be impossible to move and equip the thirty-five portable classrooms needed in time for the opening of school. Also, to offer a junior-high-school program using only portables will pose problems, although the Fern Bacon Junior High School operated with portables prior to the completion of its new plant.

Before asking for Board discussion on the matter, the superintendent reiterated the significance of the time factor. These alternatives had been evolved as emergency measures, not as long-range solutions. Because of the time factor, a large number of staff members had not been called into the planning session prior to August 19. This was, he stated, a disaster situation.

Dr. Lawson, having stressed the advantages and disadvantages of each alternative, recommended a combination of plans B and C. Specifically, he asked the Board to adopt a procedure wherein Stanford students would be housed, on a double-session basis, at the Peter Lassen Junior High School. The students would remain at Lassen until such time as thirty-five portable classrooms could be moved to the rear of the burned-out Stanford site and equipped for use. The superintendent cited three major advantages to this approach: (1) The interim double-session period would provide time needed to move and equip the portables. (2) The Stanford students would have, at Lassen, the benefit of a fully equipped plant—shortened day notwithstanding. (The entire Stanford staff would accompany the students in the move, sharing the building with Lassen on a double-session basis.) (3) Transportation costs would be kept to a minimum; only those Stanford youngsters residing in the western portions of the attendance area would need bus transportation. (See map on p. 83.) This portion would include the western extremities adjacent to Sacramento Boulevard and Broadway.

In response to the superintendent's recommendation, Mr. Schwartz inquired about the cost involved for the installation of portables on the Stanford site. The estimated amount quoted by Dr. Lawson was $50,000 to $70,000.

Mrs. Cushman's concern was for the possibility of immediately dispersing *all* of the Stanford students to the surrounding junior high schools. She cited two advantages to such an alternative approach: (1) It would eliminate the need for double sessions at Lassen; and (2) the Stanford youth would have the benefit of *full-time* education during the interim needed (perhaps two years) to replace the ruined structure.[22]

The superintendent immediately vetoed any serious consideration of the Cushman dispersal proposal for these reasons:

1. The students in the surrounding junior high schools had already been programed for the fall semester, scheduled to begin September 10. To disperse approximately one hundred students to each of these junior highs, the problem of overcrowding in some notwithstanding, would result in "administrative chaos."
2. Preservation of an entire administrative school unit, whenever possible, was Board policy. Regardless of where the new Stanford school was to be built, an attempt should be made to keep the Stanford students and faculty together as a unit.
3. Bus transportation problems, problematical under the original proposal, would now become acute.[23]

Assistant Superintendent Hall elaborated upon Dr. Lawson's statement concerning bus transportation problems which would accompany any dispersal of students to surrounding schools. He indicated that the District buses would be insufficient, hence that problems in contracting and scheduling public transportation would arise. In addition, research had proven, Dr. Hall contended, that a school district gains when its transportation circuit is oriented to *one* location (Peter Lassen).

Community Interaction—The Charge of De Facto Segregation

Several parents from the Lassen attendance area protested at this juncture. One expressed an awareness of the acuteness of the situation. However, she contended, to allow one school—that is, Lassen Junior High—to bear the entire burden caused by this emergency was unfair. Peter Lassen was willing to take its "share"—but the Stanford students should be immediately dispersed, as suggested by Board member Cushman.

In support of this contention, a second Lassen parent suggested that the expending of $70,000 to erect "temporary" portables on the Stanford site was economic folly. Money could be saved by merely dispersing the students to a number of schools, not just one, during the reconstruction interim.[24]

One of the last community speakers for the evening identified himself as Ralph Tyler, a member of the education committee for the Congress of Racial Equality (CORE). Mr. Tyler is quoted as having said the following:

Truly we have faced a disaster in terms of the burning of a school in the community. But this is also an opportunity. I have heard the superintendent speak of the possibility of rebuilding Stanford Junior High School and I would like to have the opportunity of asking him to consider the possibility of dissolving Stanford Junior High School . . . and of dispersing the students to surrounding junior-high-school areas, perhaps using the money to construct a new junior high school in another area. . . . As many of you realize, Stanford Junior High School is a symbol of *de facto* segregation. It's that simple—let's face it, because this is one of the underlying things involved in tonight's discussion. . . . If these students could be distributed to other schools, we'd have an opportunity to develop a more harmonious community. . . . Perhaps this is a residential problem. But here, we as a community have an opportunity to do something about a problem we are all aware of. . . .

The real issue is breaking up an intense pattern of segregation in Oak Park.

In response to the Tyler allegation, Board and administration reaction evolved thus:

Mr. Schwartz wondered what the Tyler proposal would do to District's neighborhood-school policy.

Dr. Hall again reiterated the housing difficulties involved in any immediate dispersal undertaking. *Capacity:* All of the present junior high schools were at or nearing seating capacity—or had school sites smaller than adequate for accommodating portables. *Scheduling:* The problems had been suggested previously by the superintendent.

Mrs. Cushman supported Mr. Tyler's idea, indicating that a few initial inconveniences would be far outweighed by the significance of such a move now—for the entire community. She then formally requested a cost analysis from the business office relative to the proposed dispersal of Stanford students.

Mr. Schwartz further emphasized the "temporary" nature of the proposed movement of portables to Stanford. Such a move, as he interpreted Dr. Lawson's original recommendation, did not preclude reconstruction on the same site. The racial issue, he further suggested, must be separated from the present emergency. "This is an emergency," he emphasized. ". . . The other [segregation] is too, but it won't be solved tomorrow or next week."

Mr. Tyler, in disagreeing with Board Member Schwartz's argument for the Lawson plan, contended that the entire evening's arguments relative to excessive transportation costs and to conflict of two student bodies at Peter Lassen Junior High School were a smokescreen. The real issue was ethnic containment at Stanford due to segregated housing in Oak Park. He rejected, without reservation, the superintendent's argument concerning scheduling difficulties which would accompany dispersal.[25]

The Board's Adoption of the Lawson Emergency Plan

Following more discussion related to the Tyler allegation, Superintendent Lawson's proposal was formally placed before the Board for adoption. The motion, in effect, asked that the superintendent be given the authority to move quickly in these areas:

A. To initiate double sessions at Peter Lassen Junior High School, housing both Stanford and Lassen students. Sessions would end by the fall of 1964 if not sooner.
B. To move portable classrooms to the Stanford site, equip them, and reestablish Stanford Junior High School in these structures until an adequate long-range plan could be adopted.
C. To evaluate the situation for long-range study, determining such factors as: (1) Where to rebuild? (2) Whether or not to rebuild? (3) Anticipated cost, if rebuilt. (4) What attendance area, if rebuilt, should be serviced?[26]

Discussion on the motion was followed by adoption of the plan by a margin of six to one. Mrs. Cushman, continuing to support Mr. Tyler's contention, voted in the negative.[27,28]

CHALLENGES AGAINST ALLEGED *DE FACTO* SEGREGATION

The following morning, one of the two local newspapers, in summarizing events of the previous evening, capsulized the seeming inevitability of pending crisis when it said, "Suddenly out of the smoke and ashes appeared the spectre of discrimination. . . . School administrators who had thought they were conducting an educational program free of bias found themselves on the defensive."[29]

The Initial NAACP Thrust

The interim between the Board's adoption of the emergency plan on August 19 and the next meeting scheduled for September 3 was filled with increased community involvement in the problem. Board minutes for September 3[30] indicate that a letter was sent to Board President Blucher and to other Board members as well as to officers of the administration from the Sacramento Chapter of the National Association for the Advancement of Colored People. The letter was signed by the Reverend Cyrus Keller, chapter president and the father of a Stanford student. Copies of the letter, dated August 21, were also sent to the local newspapers.

In summarizing a resolution passed by the local chapter's executive board, the letter made two points: (1) The School Board was asked to reconsider its adoption of the emergency plan. (2) The District was asked to call an emergency meeting so as to seek a more equitable solution to the problem.

In addition, the Keller letter stated:

As you know, there is a grave problem of ethnic imbalance at Stanford, and it seems to us that this problem should now be met by approaches which are not pre-ordained to an immediate return to the *status quo*. Clearly, a temporary transfer of the students to Peter Lassen on a half-day session basis for a few months, and their return at the end of this year to bungalows on the Stanford campus will solve no problem but may well aggravate existing ones.[31]

Keller emphasized, in continuing, the fact that the NAACP was making clear its position with respect to ethnic imbalance in the schools. As far as that organization was concerned, the erection of temporary portables on the Stanford site was merely a prelude to permanency. The propagation of the racial *status quo*, he contended, would not go unchallenged.

Political Pressure

After receiving the Keller letter and before the September 3 meeting, Superintendent Lawson also received an open letter from

State Senator Albert S. Rodda. The letter urged the Board to reconsider its decision. Senator Rodda suggested that it was imperative that those concerned with the elimination of *de facto* segregation be heard. Rodda also pointed to the legal implications involved by referring to the State Administrative Code, Sections 2010 and 2011, which clearly stated that California school districts were obligated to consider the *ethnic factor* when planning for administrative decisions concerned with school attendance boundaries.[32]

In addition, he pointed to the *Jackson* v. *Pasadena* decision in the State Supreme Court, which had stated in no uncertain terms:

. . . even in the absence of gerrymandering or other affirmative discriminatory conduct by a school board, a student under some circumstances would be entitled to relief where by reason of residential segregation, substantial racial imbalance exists in his school. . . . The right to an equal opportunity for education and the harmful consequences of segregation require that school boards take steps insofar as reasonably feasible, to alleviate racial imbalance in schools regardless of cause. . . . School authorities are not required to attain an exact apportionment of Negroes among the schools . . . consideration must be given to the various factors in each case, including the practical necessities of governmental operation. For example, consideration should be given, on the one hand, to the degree of racial imbalance in the particular school and the extent to which it affects the opportunity for education and on the other hand, to such matters as the difficulty and effectiveness of revising school boundaries so as to eliminate segregation and the availability of other facilities to which students can be transferred.[33]

Based on the material presented in the main body of his letter to the Superintendent, Senator Rodda concluded with these formal recommendations:

A. The District was obligated to consider the matter of ethnic imbalance in any of its planning.
B. The District should confer with experts on *de facto* segregation, then intensively study the problem. Specifically, it should confer with Mr. Wilson Riles, State Department of Education Consultant.
C. Any planning should be accomplished within the framework of the State Administrative Code and the *Jackson* v. *Pasadena* decision.

Press Support of Emergency Plans

The same day on which the NAACP letter to the District was made public, one of the largest Sacramento newspapers, the *Sacramento Bee*, editorially supported the Lawson plan by stating:

This arrangement will distress some. It is not perfect. Double-sessions instruction is not ideal. But an emergency exists here and the community has to face it, and all factors weighed, this solution seems best . . . it would be improper to exploit the crisis presented by the emergency relocation of Stanford pupils to raise a segregation issue without basis of fact. The first challenge remains clear: present adequate housing of dislocated pupils. The second challenge, that of dealing with any segregation patterns, if they exist, must await the Board's analysis of what is real, what is imagined.[34]

Several days before the publicizing of the Rodda letter, the second large daily, the *Sacramento Union*, editorially supported the Board's adopted plan thus:

. . . Considering that Stanford's student population is fairly evenly divided, it cannot be said fairly that there is any more segregation of its Negro members than of its white members. . . . Yet, this point should be taken into consideration in planning the rebuilding of permanent facilities, but time does not permit any proper planning or arrangement for dispersal— even if desirable.[35]

THE BOARD MEETING—SEPTEMBER 3, 1963

Consideration of the Ethnic Factor

During the opening phase of the meeting, Superintendent Lawson mentioned his participation in a conference with State Department of Education Consultant Wilson Riles. This conference, held prior to the September 3 Board meeting, had been exploratory in nature. Mr. Riles had made clear the Department's position with respect to the Administrative Code, Title 5, concerning the need for a District's consideration of the *ethnic factor* when planning school boundaries and/or buildings. In addition, the significance of the Supreme Court's *Jackson* v. *Pasadena* precedent had been discussed.[36]

Following his résumé of the conference with Riles, Dr. Lawson formally acknowledged the Board's receipt of the NAACP letter written by Reverend Keller. On the basis of an informal poll taken before the Board meeting, wherein the majority opinion upheld the Board's original action of August 19, Superintendent Lawson stated that it was his feeling that a "special meeting"—as requested by the NAACP— would serve no useful purpose. Such a session would, at best, be only a crash-oriented conference and certainly would do nothing to eliminate the negative aspects of alternative approaches to the problem of housing the Stanford student body for September.

The real problem now, Dr. Lawson stated, was the evolving of a long-range plan which would, in fact, permanently resolve school housing for Stanford students. Such a long-range study would require, for the first time in Sacramento's history, a District-wide racial census. Dr. Hall's office would be directed to handle the details. The superintendent implied that if alleged *de facto* segregation was indeed a problem in the Stanford attendance area, it might also be a potential problem elsewhere. Hence a city-wide school census was imperative. Apparently, said Lawson, the thesis of color-blindness was no longer valid.[*]

The superintendent reemphasized that any long-range study would have to be in depth. It would have to consider previously mentioned factors including: whether or not to rebuild Stanford; if so, where; anticipated costs; attendance area to be served. During the interim between September and the completion of long-range plans, therefore, double sessions would proceed, on September 10, as planned. Stanford students would then be transferred, by the end of the first semester, to forty to-be-moved portables.

Dr. Lawson then presented for the Board's perusal a prepared document designed to demonstrate what could have been anticipated if the Board had adopted another plan as recommended by Mr. Tyler, some Lassen parents, and others. He referred to the "immediate dispersal" idea. Subsequent analysis of the data indicated these facts:

A. Some of the receiving junior high schools would have gained 200 Stanford students, raising optimum enrollments above desired number.

---

[*] The concept of "color-blindness" was advanced by Justice John Marshall Harlan in the case of *Plessy* v. *Ferguson*, 163 U.S. 537 (1896). Justice Harlan, in his dissenting opinion, maintained that our Constitution was "color-blind" (at p. 559) and neither knew nor tolerated classes among its citizens.

B. Five of the anticipated "receiving" schools would require portable additions. At least one had insufficient land for such structures.
C. If race was to be a factor, the 200 Stanford students assigned to
Will C. Wood Junior High School would all have to be Caucasian
so as to avoid any increased concentration of Negro students at that
school. Conversely, the 200 students assigned to California Junior
High School would have to be Negro because of the obvious
Caucasian homogeneity at California at that time. With such a
number problem evident, what would happen in the event of new
pupils moving in and out? (These two schools were cited by the
Superintendent as two examples.)
D. Bus transportation costs ($37,000 annual, minimum) had already
been referred to.
E. Movement of portables to those "receiving" schools with land room
would involve costs of $20,000, plus possibly an additional $20,000.

Mr. Schwartz, in agreeing with the superintendent's proposal for
a District-wide racial census, recommended that the Board hold a
public hearing prior to the adoption of any to-be-conceived long-range
plan.

Mrs. Cushman asked for clarification relative to the nature of the
word "temporary" as it pertained to the housing of Stanford students
at the old site for the second semester. In addition, she strongly
insisted that it was still possible to immediately disperse the Stanford
students (administrative problems notwithstanding). Recent events,
including the NAACP letter, the Rodda letter, and the pending ethnic
study made it imperative—said Mrs. Cushman—that the Board reconsider its August 19 decision. She envisioned a sequence thus: (1)
Peter Lassen double sessions; (2) an interim decision-making period
concerning what to do about the portables, that is, whether to move
them to the old Stanford site or attempt something else before the
installation of portables—such as student dispersal; (3) the movement of portables as a last measure.

Dr. Lawson's reply again was in reference to the necessity of
portables, at Stanford, prior to the initiation of any long-range plan.
The longer the District waited to transfer the Stanford youth to the
old site, the longer double sessions—with all of their disadvantages—would have to remain in effect at Peter Lassen. Time was now
significant. Hence, the original plan would be initiated September 10.

Community Pressure and the Board's Response

At this juncture, several persons, speaking for groups or individually, formally presented remarks related to the problem before the School Board.

Mrs. Verna Carson, NAACP representative, speaking unofficially, urged the Board to reconsider its August 19 decision—to avoid the racial strife experienced in other cities. She suggested that immediate consideration be given to the points made in the Rodda and NAACP letters respecting consideration of the ethnic factor in any decision made. In conclusion, she stated that "it would be a mistake for the Board to move the portables back to the Stanford campus . . . such a move would be at odds with many of us who oppose this action. . . . This would be a strong case for those desiring that Stanford be rebuilt on the old site." Board Member Schwartz seemed concerned, at this point, about the sudden interest in *de facto* segregation. Why was the issue being raised now and why had it not been raised in the past?

Dr. Paul Mueller, psychologist, research director for Sacramento's Fair Housing Committee, reviewed the Leonard Cain study relating to the containment of the majority of the Negro populace in Oak Park—a major Stanford "feeder" area. He called for a dispersal of Stanford students, following the ending of double sessions at Peter Lassen. Portables should be used only to accommodate the students once they were dispersed. The portables should not be returned to Stanford.

Following further discussion of the remarks made by these and other speakers, the Superintendent's proposal for a District-wide racial census was adopted by the Board.[37] The following day, a public announcement indicated that about half of the Stanford students going to Lassen Junior High School would be eligible for District transportation.

Increased Involvement of Community Pressure Groups

During the days following the Board's decision of September 3 to move ahead with its original plan (double-sessioning of Stanford students at Lassen with subsequent use of portable classrooms at the old site), numerous groups increased their involvement in the crisis. Summarized briefly, they included the following:

On October 14, 1963, Reverend G. Chilton Christian, President of the Oak Park Neighborhood Council, sent a letter to the Board president. He strongly recommended that the Board include members from his Council in any decision-making body formed to evolve a long-range solution to the Stanford problem. Christian was willing to accept the District's initial double-sessions plan as "reasonable" for the interim solution. However, a return to Stanford in portables was not considered a final means of attacking the problem, even on a temporary basis.

The Social Relations and Action Commission of the Sacramento Council of Churches (without the endorsement or open support of the parent Council), forwarded a formal request to the superintendent with these recommendations:

1. End Peter Lassen double sessions as quickly as possible.
2. Do not relocate Stanford students on the old site in portables.
3. Do not rebuild on the old site.
4. Fully explore the *dispersal-of-students* idea. Those students living within the two-mile range could certainly attend Lassen, Sutter, Carson, and California Junior High Schools. Those living outside the zone could go to other junior high schools. Any transfers should be designed to minimize the possibility of *de facto* segregation.[38]
   (See map on p. 83.)

THE BOARD MEETING—SEPTEMBER 16, 1963

Increased Demands for Dispersal

At this Board meeting, the superintendent, after acknowledging receipt of correspondence from the Oak Park Neighborhood Council and the Social Relations and Action Commission, yielded the floor to the following viewpoints:

The American Civil Liberties Union, as represented by James Lucas, indicated that the Board's moral mandate under *Jackson* v. *Pasadena* was clear. Dispersal was demanded.

Dr. Paul Mueller, representing the Fair Housing Committee, indicated that to return the Stanford youth to the old site would be to disavow the 1954 *Brown* v. *Board of Education* Supreme Court decision. Attendance area lines could be redrawn so as to consider, more positively, the factor of race.

The Sacramento Council of Democratic Clubs was represented by John Fourt. He stressed five points:

1. The proposed District-wide ethnic census is a step in the right direction.
2. Stanford Junior High is at least 50 percent Negro. Therefore, it is *de facto* segregated.
3. The Board has the responsibility to appoint a broadly representative Citizens' Advisory Committee for the purpose of investigating the entire problem of racial imbalance in the Sacramento schools.
4. Stanford youngsters, because of inequality of opportunity and disadvantaged conditions, have done poorly on recently administered California Achievement Tests. (See Table 1.)
5. The patterns of housing segregation are creeping gradually southward. Unless the School District does something, the *de facto* segregation phenomenon of Stanford would spread to Peter Lassen and Will C. Wood.

Dr. Lawson's response to the group demands included assurance that the central administration would plan immediately to confer with Wilson Riles of the State Department of Education; the schools could not possibly hope to solve, in a short time, a problem caused by years of growth in the housing area; Sacramento has never gerrymandered its attendance boundaries; and finally—research has never proven that students attending "racially imbalanced" schools inherently score lower on achievement tests.[39]

THE APPROACH OF LITIGATION

The NAACP Lawsuit and Increased Pressure

On September 16, the NAACP publicly indicated its intention to force the Sacramento Board, by means of a court-ordered injunction, to have the Stanford students dispersed.

As the pressure of a pending lawsuit, now seen by the Board as inevitable, began to build up, two community groups initiated moves destined to place an even greater amount of pressure on the District's decision makers.

The date September 24, 1963, is significant. It was on this day that the organization known as the Sacramento Council for Equal Education formalized itself as an entity. Consisting of representatives from eleven community groups—including NAACP, CORE, American Civil Liberties Union, the National Council of Jewish Women, and others—it elected John Fourt as its president. This group agreed that it

TABLE 1. RESULTS OF THE STANDARDIZED ABILITY AND ACHIEVEMENT TESTS ADMINISTERED TO EIGHTH-GRADE PUPILS DURING THE FALL SEMESTER, 1962

School	No. of Students	Language			Nonlanguage			Total			Mean I.Q.
		% in Low Group	% in Mid. Group	% in High Group	% in Low Group	% in Mid. Group	% in High Group	% in Low Group	% in Mid. Group	% in High Group	
Junior High:											
California	204	12	42	46	14	55	31	9	57	34	107
Charles M. Goethe	398	24	50	26	19	55	26	17	59	24	102
Fern Bacon	389	16	49	35	16	54	30	11	59	31	105
Joaquin Miller	347	15	44	41	15	50	35	11	50	39	107
Kit Carson	372	10	50	40	14	57	29	9	59	32	107
Lincoln	106	45	44	11	22	60	18	34	56	10	95
Peter Lassen	359	16	43	41	16	52	32	10	57	33	106
Sam Brannan	275	12	40	48	11	52	37	7	50	43	109
Stanford	209	39	52	9	34	52	14	34	59	7	94
Sutter	315	23	47	30	13	52	35	15	54	31	104
Will C. Wood	210	26	51	23	20	62	18	22	60	18	100
District (Jr. High)	3,184	20	47	33	17	54	29	14	56	30	104
Natl. Norm		23	54	23	23	54	23	23	54	30	100

Source: Office of Assistant Superintendent in Charge of Planning and Research Services, Sacramento City Unified School District, May 22, 1963. Research Report No. 12, Series 1962–63.

would do nothing to alienate the business community in the city; that
it would press for an elimination of alleged *de facto* segregation in the
city's public schools; that equalization of educational opportunity was
a must; and that the Board and the administration would have to
evolve solutions—not the community pressure groups.[40]

Immediately before the Board meeting of September 30, 1963, the
second group, the Sacramento Chapter of the National Association of
Social Workers, strongly urged the Board to have Stanford students
immediately dispersed, thereby requiring all surrounding junior high
schools to bear the burden during the remaining interim required to
secure a permanent solution to the problem.[41]

THE BOARD MEETING—SEPTEMBER 30, 1963

Pre-Litigation Session

At the September 30 meeting, referring to the recently completed
"Preliminary Report on the Ethnic Composition of Pupil Population of
the Sacramento City Unified School District," Superintendent Lawson
drew the Board's attention to the racial breakdown for the district as a
whole: Negroes 9.9 percent; Orientals 7.9 percent; Caucasians 72.3
percent, and Mexican-Americans 8.8 percent; the remaining 1.1 percent classified as "other." The greatest concentration of Negro youth
was at the elementary-school level; the least (7 percent) at the sen-
ior-high-school level. Enrollment statistics for Stanford Junior High
showed 70.5 percent of the student body as non-Caucasian, so there
was a clearly disproportionate number of minority-group students at
Stanford. (See Table 2.)

After concluding the discussion on the racial census, Dr. Lawson
announced receipt of a preliminary statement for the NAACP court
injunction against the School District from Robert Carter, chief
NAACP counsel for the plaintiff. The injunction stipulated that Stanford was *de facto* segregated; the NAACP sought, specifically, to
prevent the Board from

1. Erecting a campus of temporary bungalows on the site of the
   burned Stanford Junior High School and from returning the students of the said school to the said site in such facilities.
2. Selecting the old Stanford . . . site as the proper place for construction of a permanent junior high school.
3. Failing to evolve and execute, forthwith, but in no event later than

TABLE 2. ETHNIC COMPOSITION OF THE PUPIL POPULATION OF SACRAMENTO JUNIOR HIGH SCHOOLS—SEPTEMBER 1963

School	Ethnic Composition										Total
	White-Caucasian (not including Mexican)		White-Caucasian (Mexican)		Negro		Oriental (Japanese, Chinese, and Korean)		Other Nonwhite		
	Enroll.	%	Enroll.	%	Enroll.	%	Enroll.	%	Enroll.	%	
California	567	65.5	50	5.8	52	6.0	193	22.3	4	.4	866
Charles M. Goethe	1,143	85.4	81	6.0	45	3.4	55	4.1	15	1.1	1,339
Fern Bacon	1,205	89.8	80	6.0	18	1.3	24	1.8	15	1.1	1,342
Joaquin Miller	696	70.6	75	7.6	40	4.1	174	17.7			985
Kit Carson	1,114	89.4	36	2.9	7	.6	48	3.8	41	3.3	1,246
Lincoln	95	17.0	169	30.2	79	14.1	204	36.4	13	2.3	560
Peter Lassen	1,327	89.7	83	5.6	33	2.2	27	1.8	10	.7	1,480
Sam Branman	633	72.4	6	.7	78	8.9	151	17.3	6	.7	874
Stanford	228	29.5	106	13.7	386	49.9	46	6.0	7	.9	773
Sutter	631	64.8	153	15.7	35	3.6	137	14.1	18	1.8	974
Will C. Wood	448	63.4	93	13.2	148	20.9	12	1.7	6	.8	707
Total	8,087	72.6	932	8.4	921	8.3	1,071	9.6	135	1.1	11,146

Source: "Preliminary Report on the Ethnic Composition of Pupil Population of the Sacramento City Unified School District," September, 1963.

January 7, 1964, an ethnically nondiscriminatory plan for the disposition and distribution of the student population of the Stanford
Junior High School, without double sessions or *de facto* racial
segregation, and in facilities comparable to those provided in the
junior high schools maintained, operated, and administered by the
defendants.

The public hearing would be held October 7, 1963, in Sacramento
Superior Court, Judge Perluss presiding.[42]

THE INJUNCTION

On the morning of Monday, October 7, 1963, a public hearing was
held in Superior Court for Sacramento County. The case involved legal
proceedings instituted against the City School District by Reverend
Cyrus Keller on behalf of his son, Cyrus, Junior.[43]

Robert Carter, attorney for the plaintiff, initiated proceedings
by charging that not only had the Board failed to adhere to California
state law in providing for housing for these students on an integrated
basis, but it had also made plans, double sessions notwithstanding, to
house them in substandard facilities—portable classrooms. This plan,
Carter asserted, was a denial of equal educational opportunities even
apart from the issue of race. Furthermore, said Carter, "the Board
has the obligation to plan and draw attendance zones and to re-
organize the school system to get rid of the concentration of the
Negroes and nonwhites in a particular school, that it has the obligation under the law and that it has an educational responsibility to
do this."[44]

The Board of Education attorney, Mr. Heinrich, contested the
plaintiff's assertion by arguing that the statements made would make it
appear that the *ethnic factor* was the only factor, under California
law, to be considered in terms of the drawing of attendance boundaries. There never has been, he challenged, any overt attempt on the
part of the Board to discriminate against any group in the community.

The superintendent's later testimony is significant at this point.
The record shows that in response to Judge Perluss's question concerning the educational desirability of portable classrooms on a separate
site, on the one hand—as opposed to double sessions at *one* school, on
the other—Dr. Lawson responded that regular sessions, even in
portables, were preferred. His reasons included the numerous dis-

advantages previously noted by him. He also reemphasized the disadvantages that would have issued from the immediate dispersal of Stanford students to surrounding junior high schools.

Following the examination of a number of other witnesses, including Board President Blucher and a Sacramento State College professor, the court deliberated.

Added to the stepped-up tempo were demands from a newly organized Peter Lassen parent group which vigorously protested the apparent delay in plans for ending the double sessions. Such was the setting at the end of the court hearing on October 7, 1963.

The Ruling of De Facto Segregation

The Perluss ruling was issued as a memorandum opinion on October 8, 1963. Prior to rendering a decision, the court reviewed the significance of *Brown* v. *Board of Education*. Concerning itself with the matter of "affirmative integration," the court referred also to the New York decision:

The educational system that is thus compulsory and publicly afforded *must* deal with the inadequacy arising from adventitious segregation; it cannot accept and indurate segregation on the ground that it is not coerced as planned but accepted.[45]

Perhaps the most significant part of the preliminary statement issued by Judge Perluss was his reference to the legal precedent offered by the California State Supreme Court in *Jackson* v. *Pasadena*. The latter had, in effect, stated that "school boards [must] take steps, insofar as reasonably feasible, to alleviate racial imbalance in the schools regardless of cause."[46] In addition, the court referred to the mandate made clear in the California Administrative Code, Title 5, Sections 2010–2011, relative to the consideration of the ethnic factor when administering attendance boundaries.

In finding that Stanford Junior High was, in fact, "a racially segregated school," the Superior Court Justice ruled the following:

A. The temporary restraining order was dissolved. The Board had acted in good faith in establishing an emergency plan necessitating eventual use of portables on the burned-out site. Hence, on a temporary basis only, portables could be sent to the Stanford campus.

B. The order restraining the Board from building in the future, on the Stanford site, was dissolved. It was assumed the Board would act in good faith, if such was decided after evaluation.

C. The evolving of a study and a plan by September, 1964, was considered a reasonable request by the court. The school district would, therefore, prepare for such action.

Three days later the court issued its final disposition in the form of a court order and stipulated in part "that defendants, on or before September, 1964, complete a study and evaluation of the ethnic composition of the student population under their control and jurisdiction and evolve a plan for the correction of any racial imbalance in the Stanford Junior High School by said defendant."[47]

Community reactions to Judge Perluss's decision were varied. The *Sacramento Bee* quoted NAACP attorney Nathaniel Colley's pleasure with the decision: "Our main fear was that the portable classrooms on the Stanford campus would become permanent. We no longer have that fear." According to the *Bee's* education staff writer, Leo Rinnert, a number of letters condemning Perluss for his decision were received by the newspaper. Conversely, others suggested that the decision had been rendered inevitable because of the Pasadena precedent. One key point: most letters, regardless of the initial opinion expressed, hoped that community friction would be avoided—that Sacramentans would support whatever desegregation plan the Board might adopt by September, 1964.

Administrative Planning for Compliance

A series of conferences was held—involving key administrative personnel—prior to the October 14, 1963, Board meeting. Chief factors considered in the formation of a desegregation plan were:

A. Financial feasibility of moving portables, at a cost of $70,000 maximum, to Stanford for such a short period.

B. Possibility of a to-be-designed desegregation plan being implemented by September, 1964.

C. Justification for consideration of race at the elementary-school level.

D. Possibility of dispersal of Stanford students in the spring of 1964.

E. Alternative desegregation plans.

THE BOARD MEETING—OCTOBER 14, 1963

Decision Making and the Desegregation Plan

In the Board meeting of October 14, 1963, Superintendent Lawson suggested the Board members consider and choose among the alternative proposals developed by the staff. The Board agreed to this proposal and Dr. Lawson formally presented two alternative solutions:

Alternate Plan 1: Dispersal of the Stanford student body to other junior high schools without adding an additional school plant.

Alternate Plan 2: Building a new junior high school in the eastern end of the city, not at the Stanford site (the "Einstein plan").[48]

The administration preferred the Einstein plan, whose substantive content and advantages were put forth as follows:

A. With the building of Einstein Junior High School, transportation problems would be few. Kit Carson would be relieved of the necessity of handling the entire eastern area. Most of the students in the Rosemont area would be within walking distance of Einstein.

B. The building of Einstein would make possible the retention of the Board's adopted policy of two miles as a maximum walking distance for junior-high-school youngsters.

C. There would be fewer students at Einstein, during the projected building period, than there had been at Stanford. Hence, fewer portable classrooms would be needed.

D. The implementation of the Einstein proposal would probably be accompanied by junior-high-school redistricting. Such action would, no doubt, be in compliance with the court mandate. It would also avoid:

1. The additional expenditure involved in dispersal without redistricting; that is, extra transportation costs for Stanford students living beyond the two-mile limit.
2. The massive rescheduling problem which would accompany such a move, as suggested by the top administrator of the junior high schools.
3. Lack of counseling and difficulty in handling teacher assignments under an immediate-dispersal plan.[49]

THE BOARD MEETING—OCTOBER 16, 1963

Resolution of the Conflict

The superintendent informed the meeting that several top-level administration conferences had elaborated upon and evaluated the Einstein plan presented during the last session. He pointed out the following advantages of this plan:

1. The plan would allow for the immediate construction of a junior-high-school plant which would be needed by the fall of 1966 anyway. The entire eastern area was expected to develop rapidly.
2. The Board could not only adopt, but could also place into operation, a long-range desegregation plan by the fall of 1964.
3. Once effected, attendance boundaries would then be stabilized for a number of years.
4. Greater building utilization would evolve with the realignment of attendance boundaries of the California, Kit Carson, Joaquin Miller, Peter Lassen, and Will C. Wood Junior High Schools. This result would follow because California and Will C. Wood, located in the older sections of the city, had experienced declining enrollments for several years.[50] (See map.)

The superintendent pointed out that an accelerated building program, made possible through the eventual use of Stanford insurance funds, would provide the necessary money for initial buildings. He and Assistant Superintendent Hall further detailed the technical aspects of the plan. Concerning the ethnic factor, Hall explained in some detail the significance of Alternate Plan 2. The projection table indicated that

the maximum concentration of Caucasian-Mexicans in any of the junior high schools would be no greater than 16 percent . . . maximum Negro concentration reduced from 50 percent to 16 percent . . . maximum Oriental concentration reduced from 27 percent to 19 percent.[51] [See Table 3.]

In this Board meeting the superintendent also made reference to Alternate 3. This plan involved reconstruction of Stanford Junior High School on its present site. Among a number of drawbacks to this plan, it would not eliminate *de facto* segregation at Stanford. Population studies showed the Oak Park area to be increasing in minority population.

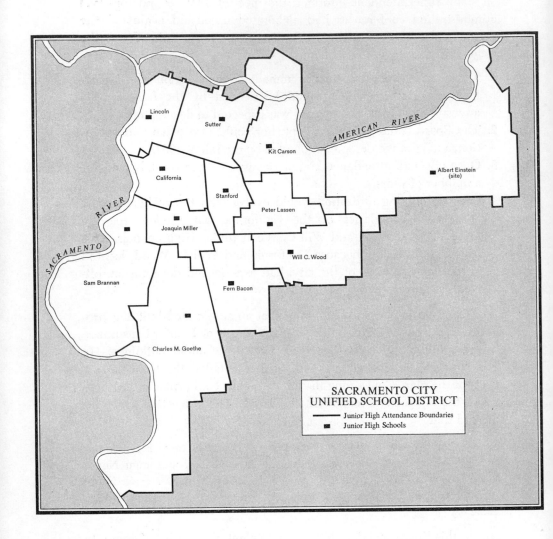

Lincoln

Sutter

Kit Carson

Albert Einstein
(site)

California

Stanford

Peter Lassen

RIVER

Joaquin Miller

SACRAMENTO

Will C. Wood

Sam Brannan

Fern Bacon

AMERICAN RIVER

Charles M. Goethe

SACRAMENTO CITY
UNIFIED SCHOOL DISTRICT

—— Junior High Attendance Boundaries
■ Junior High Schools

TABLE 3. PROJECTED ENROLLMENT AND ETHNIC COMPOSITION OF PUPILS IN JUNIOR HIGH SCHOOLS OF SACRAMENTO, CALIFORNIA, UNDER PROPOSED DESEGREGATION PLAN—SEPTEMBER, 1964

Name of School	September 1963 Enrollment	Projected Enroll. for Sept. 1964 after Redistricting	Ethnic Composition, September, 1963					Projected Minority Composition, September, 1964		
			Caucasian	Mexican	Negro	Oriental	Other Nonwhite	Mexican	Negro	Oriental
California	866	967	65.5%	5.8%	6.0%	22.3%	.4%	7.0%	16.0%	19.0%
Einstein		473						2.0	0	6.0
Joaquin Miller	985	963	70.6	7.6	4.1	17.7	0	9.0	6.0	18.0
Kit Carson	1,246	1,088	89.4	2.9	.6	3.8	3.3	4.0	8.0	2.0
Peter Lassen	1,480	1,245	89.7	5.6	2.2	1.8	.7	8.0	13.0	3.0
Sutter	974	947	64.8	15.7	3.6	14.1	1.8	16.0	3.0	14.0
Will C. Wood	707	892	63.4	13.2	20.9	1.7	1.8	12.0	16.0	2.0

Source: Compilations based on data secured from Research Report No. 2, Series 1963–64, "Revised Junior High School Attendance Boundaries," November 4, 1963, Sacramento City Unified School District.

Note: Four junior high schools were expected to have the same ethnic composition displayed in the preceding table; these were Charles M. Goethe, Fern Bacon, Lincoln, and Sam Brannan.

Audience reaction to the Lawson-Hall proposals was, in the main, favorable. Board members generally expressed satisfaction with a proposal which could resolve the racial crisis and also settle the problem of housing for students in the eastern area. Board agreement was unanimous. With the signing of contracts for the movement of the portables, stage one of the desegregation plan would begin immediately. As indicated by Member Schwartz, the Board's decision to desegregate Stanford would require great community understanding and cooperation, for which it was urged that the P.-T.A. groups of the schools involved, as well as the numerous community organizations heretofore concerned in the decision making, help to lay the groundwork.[52,53]

THE CITIZENS' ADVISORY COMMITTEE

At its November 26 meeting, the Board decided that a Citizens' Advisory Committee on Equal Opportunity would be formed. A number of responsibilities were chalked out for the Advisory Committee to undertake.

Discussions relative to criteria to be used in selecting committee members were held December 9, 1963. Each Board member was to come prepared to submit the names of five persons who qualified for consideration as members of the committee. December 17 was designated as the date for final selection of the broadly representative committee which, following confirmation in January, 1964, consisted of ten Caucasians, two Negroes, and one person each of Chinese, Japanese, and Mexican-American ancestry.

After deliberations of more than a year, the Advisory Committee submitted its report on equal educational opportunity in the Sacramento City Unified School District.[54]

Committee Report's Findings[55]

The Committee's findings in this specific area of its concern were dependent upon the following definitional agreement: "De facto segregation is defined as a condition in which the ethnic composition of student population in a particular school differs markedly from the ethnic composition of the total school-district population."

Census figures made available after those presented for September, 1963, revealed the total ethnic-minority composition of the District to be about 30 percent. Hence, reasonable men would agree that if the ethnic minority of a particular school exceeded 40 percent, that school was, in fact, segregated. In like manner, if the ethnic composition of a single minority group was placed at 12 percent of the total student population in the District, then a concentration of 25 percent or more of group members in a school would render that school *de facto* segregated. Operating under these guidelines, the Committee found:

I. *Segregation*

A. An obviously heavy total minority concentration at Lincoln Junior High School: Mexican-American 35.9 percent, Negro 12.7 percent, Oriental 31.2 percent.

B. An absence of ethnic-minority students at the new Einstein Junior High School: 92.8 percent Caucasian, 0.3 percent Negro, 0.9 percent Mexican-American, and 6.0 percent Oriental.

C. A significant concentration at Will C. Wood Junior High School: Mexican-American 12.0 percent, Negro 20.2 percent.

D. An elementary-school situation showing pronounced trends:
   1. A total of 23 schools had total ethnic-minority enrollments in excess of the number for reasonable integration, that is, 40 percent.
   2. Of these *de facto* segregated schools, 7 contained a single ethnic-minority enrollment exceeding 50 percent.
   3. In 7, the total ethnic-minority population exceeded 50 percent.

II. *Compensatory Education*

A. An intense need for accelerated programs designed to handle the needs of disadvantaged youth in at least six of the *de facto* segregated elementary schools.

B. A need for approaches to the same problem for low-achieving, poorly motivated secondary-school students.

III. *Personnel Practices*

A. Of the 1700 employed teachers in the District, only 44 Oriental, 42 Negro, and 4 Filipino.

B. Only one Negro principal in the District.

C. Few teachers requesting assignments in schools which were ethnically imbalanced.

D. Nearly *all* school principals promoted from within the system.

E. The complete absence of any organized program for the in-service training of teachers in working with minority youth.

Committee Report's Recommendations[56]

Based upon a detailed analysis of the findings gained by the Citizens' Committee, a number of specific recommendations were made. These included:

Recommendation 1. De facto segregated schools should be identified as such (based upon the established criteria reviewed).

Recommendation 2. The School District should assist private and public agencies and groups seeking to reverse acute housing segregation trends.

Recommendation 3. The District should establish a policy designed to develop within each school an ethnic composition comparable to that in the city.

Recommendation 4. De facto segregation must be dealt with as the primary obstacle to equal educational opportunity.

Recommendation 5. In dealing with *de facto* segregation in the schools, broadly defined attendance areas should be established. These areas should include "clusters" of elementary schools whose total ethnic balance is approximately the same as that, currently, of the entire District. Schools within each cluster should be given attendance-boundary assignments tending to contribute to an integrated school setting. *De facto* segregated schools should be abandoned.

Recommendation 6. The Board should create an administrative position for the coordination and supervision of all activities related to the matter of equal educational opportunity. In addition, a fully organized program of compensatory education should be established for the benefit of disadvantaged youth.

Recommendation 7. A pronounced effort should be made to insure that parents are free to communicate in all relationships with teachers, counselors, and administrators.

FINAL PREPARATIONS FOR DESEGREGATION

With respect to implementation procedures for the Einstein program, Dr. Hall felt strongly that the March-through-June period was

crucial. In relationship to this concern, the Assistant to the Special
Services Deputy maintained:

. . . with the impending changes accompanying the redistricting of the
junior high school attendance boundaries . . . it was apparent that a
program of orientation and assimilation for all people involved, unlike
anything this district had yet experienced, was needed. A District-wide
committee was appointed to plan for and activate the orientation and
essential information for pupils, staff members and parents, in order that all
efforts be made to achieve the goal of equality of educational opportunity
to the greatest extent possible.[57]

7 INTEGRATED VS. COMPENSATORY EDUCATION IN THE RIVERSIDE– SAN BERNARDINO SCHOOLS

NATHANIEL HICKERSON

Assistant Professor of Education, University of Southern California

Dr. Hickerson was, at the time this article was written, Director of Education, Pacific South West Regional Office, Anti-Defamation League of B'nai B'rith. As part of his duties, he served as a consultant to the towns of Riverside and San Bernardino, as they struggled with the problems of education under conditions of segregated housing. He, too, holds an Ed.D. from Berkeley, and has recently published a successful book, *Education for Alienation* (New York: McGraw-Hill Book Company, 1966). In it he summarizes the findings of his dissertation concerning racial discrimination in a local high school.

Desegregation and compensatory education are the two remedies urged by students of educationally handicapped ghetto children. Frequently the two remedies are viewed as mutually exclusive. Such was the case in San Bernardino, which has a comprehensive system of compensatory education but has made only a token beginning toward desegregation. Neighboring Riverside has gone almost as far in compensatory schooling—and also has nearly complete desegregation.

Remarkably similar in socio-economic composition, these two small cities also resemble each other in political outlook. San Bernardino tends to be somewhat more liberal in national and state-wide elections, whereas Riverside has a more active civic leadership and a somewhat richer cultural life.

Opposition to *de facto* segregation in both cities was spearheaded by Negroes, with little apparent support from the Mexican-Americans, the other sizable minority group. The Negro opposition in Riverside was better organized and seemed to have deeper roots in the community. School boycotting was the chief form of protest in both cities, and was used only sparingly. Neither school board was called upon to defend itself in court.

In San Bernardino, the board of education, the superintendent, and most of the school-district staff were strongly committed to the neighborhood-school concept. In Riverside, school officials and staff were prepared to meet changing conditions, despite a bias in favor of neighborhood schools.

■■■

As more and more interest has focused on the education of the economically deprived in America, a polarization has emerged in the thinking of many concerned with the problem. One group of educators has turned increasingly to compensatory education for the children of the poor as the principal means by which their educational deficiencies could be made up. Another group of educators has become convinced that though compensatory education may be of value, the end of *de facto* segregation in public schools must be the first target if quality education is to be made available to the disadvantaged children of what has come to be termed "the ghetto."

Defenders of the first position maintain that it does not matter where a child goes to school, as long as the conditions of that school are such that children are motivated to learn. They say further that compensatory-education programs—if, for example, they reduce class sizes, make the latest equipment available, use the newest curricula, place the best teachers in the classrooms, provide more comprehensive counseling services, allow children interesting and informative field trips, and involve teachers and parents in a common effort to raise the levels of aspiration of the children—will result in measurable upgradings of performance levels in the ghetto schools. They envision that through compensatory education the children of the ghetto will acquire sufficient skills to enable them to enter into competition with their non-ghetto peers, when both reach adulthood, for the available skill-demanding jobs.

On the other hand, numerous educators maintain that the existence of *de facto* segregated schools in multi-racial or multi-ethnic cities precludes quality education. They argue that Negro or Mexican-American children are denied equal opportunity simply by being forced to remain in a *de facto* segregated school. Their principal argument is similar to that of the Supreme Court in 1954, that separate is never equal, and equal cannot be separate. They contend that children who grow up in the ghetto, and attend school in the ghetto, come to think of their ghetto as the world, and suffer from feelings of isolation and rejection that cannot be erased by compensatory-education programs given within the context of the ghetto school. Many further suggest that ghetto schools make it impossible for young children of differing racial or ethnic backgrounds to come to know each other. This, they say, contributes to the continuation of the race- and caste-consciousness that have been so much a part of American behavior since our beginnings.

As a result of this dichotomy in thinking, many school districts in the North and West have resorted to one type of program or the other. As is often the case when two distinctly different ideas are available for implementation, there seems to be a tendency to take Peter at the expense of Paul. Some school districts have accepted compensatory education and insisted upon maintaining the neighborhood school at all costs, even if the neighborhood school meant *de facto* segregation. Other districts have broken *de facto* segregation patterns, through partial busing, the use of the Princeton plan, and so on, and have done little in the area of compensatory education. Needless to say, the advocates of both approaches are convinced that they are right.

THE TWO CITIES—COMPARISONS AND CONTRASTS

A remarkable example of the two positions can be found in two school districts located in Southern California, about sixty miles east of Los Angeles. These two districts, San Bernardino and Riverside, serve twin cities, lying only ten miles apart. Both have populations of somewhat over 100,000 and both are relatively non-industrial. Both have air bases just outside the city, and the two have similar popula-

tion patterns. San Bernardino has about a 10 percent Negro population and a 15 percent Mexican-American population, while Riverside
has Negro and Mexican-American populations of about 7 percent and
11 percent, respectively.

Some differences between the two cities should be emphasized at
the outset. San Bernardino tends to be a little more liberal in its
political thinking, as far as voting in national and state-wide elections
is concerned. However, San Bernardino has had a history of right-
wing attacks upon the Board of Education and the school district,
culminating in the 1950's in charges that the schools and the superintendent's office were Communist-oriented. Higher education is represented by the San Bernardino Valley Junior College, situated in the
heart of the city, and a newly opened state college. The local newspaper tends to be quite conservative.

San Bernardino's school board and school administration are committed to neighborhood schools. San Bernardino has an extensive,
expensive, and thorough compensatory-education department. One
kindergarten teacher visited seventy-five homes during the last school
year. To fund its program, San Bernardino has applied for nearly one
million dollars in federal and state monies. Seminars for elementary
and secondary teachers dealing with compensatory education and
education of the disadvantaged are funded by adult-education funds.
The superintendent, who devoted eight months to a research study,
concluded that there was no evidence to indicate that *anyone* would
profit if Negro and Mexican-American and other Caucasian children
went to school together. This study was interpreted to support the
contention that compensatory education met the needs of the minority-
group children of San Bernardino far better than would the ending of
de facto segregation. At least until 1967 San Bernardino has chosen
compensatory education and denied the concept that school desegregation is necessary in order to insure quality education for all.

Riverside's minority-group population has a somewhat higher
median income than San Bernardino's, possibly because the Negro
and Mexican American people of Riverside have, for the most part,
lived longer in their city than have their counterparts in San Bernardino. Right-wing activity in Riverside has been minimal. Higher education is pursued on the local campus of the University of California,
which is noted for its strong orientation toward the humanities. Riverside's local newspaper has a liberal tradition and has won human-

relations awards from various liberal-thinking organizations throughout Southern California.

An elaborate compensatory-education program, set up in Riverside in 1963, has been all but lost from view as the battleground has
shifted to the field of *de facto* segregation. This is not to imply that
Riverside has not had a compensatory-education program, but merely
to note that, unlike in San Bernardino, emphasis requiring the full-
time concentration of an administrator has not been evident. In no
way can the interest of Riverside in this approach compare with the
thorough and elaborate manifestation of reliance on compensatory
education exhibited by the San Bernardino school system. Rather,
Riverside has moved quickly and completely to end *de facto* segregation in its schools and has placed far less emphasis, either in time or
money, on compensatory education.

As a review is made of the events and conditions leading up to the
different positions ultimately taken by the two districts, note will be
made of what is considered by the writer to be the most significant
factors leading to the contrasting choices. All must be conjecture,
however, because there is no way to determine what kinds of intangi-
bles have been at work helping to point direction. One thing is
certain: there are enough significant differences in what has happened
in the two cities with regard to the education of the disadvantaged to
allow some conclusions to be drawn as to why one city went one way
and the other city the other way.

SAN BERNARDINO OPTS FOR COMPENSATORY EDUCATION

In San Bernardino, nine of forty-two elementary schools have
enrollments exceeding 89 percent Negro and Mexican-American.
Eight are more than 95 percent Negro and Mexican-American. These
schools are located on the west and south sides of the city. At the same
time, twenty-four elementary schools have an 80 percent or higher
enrollment of non-Negro and non-Mexican-American children. Nine-
teen are 90 percent or more non-Negro and non-Mexican-American.
Eleven are 95 percent or more non-Negro and non-Mexican-American.
None of the high schools approaches 90 percent minority-group enrollment, although San Bernardino High School, the oldest in the city, is
nearly 50 percent Negro and Mexican-American. It is interesting to
note that a new high school, now under construction in the northern

part of the city, will siphon off numbers of non-Mexican-American Caucasians from the San Bernardino High School attendance area so that in future years, unless housing patterns change, this school may truly qualify as a *de facto* segregated ghetto school.

In the spring of 1964, a group of Negro parents attended a school board meeting and requested that *de facto* segregation in the San Bernardino schools be ended. They argued that as long as their children attended separate schools, their chances of achieving educational success were greatly diminished. They suggested that poorer teachers were placed and kept in these schools. They charged that facilities in the ghetto schools were inferior to those in elementary schools elsewhere in the city. They insisted that the atmosphere in any ghetto school was not conducive to meaningful learning. In the next six months, the complainants returned to board meetings on a number of occasions, and the board finally agreed to make a study of their charges. The superintendent undertook this assignment.

In the meantime, the board continually reminded the complainants that a massive compensatory-education program was under way and that the San Bernardino school district would spare no effort in upgrading the education of the ghetto children. After eight months, the superintendent issued the results of his findings. He categorically denied that inferior teachers were placed in ghetto schools. He denied that ghetto facilities were not equal to those elsewhere in the city. He insisted that a large majority of the people in the west-side ghetto were not dissatisfied with the schools. He concluded with a staunch defense of the concept of the neighborhood school and maintained that in the eight months of research he had just completed, he could find no evidence that Negro or Mexican-American or other Caucasian children profited educationally by going to school together.

Shortly thereafter, the board reaffirmed its support of neighborhood schools. The board, however, did announce an open-enrollment policy, to be put into effect for one junior high school with more than 90 percent minority-group attendance. The board defended this departure from a neighborhood-school policy on the ground that three junior high schools in the city were underattended. Within the first month after the announcement, about forty children had transferred. The majority of these were Mexican-Americans who asked for a transfer to a junior high school with a large Mexican-American enrollment. (Many have since returned to their original schools.)

Shortly before the opening of the 1965 school year the San Bernardino superintendent's office announced a drastic curtailment in bus service for children. The superintendent maintained that with the closing of the local air base a major source of revenue for the schools had been lost. The superintendent showed that the new bus regulations were in keeping with common practices throughout much of California and that the previous service had gone far beyond typical service available to children elsewhere in the state. After this announcement, a group of Negro women formed an organization called "The Community League of Mothers," and threatened to call a boycott of the public schools if the new bus regulations were not rescinded. As school opened, about three hundred children, almost all of them Negroes, were absent from their classes, attending a Freedom School system. A month and a half later the number of children absent from public school had diminished sharply, with no actual count available. Although it would appear that curtailment of bus service was the immediate cause of the boycott, the reasons apparently ran much deeper.

The acting principal of the Freedom School system says that the Community League of Mothers was really in pursuit of the right to enroll their children in any school in San Bernardino. Further, he says, the women maintain that the contribution of Negroes to American culture is not being given proper consideration in the history and civics classes in the schools. But many observers feel that the boycott was primarily the result of a strong sense of frustration stemming from the refusal of the San Bernardino school board to consider ending *de facto* school segregation in the city's public schools.

Just how much support exists in the Negro and Mexican-American communities for the move to end *de facto* segregation is difficult to determine. Certainly, there has been little or no interaction between the Negroes and Mexican-Americans for the purpose of presenting a common front. In fact, quite the reverse was the case. When offered the choice to transfer to a junior high school that was better balanced racially, few from either group took the opportunity. There is little evidence to indicate that the two ethnic groups have ever worked together at all, despite common problems facing them as the low socio-economic groups in the city. In addition, the various Negro organizations in San Bernardino apparently have not been able to agree on a common program.

As of 1967, the city of San Bernardino has rejected the efforts of some members of the Negro community to put an end to *de facto* segregation in the San Bernardino schools. A high school is under construction that will increase *de facto* segregation—for the first time on the high-school level. In San Bernardino, school board, superintendent, and administrative staff are committed to the concept of neighborhood schools and compensatory education.

RIVERSIDE CHOOSES DESEGREGATION

In Riverside, three out of twenty-eight elementary schools had a 97 percent or higher enrollment of Negro and Mexican-American children in 1963. One school had a 100 percent minority enrollment. At the same time, nine of twenty-eight elementary schools had a 95 percent or higher enrollment of non-Negro and non-Mexican American students. Thus, twelve of the twenty-eight elementary schools in Riverside had a marked racial imbalance. No junior or senior high schools in Riverside can be identified as racially imbalanced. As in San Bernardino, racial imbalance in schools resulted from housing patterns. In September, 1963, the Riverside Unified School District, prodded into a formal self-examination by complaints from Negro parents, officially recognized that low achievement by minority-group children had become a serious problem.

The superintendent's office recommended to the board that an intensive compensatory-education program should be instituted in those schools where levels of achievement of students were low. This program was to include informational and cultural field trips, special reading help, teacher's aides, tutors, increased library services, and preschool education. The board quickly adopted the recommendation. As the year progressed, it became increasingly evident to some people in the Negro community, and apparently to certain members of the administrative staff, that this program of compensatory education was not producing the desired results. Achievement of minority-group children was not being raised in any appreciable amount. Criticism of *de facto* segregated schools continued to emanate from the ghetto communities, particularly from Negro citizens. By the end of the 1963–64 school year, disenchantment with the compensatory-education program was widespread among both lay people and some members of the administrative staff.

At this time, an exceptionally articulate young man, a former president of the local NAACP and a teacher in the Riverside schools, was placed in the administrative offices of the school district to develop a Human Relations Council in the city, to expedite compensatory education, and to work closely with the Negro community to bring about a closer understanding between the schools and minority groups. This man, a Negro and a resident of Riverside for twenty years prior to his appointment, was to be directly responsible to an assistant superintendent of schools. Apparently the superintendent took little active part in supervising these two men.

During the school year 1964–65, the director of the Human Relations Council and the assistant superintendent worked hard to convince local civic leaders that compensatory education was not the answer to the low-achievement problem of minority-group children. They directed the thinking of some community leaders toward the ending of *de facto* segregation. The newspaper lent its support. The chairman of the board of education became interested, as did one of the local bank officials and one of the city's most prominent business executives. Meanwhile, the compensatory-education program had begun to deteriorate and the Negro community became more and more insistent, strengthened by allies, that *de facto* segregation be ended.

As the opening of school for the 1965–66 year neared, some leaders in the Negro community announced plans for a boycott of the public schools unless the three ghetto schools were shut down. The board took no action, although members talked at great length with Negro leaders. Then, on September 7, a petition was presented to the school board asking that two of the three schools be closed immediately. Spokesmen for the petitioners said that the compensatory-education program was not bringing about the educational improvement they sought. This petition was presented on the same day that an early-morning fire had destroyed some of the older buildings on the site of one of the *de facto* segregated schools. The board, as a result of this fire, had authorized the transportation of kindergarten, first, second, and third graders from the burned-out school to other schools in the district. This did not satisfy the petitioners, who then renewed the threat of boycott unless two of the three *de facto* segregated schools were closed entirely. On September 13, when school opened, attendance at the two schools was only one-third of normal, as "Freedom Schools" went into operation.

That afternoon the board met and agreed to work immediately toward total desegregation in the Riverside schools. The boycott was ended. October 18 was the date set for the plan of desegregation to be presented to the school board. On September 30, the names of a seventeen-member advisory committee, appointed by the board to work with the superintendent's office, was made public. The advisory group was comprised of original petitioners and other leading citizens, both laymen and professional educators. The plan of the advisory committee was accepted unanimously by the board, and the Riverside School District moved to eliminate the three *de facto* segregated elementary schools by September, 1966.

WHY THE DIFFERENCES IN APPROACH?

Undoubtedly many factors helped to determine the differing commitments toward education of minority-group children in the two communities. It would be difficult to make a case that any one of these factors was the most important. A review of specific differences appears to highlight a number of societal factors with significant bearing upon public education.

1. The power structure in the two cities played a key role. In San Bernardino, apparently no representatives of the city's decision-making group took any part in pushing for school desegregation. Indeed, there is little indication that any of the "important" people in San Bernardino are even aware of the existence of a problem. The protests for the most part are attributed to a handful of Negro dissidents who do not seem to reflect the majority of the Negro population and do not speak *at all* for the Mexican-American group.

In Riverside, certain members of the power structure recognized the need for change and lent their support. Whether this was because of altruistic motives or a desire to avoid further dissatisfaction in the community is not really important. What *is* significant is that the newspapers and at least half a dozen leading citizens helped directly in effecting desegregation.

2. In both cities, only intense pressure from elements in the Negro population succeeded in producing movement. In San Bernardino, the board, after a year and a half of difficulty, reluctantly appointed a citizens' advisory committee to investigate charges leveled against the school district by Negro citizens. Even this move was achieved only after prodding from the State Department of Education. There is little

indication that, even if the advisory committee recommends desegregation, the board will act decisively on the report.

In Riverside, the pressure of the Negro community was reinforced by a coincidental event: a fire in one of the ghetto schools. This, together with receptiveness from a portion of the power structure after continuous effort by Negro leaders to bring the difficulties into the open, was enough to set rolling the wheels of change. However, had not some leaders of the larger community seen fit to lend their support to desegregation, one may speculate as to how long it would have taken for changes to be made even with the pressure of the Negro community and the school burning.

3. The local press in the two cities appears to mirror the commitment of the local power structures. In San Bernardino, the newspaper, like the power structure, has been almost totally silent concerning the need for desegregation. In Riverside, the local newspaper was sensitive to the expressed thinking of certain key people in the community and reinforced their point of view through editorials and news coverage. The newspaper in Riverside not only reacted to what was already evident in the thinking of part of the power structure, but also influenced the attitudes of others by its forthright stand.

4. The superintendent's office is a most important force in effecting change in the policies and procedures of the schools. This office is, as well, a crucial instrument in providing direction for the local citizenry as they develop commitment to particular educational policies and procedures.

In San Bernardino, the superintendent's office has led the power structure and indeed a large segment of the Caucasian population in rejecting desegregation. The superintendent's office also has reacted to the absence of pressure from the power structure by assuming that there is no need to think in terms of desegregation. In Riverside, the superintendent's office provided leadership in convincing citizens of the community of the need for the change. In turn, the superintendent's office reacted to the already favorable attitudes toward school desegregation held by leading citizens.

5. Although both school boards appear to be heavily committed to the neighborhood school, Riverside, under pressure, found a way to accommodate both the neighborhood-school philosophy and desegregation. The Riverside plan calls for the transportation of entire blocks of children to a receiving school. In this way, as many as seventy-five

to one hundred children who live on the same street are bused together to their new school. Riverside school officials maintain that this policy will not result in the destruction of the neighborhood school. On the other hand, the superintendent's office in San Bernardino has accepted the neighborhood-school concept to mean attendance in the school closest to the child and has been adamant in defense of the position that any transportation of elementary school children will be injurious to the students.

6. The individuals responsible for making school policy are extremely important in explaining the events that take place. In San Bernardino, there is no one in the superintendent's office who, at least in public, voices the need for desegregation. Much time is spent in defending the concept of the neighborhood school as a pillar of quality education on the elementary school level. In Riverside, there are articulate defenders of desegregation in the superintendent's office who worked diligently in the schools and in the community to enlist support for their position. Communication between the superintendent's office and the rest of the community was at a high level. Little was left to chance. Planning and execution were well thought out. The administrative officers at the schools, as well as important people in the power structure, parents, teachers, school children, and citizens in general, were involved in producing the desegregation.

7. The presence of a college or university, particularly one with a strong emphasis on community involvement, may be an important factor in producing change. In San Bernardino, the only post-high-school institution in full operation is a junior college. The new state college has just opened its doors, and its impact on the community has not as yet been seriously felt.

In Riverside, many faculty members from the University of California were involved in aiding the school district to meet the crises that developed. At least half a dozen faculty members served as consultants or aided the superintendent's office in some manner so as to convince the citizenry of Riverside of the need for desegregation. Now, through the university, large sums of money have become available to the school district and the university for a joint continuation of research pertaining to desegregation.

8. Both school districts recognize the need to compensate for the centuries-old neglect of the Negro in American education. San Bernardino believes that it can accomplish its purpose of raising achievement

levels of Negroes (and Mexican-Americans) through an extensive compensatory-education program. Riverside, though it in no way denigrates the value of compensatory education, nonetheless has moved to desegregate, maintaining that achievement levels can be raised for Negro (and Mexican-American) children only in an integrated environment. Riverside is continuing its compensatory-education program but only as an adjunct to desegregation.

9. Educators in both San Bernardino and Riverside deny that mere physical integration of schools will raise the level of achievement of minority-group children. San Bernardino, to judge by its actions, does not even consider desegregation important in improving motivation and opportunity for minority-group students. Riverside, though committed to desegregation, has accompanied the move toward it with a continuation of compensatory education (although not with a program of the same depth as in San Bernardino) and with in-service programs for teachers in whose classrooms minority children are placed. There is an effort to involve not only parents in school affairs but also the entire community in aiding the process of desegregation. In addition, the Riverside school district has a professional human-relations advisor who works almost entirely with the minority-group students and their parents in helping to increase student motivation and parent involvement. He also serves as a mediator in disputes with racial overtones.

In 1966, a Citizens' Advisory Committee, appointed by the San Bernardino School Board to investigate charges leveled against the schools by a Negro organization, recommended that desegregation plans be adopted by January 1, 1967, and that implementation begin in September, 1967. Instead, the school board appointed a special-relations consultant, a Mexican-American, whose major function was to coordinate efforts to implement the recommendations of the Citizens' Advisory Committee. One of his first acts was to appoint a new Advisory Committee to work with him. A policy of open enrollment was adopted for some elementary and junior high school students, permitting ghetto children to enroll in non-ghetto schools. As of September, 1967, it was too early to determine how many parents had taken advantage of this opportunity for their children.

8 | DESEGREGATION AND BEYOND: THE SAUSALITO–MILL VALLEY SCHOOL PROGRAMS

STATEN W. WEBSTER

Associate Professor of Education, University of California, Berkeley

Dr. Webster is an Associate Professor of Education at the University of California, Berkeley. During 1965–1966 he served as a consultant in human relations to the Sausalito and Mill Valley School Districts. He is also a consultant to the Urban Special Services Division of the Oakland Public Schools, and is editor of the recently published book, *The Disadvantaged Learner: Knowing, Understanding, Educating* (San Francisco. Chandler Publishing Company, 1966). He is indebted to numerous individuals who participated in the events described, especially to Mr. Charles W. Lavaroni, Mrs. Bill Garoutte, and Mrs. Joyce Gross.

In Sausalito the problem centered upon the existence of a segregated school. In Mill Valley there were almost no Negroes in attendance and some of the residents wanted their children to attend school with a variety of classmates. Mill Valley once consisted of a cluster of workers' homes surrounding a redwood-lumber mill. Now it is a suburb of San Francisco consisting almost entirely of homes, built partially of

redwood, for the well-to-do. The situation illustrates the contrast between suburban communities from which Negroes, by one means or
another, are excluded, and the urban communities from which the
middle class have largely fled. If complete integration is to take place
in the schools of northern cities, the needed number of white children
must come from the suburbs. Educational parks are regarded as a
possible solution. Schools placed on the periphery of cities might be
another. Either would require control of the schools on a metropolitan
basis. A county-wide system would not be large enough. For example,
no fewer than nine counties border on the twin Bays of San Francisco
and San Pablo, yet there is almost no break in the housing.

Still, it is very difficult, because of the long-established American
practice of local control of schools, to think about schools except in local
terms. The realization that the State of California has a measure of
jurisdiction over "our" local schools is an enlightened one. Hence a
feeling of responsibility by the citizens in one district, like Mill Valley,
for the schooling in another, like Sausalito, is engendered only with
difficulty. Paradoxically, Sausalito has twice the tax base behind each
child that Mill Valley has.

Pressures for desegregation are often mounted from outside a
district. In Sausalito, the initiation came from CORE, with both white
and Negro leadership living in Mill Valley. Some action from local
churches is noted. There was no specific court case, but *Jackson* v.
Pasadena was cited almost threateningly.

Once the local school authorities had been sensitized by the
protesters, experts from higher education and from the State Department of Education were called in to ascertain the facts, and to suggest
remedies. But Sausalito's school board election and selection of a new
superintendent underline the extent of local control over the schools
and the entrenchment of the practice. The talk is always toward larger
rather than smaller districts through either unionization, putting two or
more elementary districts together, or unification, putting elementary
and high school districts together. But, as Mill Valley's McConnell
Report shows, change in the size of a district is effected only with
difficulty and always takes from nine months to a year even when
successful. A measure of voluntary pupil exchange between Sausalito
and Mill Valley has been achieved, and this is the only case study here
(except New York City) to report this forward but inevitable step
toward racial balance in the schools. In Sausalito, as in so many urban
school districts of the North, nearly half the school children are Negro.

An impressive variety of practices aimed toward integration and
compensatory education is listed in the article that follows. Cluster

grouping is especially important. When the usual practice of homogeneous grouping is followed, children whose families are low on the socio-economic scale nearly always find themselves in the slow or low groups. Hence the ends of desegregation are largely circumvented. Cluster grouping means that fast, medium, and slow students are assigned to a class with the same teacher so that, although they will still be grouped for instruction within the class, the opportunity to move to a faster group will constantly be available. To a marked degree, opportunity for advancement will be equalized.

∎∎∎

Distinct, but related, programs have been launched in two of California's elementary school districts in efforts to deal with problems of *de facto* segregation. First, Sausalito attacked the problem in its own schools by an assault upon segregation in grades kindergarten through four. Sausalito then combined with Mill Valley to provide a desegregated learning experience for Mill Valley's Caucasian elementary school children. The plan was implemented through an interdistrict transfer program for selected students. These two programs were not undertaken easily. Before an attempt can be made to follow their trails of strife in the two communities, an examination of the geographical and demographic features of the school districts must be made. The Sausalito desegregation problem then needs consideration before the Sausalito–Mill Valley Transfer Program can be envisioned.

The Two Communities

Sausalito: This small city is immediately south of Mill Valley and north of San Francisco across the world-famous Golden Gate Bridge. Both cities are at the southernmost end of Marin County. Sausalito is noted for its *avant garde* atmosphere produced by such features as art galleries, specialty shops, expensive restaurants, and extensive marine facilities. It is a tourist attraction as well as a popular Sunday-visiting spot of Bay Area residents. In 1960, the city had a population of some 6500 persons, almost all of whom were Caucasians. The city is increasingly becoming an apartment-type bedroom community for professional and white-collar workers who commute daily to San Francisco.

The Fort Area: To the south of Sausalito and immediately adjacent to the Golden Gate Bridge lie United States Army Forts Barry, Baker, and Cronkhite. Attached to these forts is a military dependents' housing area containing a population of approximately 1400 persons. This population increases significantly during times of national emergency.

Marin City: On the north side of Sausalito lies an unincorporated area containing both public and private housing units of very recent construction. This is the almost all-Negro community of Marin City, often called the "gilded ghetto" because of its mixture of both middle- and lower-class occupants, and because of the newness of its buildings. Marin City came into existence during World War II as the site for an extensive temporary federal housing project for shipyard workers. Persons living there work throughout Marin County and in San Francisco.

Physically, Marin City is a combination of high-rise low-cost housing units, low-rent and co-op apartments, and individual homes. Private dwellings range in price from approximately $15,000 to $19,000. Presently, some 2500 persons live in Marin City. During World War II the population was approximately that of Sausalito proper at that time—slightly over 4000. Since then redevelopment programs have produced a sizable drop in Marin City's population.

Mill Valley: To the north of Marin City lies the middle-class to upper-class community of Mill Valley, with a population of some 12,000 persons. Large numbers of professionals and executives who work in San Francisco live in this quiet, semi-isolated, tree-shaded residential community. Individuals such as these help to make Marin County one of the 12 wealthiest counties in the United States on the basis of personal income. Mill Valley, largely residential, has virtually no industries located within its boundaries.

The School Districts

Sausalito School District: Sausalito proper, Marin City, the military fort area, and other unincorporated county areas comprise the Sausalito School District. The student population of this area is summarized in Table 1. Bayside, Richardson Bay, Manzanita, and Central Schools carry out the educational program of this district which, while small, does possess sufficient property resources to support a higher per pupil expenditure than is possible in the case of the Mill Valley School District. During the school year 1965–66, the Sausalito district spent approximately $845.30 on the education of each of its 925 students. The assessed valuation in the district amounts to an average of $26,292 per pupil.[1]

Mill Valley School District: The boundaries of the Mill Valley School District contain the city of Mill Valley and certain unincorporated areas of Marin County. Some 3400 children are enrolled in this elementary school district, which contains eight school plants.[2] Because of its residential character, the Mill Valley School District has fewer resources available to it, on a per pupil basis, than does the Sausalito district. The assessed valuation per pupil[3] is $13,343.

TABLE 1. POPULATION OF SAUSALITO SCHOOL DISTRICT (PRE-SCHOOL AND K-8)

Area	Population	School Population	Percentage of School Population
Sausalito and Forts Barry, Baker, and Cronkhite	7,900	427	47.8
Marin City	2,500	465	52.2
Total	10,400	892	100.0

The ethnic composition of schools in this district is also in stark contrast with that of the Sausalito schools. During the school year 1964–65, for example, only 108 non-white students were enrolled in the district. This non-Caucasian group was comprised of 11 Negroes, 75 Orientals, and 22 other non-whites.[4] Eleven Negroes out of 3400 students means a minority so small that any notice it attracts is benevolent rather than hostile.

THE EFFORT TO DESEGREGATE THE SAUSALITO SCHOOLS

In 1963, protests from the Negro community of Marin City initiated a controversy that led to desegregation in the Sausalito School District.

Manzanita, the neighborhood school for Marin City, housed kindergarten through grade four. In March, 1964, only 16 white children attended the school.[5] But the complaints of Marin City parents were not, at first, directed at segregation. Instead they protested against actions of the principal, and against the quality of the teaching, and they deplored an alleged combination of disdain and patronage leveled against their children in the classrooms and themselves when they visited the school. The Marin County Chapter of the Congress of Racial Equality (CORE), including Negroes and whites from Marin City, Sausalito, and Mill Valley, provided leadership for the dissatisfied parents.

The Negro majority at Manzanita was mirrored by an almost complete absence of Negroes at Bayside (grades 1 and 2) and Central (K, 3, 4), two of the three other Sausalito elementary schools. All students within the district then completed grades five through eight at Richardson Bay School.

At this stage of the emerging crisis, the five-member Sausalito Board of School Trustees were Mr. Harold L. Sleight, Chairman, Mrs. Juanita Cobb, Clerk, Mr. George R. Kowski, Mrs. Jessie Zimmer, and Dr. Stanley J. Wolfe. The Superintendent of Schools was Mr. Marcus F. Davis.

Persons involved in the Manzanita issue report that efforts to seek a solution of the alleged difficulties through meetings with the school board were unsatisfactory. Indeed, reports indicate that Mrs. Cobb, a Negro board member and resident of Marin City, was not in sympathy with the parents and that she failed to articulate properly the feelings of the Negro community. Tensions continued to mount as CORE and other community groups, including churches, began to voice their dissatisfactions over the board's lack of specific action to solve the alleged problems at Manzanita School.

As confrontations between citizens of Marin City and school board groups increased in intensity, attention began to shift to the all-pervasive problem of *de facto* segregation in the Manzanita School. This change of emphasis was perhaps stimulated by the *Jackson* v. *Pasadena City School District* case[6] in which exclusion of minority groups from schools by acts of school districts were reviewed. The decision made these major provisions:[7]

Where such segregation exists it is not enough for a school board to refrain from affirmative discriminatory conduct.

The right to an equal opportunity for education and the harmful consequences of segregation require that school boards take steps, insofar as reasonably feasible, to alleviate racial imbalance in schools regardless of its cause.

In late August, 1963, the Executive Committee of the Education Committee of the Marin County Chapter of CORE, also raised the issue of racial imbalance and issued a statement consisting of five demands to the Sausalito school trustees. These demands included[8]

1. a statement from the Board that it agrees in principle with complete integration of the schools in the district.
2. a plan for racial balance within all schools from kindergarten up.
3. study the problem of creating racial balance within the classes.
4. plan for integration to be presented by November 15, 1963.
5. in the interim, parents of minority groups may request transfers to other schools in the district.

In response to the demands of CORE, the Board of Trustees of the Sausalito School District on September 30 passed a resolution requesting "the advice and assistance" of the state Commission on Equal Opportunities in Education (COEOE) in resolving problems "regarding the ethnic distribution of pupils and school attendance areas." This Commission had been established in 1958 to help local school districts with problems relating to racial, religious, and other discriminations in connection with employment of certificated employees. It is interesting to note that on September 20, 1963, just ten days prior to the Sausalito school board's resolution, the educational code of the State of California was amended to authorize COEOE to assist and to advise school districts in matters relating to racial imbalance and school attendance areas.

The Riles Report: Several points of view central to the issue under consideration were in evidence at the time COEOE began to study the situation in Sausalito.[9]

1. Educational opportunity was not equal in the Sausalito School District, as was illustrated when the Manzanita School program was contrasted with programs at Central and Bayside Schools.
2. Racial integration in the desegregated Richardson Bay School (grades five through eight) would probably be more successful if interracial experience were initiated in the primary schools of the district. This belief led to demands that some Negro children be bused into the white primary schools and that some white children be transported to Manzanita.

3. Conversely, other residents of the school district viewed the neighborhood-school arrangement as essential for an adequate educational experience. They claimed that young children were not mature enough to cope with a broader environment.

The Executive Secretary of COEOE at this time was Wilson C. Riles—the first Negro citizen of California to hold a major position in the State Department of Education. During the months following the authorization of COEOE to advise the Sausalito School District, Mr. Riles held a number of meetings with the Superintendent of Schools, the administrative staff, a member of the board, and a representative from the County Counsel's Office. Additional meetings were held by the Executive Secretary with the Education Committee of CORE and with individuals in the Marin City area. Also, in February, 1964, Dr. John C. Connelly, a professor at San Francisco State College, was assigned by COEOE as consultant to the Sausalito investigation.

During these activities, the citizens of Marin City watched and waited for some word from the COEOE investigation. Feelings of impatience grew, culminating in the one-day CORE-directed Freedom School held on May 18, 1964. The situation remained tense until July 29, when Mr. Riles announced that COEOE was ready with its report and recommendations to the Board of Trustees of Sausalito. The Riles Report contained seven specific conclusions—products of the study:[10]

1. A condition of racial imbalance exists in the Sausalito School District.
2. Because of the high percentage of non-white pupils in the district, it is not possible to achieve an ideal ethnic balance in each school. In other words, if white and non-white pupils were distributed equally in each school unit, acceptable racial balance would not be achieved.
3. The staff found no evidence which would indicate that there has been a deliberate attempt on the part of the Board of Trustees to maintain or promote the segregation of pupils on the basis of race. Nor has evidence been found which would indicate that inequitable educational opportunities have been consciously promoted.
4. Amelioration of the effects of de facto segregation in the Sausalito School District can only be achieved by concentrated, creative, and sensitive approaches to the educational problems within the district. The resolution of the problems will require facilities and resources from outside the local district. The cooperation of county, state and federal agencies, all of which at the present time have involvements with the education of the children residing in the district, must be secured. Marin County especially has a major responsibility in assisting the Sausalito School

District in finding solutions to a number of the problems which over a period of time were thrust on the local district by outside jurisdictions.

5. A deterioration in school-community communications has developed over a long period of time which contributed to the alienation of the schools to substantial segments of the communities within the district.

6. Since all children in grades 5 through 8 are housed at the Richardson Bay School, desegregation has been achieved at the middle and upper grade levels in the school district.

7. School housing in the primary units—Central-Bayside and Manzanita— seems to be inadequate.

The importance of two of the above conclusions in later events necessitates some elaboration. In the second conclusion an assumption was introduced which was to provide considerable fuel for later controversy—the idea that *ideal ethnic balance could not be achieved* because of the presence of large numbers of Negro children, approximately 48 percent, in the district as a whole. This assumption, according to Mr. Riles's personal comments, was made on the basis of the often-quoted desired minority-to-majority ratio of 25 to 75. This ratio appears in a selection by the Negro social scientist Allison Davis in a work by Berelson and Steiner.[11] The magic numbers of Davis were seized upon by those persons and groups most resistant to change. Their surprising argument was that unless the ideal could be reached it would be better to leave the schools almost completely segregated.

The seventh conclusion in the Riles Report likewise had importance for later events. This statement pronounced inadequate all three primary-school plants in Sausalito and thus helped to focus the district's attention upon building needs.

In addition to these conclusions, the Riles Report made a series of recommendations:[12]

I. A CITIZENS' ADVISORY COMMITTEE OF TWELVE TO FIFTEEN PERSONS SHOULD BE APPOINTED BY THE BOARD OF TRUSTEES TO MAKE A THOROUGH STUDY OF THE EDUCATIONAL NEEDS OF THE DISTRICT.

Areas to be examined should include:
1. Equal educational opportunities
2. Problems of de facto school segregation
3. Intergroup relations
4. School building needs, and
5. School finance

The recommendation for a citizens' advisory committee is desirable because of the fact that inter-community communication and coordination are the central considerations which will allow or disallow the development of effective educational programs for the children and youth of the school district. The committee should be representative of significant community interest in Sausalito, Marin City and the military reservation. The specific problem areas for study and assessment may be handled by subcommittees.

It is suggested that the following specific areas be considered along with others that might be raised by the committee, the Board of Trustees, or interested citizens:

1. School unification proposals and their effect upon children of the Sausalito School District.

2. Present school district sites including a professional appraisal of their values and the conditions under which they have been acquired and held.

3. Prospects for the development of the Richardson Bay School site into an adequate single school, K through 8, using the concept of the "educational park."

4. In line with No. 3 above, study should be made of disposing of the Central School site and utilizing the proceeds for the development of the Richardson Bay School site.

5. Consideration should be given to the extension of compensatory programs for educationally disadvantaged pupils. The study should include an examination of the child-care center program, presently housed at Manzanita School with attention being given to the development of a parent-child pre-school education program for the entire district utilizing the Manzanita site.

6. Prospects for inter-district exchange of pupils should be investigated. A number of Marin County parents outside the Sausalito School District seem to desire inter-cultural and inter-racial educational opportunities for their children. CORE with its widespread membership in Marin County might provide leadership for encouraging and supporting such a program. The newer school facility at Manzanita School site might be utilized in such a program.

II. AN INTER-SCHOOL FACULTY COMMITTEE SHOULD MAKE A STUDY OF CURRENT SCHOOL TESTING, PUPIL CLASS ASSIGNMENT AND CURRICULUM PRACTICES WITH RECOMMENDATIONS FOR CHANGE AS APPROPRIATE. SUCH A COMMITTEE MIGHT FUNCTION AS A SUBCOMMITTEE OF THE CITIZENS' COMMITTEE.

Dissatisfaction among certain citizens regarding racial imbalance at Manzanita School had been the basic pressure which finally led the Sausalito Board of Trustees to seek the assistance of COEOE. Yet the recommendations of the Riles Report offered no quick solution to the problem. In light of later events the most significant of the ideas advanced by Riles was that an inter-district exchange of pupils be explored. Also important was Riles' suggestion calling for the creation of a broadly constituted citizens' committee. This gave those groups critical of the school district an opportunity to seek actively the changes they desired.

The Work of the Citizens' Committee: On October 19, 1964, the Board of Trustees created a 17-member Citizens' Committee on the educational needs of the Sausalito School District. Dr. Connelly, who had coordinated the COEOE investigation, was hired as consultant to the group. A charge was issued to the Committee that its report and recommendations for change within the Sausalito School District be in the hands of the Board not later than June 1, 1965.[13] One week later the Board of Trustees issued a Letter of Instructions to the Citizens' Advisory Committee which was very specific in defining certain ways in which the group should work.[14] The Advisory Committee was reminded of the necessity that their proposals respect Board rules, regulations, by-laws, and areas of jurisdiction; that subcommittee reports should be made to the Committee as a whole and not to the general public; and that participants in the group must act independently and not be committed to a sponsoring organization. Finally the members of the Committee were instructed to bear in mind the importance of submitting only a majority report. Minority reports could be submitted only in those cases where there were wide differences or basic differences in principle.

With its charge and instructions in hand the Citizens' Advisory Committee began deliberations. This group of citizens representing the district's three communities (Sausalito, the forts, and Marin City) conducted most of its work as a committee of the whole. But still another crisis faced the Sausalito community.

School Board Election, Spring 1965: Earlier confrontations (1963) over the status of the Sausalito schools had resulted in a polarization of the white citizenry of Sausalito itself. At one end of this division were those groups in favor of children attending the neighborhood school, while at the other end were those favoring some swift move to end de facto segregation. In April 1965, with this polarization still prevalent, a school board election was held to elect three members. Dr. Wolfe and Mr. Kowaski were the incumbents seeking reelection. Mrs. Cobb, a board member from Marin City, had decided not to run.

Among the new candidates for seats on the board were three young liberal residents who campaigned on the educational issues before the school district. These candidates were Mr. Dave E. Freedheim, Mr. Bruce Woelfel, and Mr. Nathaniel Johnson, a Negro resident of Marin City.

Informants report that Mr. Woelfel entered the contest with little hope of winning and saw his role as one candidate in a position to freely bring out the issues at hand. Indeed, Woelfel was very candid on such matters as opposition to *de facto* segregation in the schools, the quality of the educational program in the district, especially at Manzanita School, and the performance of the Superintendent at the time, Mr. Davis.

Two other issues were before the community and Board of Trustees during the campaign for this election. First, the Human Rights Commission of Marin County had been assigned, because of public pressure, the task of looking into questions that had been raised regarding the Sausalito schools. This group made extensive demands upon the Sausalito Board of Trustees for information regarding its program and placed the Board in a crossfire between the Commission itself and the CORE and Marin City groups.

Second, confronting the citizens in southern Marin County was the question of whether the eleven school districts feeding into the Tamalpais Union High School District should be unified. This unification issue contributed to tensions already present in the Sausalito School District over issues of *de facto* segregation. As a subsequent vote on the question showed, although enough citizens of Sausalito, Mill Valley, and Marin City were in favor of unification, it was defeated because of strong opposition in those areas of the high school district containing few, if any, Negroes.

In a hard-fought contest the Freedheim, Woelfel, and Johnson slate was victorious over the incumbents and other candidates. Surprisingly, Mr. Woelfel won over the next candidate—though by a close margin of only 12 votes. Woelfel's outspoken position had served to arouse even greater opposition to change from the more conservative elements in the district. Despite the controversy over the assignment of school attendance, the citizens of the Sausalito School District passed a proposition calling for a significant increase in the District's tax rate.

The final meetings of the retiring Board of Trustees were held under frustrating circumstances. Three members were about to retire;

the report of the Citizens' Advisory Committee, scheduled for June 1, was not made until June 29, 1965; and Superintendent Davis turned in his resignation at the last meeting but one, on June 17. His resignation was accepted by unanimous vote and at the June 29, 1965, meeting he was awarded a compensatory salary adjustment of 120 days of unused vacation time with pay. Thus ended Mr. Davis's seven-year tenure with the district, and the community found itself facing an eventful summer without a chief administrator.

The Citizens' Advisory Committee Report: As has been stated, the Citizens' Advisory Committee (CAC) grew out of the suggestions presented in the Riles Report, and chose to conduct most of its work as a committee of the whole. During the CAC's deliberations, spread over nine months, attention was devoted to the topics of School District Boundaries, Desegregation and Integration within the Present School District, Special Programs and Integration Efforts in the Schools, Educational Issues, and School Sites and Finance.

These differ slightly from the topics suggested by Mr. Riles. Despite minor discrepancies between the two lists, the committee did come to grips with the central problem of *de facto* school segregation. This fact is illustrated in an excerpt from the summary portion of the CAC's final report:[15]

In its efforts to seek out the central provocateurs of many problems, in its desire to make a contribution to the betterment of educational opportunity, to aid in promoting an education of the highest quality for all children of the community, the Committee has had to face the reality that racial imbalance and racial segregation are the focal problem out of which boil many specific problems. The Committee has had to accept that eradication of these undemocratic and destructive circumstances must be pursued with force, vigor, and the sacrifices essential for disciplined constructive effort. Changes have taken place in the community and in the schools which require new views and new assessments if the ethical values of a democratic society are to be maintained. We no longer have a choice in the matter of whether change will or will not occur. We have only the choice of whether our confrontation with the fact of change will be well or poorly done. We cannot expect that a disciplined program of study or a disciplined association of our children and youth in the schools can be achieved by regulative edicts or policies unless the adult community demonstrates a disciplined courage in their feelings, aspirations and actions, in their rational viewing of problems and in intelligent, sensitive regard in acting upon them. We do not believe the cancerous growth of an undemocratic virus can be curtailed by "first aid" expediencies. We know that some pain, some fear, some ambivalence and reluctance, some doubt will attend the planned efforts to eliminate causes of malfunction and deterioration which plague our schools and prevent a healthy revitalization of our educational enterprise. We know also that it is beyond the competence of a lay committee to prescribe the details of procedure essential to effect the necessary cure for our school problems.

Within the final CAC report were ten specific suggestions to the Board of Trustees, five of which relate to actions later taken.[16]

The Committee, recognizing that racial imbalance, segregated schooling and certain social, economic and culturally disadvantaged conditions exist, recommends:

1. A professional study of our entire school system including policies, procedures, administration, curriculum content and method, personnel qualifications, and community relations, as an initial diagnostic assessment.

4. An immediate desegregation and integration of the primary schools and to the extent necessary a vigorous program of integration in the desegregated upper-grade school.

5. Cooperative effort with the Mill Valley School District and other neighboring school districts to aid in the elimination of racial imbalance in the Sausalito School District, with the expectation of early unionization of school districts and ultimate unification of school districts, with mutual benefits to all.

7. Development of effective communication between all schools in the district, between neighboring districts, between faculty, administration and community.

8. Authorizing the establishment of a permanent Citizens Advisory Committee to serve as liaison between the community and schools and the various communities of the school district.

Summary: The Sausalito School District on July 1, 1965, faced two major problems for which solutions had to be sought before the opening of school in September. First, it had to locate a new superintendent to replace Mr. Davis. Second, it had to decide what was to be done about *de facto* school segregation in the district. Both problems were solved.

THE SOLUTIONS FOR SAUSALITO

Obtaining a Superintendent: In California, the County Superintendent of Schools seeks to provide assistance and leadership to local districts having difficulties within his county. Thus, at the June 29, 1965, meeting of the Board of Trustees a letter was read from Dr. Virgil Hollis, County Superintendent. Dr. Hollis offered the services of both himself and his office for the screening procedure required in seeking a new district superintendent. Dr. Hollis also expressed his willingness to assist the district in answering certain questions which had been placed before it by the Human Rights Commission of Marin County. He suggested that the commission submit such questions to his office and that the Sausalito District supply the information to him for evaluation. After this, he proposed, the information should be sent to the Human Rights Commission via the County Superintendent's office. During the meeting of June 29, the Board of Trustees voted unanimously to ask Dr. Hollis to serve as interim superintendent until a new district superintendent could be appointed.

The new Board of Trustees met for the first time on July 2, with Mr. Freedheim, the elected chairman, presiding. Attention was devoted to the question of procedures to be followed in seeking a new superintendent. A screening committee was appointed to serve under the direction of Acting Superintendent Hollis, the non-voting coordinator of the committee; the committee to be composed of Dr. Richard L. Foster, Chairman, Mr. Wilson C. Riles (COEOE), and Dr. Aubrey Haan, Professor of Education, San Francisco State College. Much discussion produced the decision that Dr. Hollis should delineate a job specification for the superintendency position.

This he did; the screening proceeded; and the selection fell to a native of Marin County who had served as teacher and principal in a neighboring district, Mr. Charles W. Lavaroni. On August 23, 1965, he was appointed District Superintendent for Sausalito. It was under Mr. Lavaroni's leadership that the desegregation program was implemented.

The End of De Facto School Segregation in Sausalito: Prior to the termination of its tour of duty on June 29, the old Board of Trustees of the Sausalito School District had been considering the possibility of remodeling the Manzanita plant. Most of the buildings were of wood frame hurriedly constructed during the years of World War II. In the spring of 1965, when the public became aware of the old board's proposed plan to remodel the Manzanita School (with the exception of a new four-classroom unit which had been built in 1962), immediate protests arose. Spokesmen from CORE and other groups demanded that the old Manzanita plant not be improved because of its location within the Negro community. Under such pressure, on April 26, 1965, the board agreed to delay the matter of remodeling until the new board had been installed. This decision marked the end of any attempt by the old Board of Trustees to maintain *de facto* school segregation in the Sausalito School District.

The Citizens' Advisory Committee's report, transmitted to the Board on June 29, 1965, paved the way for the new trustees to solve the problem of *de facto* segregation in the district. The committee members recognized their lack of knowledge concerning curriculum, finance, school-building program needs, and actual steps to be followed in desegregating the schools; hence the final report included suggestions for securing expert assistance. The Sausalito Board, on July 7, considered recommendations from the CAC regarding the selection of consultants to assist in creating a Master Plan for educational change in the district. A decision was made to ask Dr. Bernard McKenna of San Francisco State College to suggest a panel of consultants for the district. A week later Dr. McKenna brought with him a team of staff members from the college. The chairman told the team of the board's desire for evaluations of (1) the curriculum, (2) the interracial and discipline situations, and (3) the district's four elementary school facilities. Dr. McKenna and other members of the team expressed concern about the short time allotted for such a study; the fact that school was not in session; and the fact that the investigators would not be able to view the schools in actual operation! Seemingly little was accomplished by this encounter inasmuch as the team headed by Dr. McKenna was not employed.

Later in this meeting, with much discussion, the board sought another solution to the problem of obtaining a consultant-directed study of the district. Trustee Sleight held that consultants should not be hired until (a) the district had received a legal statement about what it could and could not do and (b) the new superintendent had been appointed. Chairman Freedheim countered with the argument that integration was the goal of the district and that the times demanded that the district move toward desegregation. Finally the board decided to request that Acting Superintendent Hollis conduct a 30-day study to show what desegregation would mean physically to the schools. The board allotted $750 to Dr. Hollis for assistance and requested that the report be presented on August 9. Mr. Sleight was the only Board member who opposed the motion. At the next meeting Dr. Hollis announced that Drs. David F. Shapiro and Richard L. Foster had been engaged to begin immediately with the study, which introduced them to a wide array of individuals associated with the Sausalito School District. Operations of all schools, even though closed, were examined as well as the physical status of each.

This 30-day study, officially entitled the Foster Report, was presented to the board on the day stipulated, August 9. It encompassed a wide variety of topics. Concerning the end of *de facto* school segregation the Foster-Shapiro team recommended that the Board:

1. Discontinue use of the old Manzanita Plant as a K-4 school, adapting it to house the preschool program and all of the district's kindergarten students.
2. House all first-grade students in the district in the Bayside School.
3. Hold all second- and third-grade classes in the Central School.
4. House all fourth through eighth grades in the Richardson Bay School.

To fully appreciate the nature of these proposals, it should be recalled that at the end of the 1964–65 school year the schools contained these grades:

Manzanita (Marin City)	K–4
Central	K, 3–4
Bayside	1–2
Richardson Bay	5–8

The Foster-Shapiro recommendations provided a way of ending *de facto* school segregation in Sausalito. Now, with less than a month before the opening of school, the Board of Trustees was confronted with implementation. Despite the fact that the district was still without a superintendent, the trustees wasted no time. Two days after receipt of the Foster Report, at a meeting held on August 11, 1965, the board voted unanimously to accept and effect the recommendations regarding desegregation. Significantly, from records and reports of this meeting it is evident that a majority of the citizens of Sausalito were committed to the end of *de facto* school segregation.

On the essential issue of precisely how students were to be

grouped for instruction, however, a consensus was lacking. For example, Trustee Sleight went on record as supporting desegregation and the improvement of school facilities but stated that he could not support the idea of cluster grouping,* which had been strongly advanced by Dr. Foster. This question of grouping practices was crucial—if it were not answered, any desegregation effort might prove ineffective. Steps would have to be taken to insure integrated groupings within desegregated school settings, for social class and ethnic factors have been found to reduce the scores of certain pupils on tests of achievement and intelligence, measures traditionally used to group students. Records of the Board of Trustees contain no evidence that the question of cluster grouping was ever put to a vote. Nonetheless, when the schools opened in September, a program of cluster grouping was in effect, accomplished through the use of the Data Processing Services facilities available to Marin County schools. This program was not ideal since judgments of teachers on vacation were unable to be used in placing students, an omission that generated some staff and public dissatisfaction later.

At the historic August 11th meeting another decision of some importance was made: funds were provided for hiring a Consultant in Intergroup Relations to assist the district in achieving desirable levels of integration within the newly desegregated school setting.

Summary: The termination of *de facto* school segregation in Sausalito is an example of what progress can be made when the citizens of a community, its elected officials, and its school personnel become committed to important needed social change. Indeed, in less than a month the Board of Trustees of this district and their administrative staff were able to cope with the problems involved in opening a school system with a completely desegregated student body in all grades and with a process of cluster grouping which further enhanced desegregation within the schools. In addition to these accomplishments, some 110 white students from the neighboring Mill Valley School District benefited from a desegregated learning experience not available to them in their own district.

---

* Cluster grouping is the process of assigning to each class a group of students who represent a range of ability on criteria variables (for example, reading achievement, arithmetic ability, I.Q., and teacher's recommendation), in order to assure a broader range of student ability in each class than is possible with traditional homogeneous-grouping practices.

THE SAUSALITO–MILL VALLEY TRANSFER AGREEMENT

Background

When Wilson Riles of the California Commission on Equal Opportunities in Education reported to the Sausalito Board on July 27, 1964, the results of his investigation of *de facto* segregation in the district, he made two points which were to influence later events:

1. That an ideal ratio of Negro to white students (25% Negro or non-white to 75% white) could not be obtained in the Sausalito schools;
2. That any real solution to the problem of *de facto* segregation in the district would require resources and facilities outside the district.

Lengthy discussion is reported to have followed Riles' presentation. According to one source,[17] a member of the audience, whose community of residence is not identified, proposed an exchange of students between Mill Valley and Sausalito in order to assist in correcting the evident racial imbalance of the two districts. The idea advanced called for sending some white children from Mill Valley to Manzanita School, which was almost all Negro, while some Negro children should be sent to school in the virtually all-Caucasian Mill Valley district.

A week later, on August 3, 1964, several citizens of Mill Valley approached the local Board of Trustees, and repeated the suggestion already presented to the Sausalito Board. Furthermore, suggestions were made that Mill Valley explore the possibilities of annexation of Marin City (and Manzanita School) or the unionization of Mill Valley with the Sausalito School District. The Mill Valley Board expressed interest and promised to call a special meeting. The board also instructed its chairman, Mrs. Joyce Gross, to attend the August 13 meeting of the Sausalito Board and to express the Mill Valley District's interest in assisting with the problem of racial imbalance in Sausalito.[18]

On August 20, 1965, the Mill Valley Board held a public hearing to discuss the proposed involvement of that district in the *de facto* segregation situation in Sausalito. While several persons among the thirty addressing the board opposed the involvement of Mill Valley in the issue, most speakers supported the idea of some positive action in seeking remedies for the situation at Manzanita School.[19] At the conclusion of the meeting the Board of Trustees instructed Superintendent G. R. McConnell to submit within thirty days a study of the financial and practical implications of three possible courses of action with Sausalito: inter-district attendance, annexation, or unionization.

The first possible course of action, *Inter-district Attendance*, involves an agreement between school boards whereby children residing in one district are allowed to attend school in the other. *Annexation*, or the changing of boundaries, is the transfer of territory from one district to another. *Unionization*, or elimination of boundaries, is the process of merging school districts. The comprehensive report evaluating these alternatives (termed the McConnell Report) was presented to the Mill Valley Board on September 18, 1964. This report contained an excellent summary of the superintendent's findings (see Table 2).

Why would Mill Valley seek to assist Sausalito in improving the ethnic balance of its schools? One answer is that a number of Mill Valley citizens, as members of CORE committed to desegregation in education, had been deeply involved in the struggle over the Manzanita School issue. From among this group of people leadership emerged, encouraging the Mill Valley Board to become involved in the Sausalito predicament. Another answer was the availability of vacant classrooms in the Sausalito District, desirable because of the somewhat crowded conditions in Mill Valley schools, the Mill Valley District's bonded indebtedness at that time, and the higher per pupil expenditure available in the Sausalito schools.

Whatever the reasons, negotiations between the districts over the possibility of transferring Mill Valley students into Sausalito appear to have been conducted on an informal basis during the remainder of 1964 and on into the spring of 1965. An inter-district attendance program had been in existence before, although the number of students involved was never more than twenty. Not all Mill Valley citizens supported the proposal to send children into the Sausalito District, for two reasons: resistance to the increased transportation and other costs of transfers, and the assumption that the quality of the Mill Valley educational program was superior to that of Sausalito. Under inter-district attendance agreements, state-aid funds are awarded to the district in which a child attends school. If the usual procedure were to be used in the proposed mass transfer plan, Sausalito would stand to gain funds which the state would normally have paid to Mill Valley.

TABLE 2. SUMMARY OF ALTERNATIVES FOR MILL VALLEY SCHOOL DISTRICT

Factor	Inter-district Agreement	Annexation (Partial)	Unionization
Procedure	Simple contract between boards. Could be arranged in a matter of days.	Petition by 25% of registered electors of deannexed area or by majority of that area's board. Receiving board may agree to accept. County committee reports to Supervisors, who hold hearing, then grant, deny, or order election. Minimum time estimated at 9–12 months.	Petition by 25% of registered electors of each district or by both boards. County Superintendent must call election. Majority vote in each district required. Minimum time estimated at 9–12 months. (Vote is held only in district to be absorbed when done by annexation method.)
Finance	Expensive for Mill Valley if additional staff is needed. Additional costs of training and materials anticipated. Transportation costs would rise, if provided by district.	Heavy expense for Mill Valley, unless area annexed included large amounts of assessed valuation. Requires negotiation relative to existing properties and liabilities.	Slight loss in state aid over-all. Union district tax limit ample to support existing program. Requires agreement relative to outstanding indebtedness. Spreads maintenance costs over broader base.
Space	Virtually no space in Mill Valley, much in Sausalito. Large-scale operations would have to be one-way or straight exchange.	No problem if annexed area included school buildings except that some of Sausalito's buildings have been termed inadequate.	Offers greatest flexibility in pupil assignment and would forestall additional construction for some time.
Transportation	Optional exchanges need not concern either district. If district transportation considered, additional equipment required.	Heavy expense of busing large numbers would be borne by Mill Valley.	Heavy expense of busing would be shared by entire area.
Other	Requires inter-district liaison, planning, public information, in-service education, supervision, and evaluation.	Same as at left, plus election efforts.	Same as annexation.

Source: McConnell Report, p. 16.

The Mill Valley Board held a series of public hearings. The board realized that in order to move ahead with some kind of transfer program it would have to make concessions to the more vocal and anxious elements of the community. Therefore, the following conditions were established by the board:

1. Mill Valley would *rent* classroom space from Sausalito for approximately four classes.
2. Students would remain together and be taught their basic academic subjects by Mill Valley teachers who would accompany them there.
3. Students would join Sausalito students in music, home economics, shop, and physical-education courses.
4. Only students who were volunteers (with mandatory permission, of course, from their parents) could participate in the program.

Thus, the program proposed by the Mill Valley Board involved a transfer of one class of students in each of grades five through eight. Also, since this was not an inter-district attendance agreement, state funds would still go to the Mill Valley District. Mrs. Gross attended the Sausalito Board's meeting of July 13, 1965, and announced her district's readiness to engage in this program.

The Transfer Agreement

The proposal to transfer Mill Valley classes to the Sausalito District was approved by the Sausalito Board of Trustees on July 26, 1965. What was significant about this agreement? First, two adjacent school districts found a means of providing an ethnically better integrated learning experience for several hundred children. Second, the transfer agreement, while not an ideal program because of the restrictions imposed, provides evidence that people of goodwill can find solutions to educational problems when they approach them with creativity and determination.

As has been intimated, the program bringing Mill Valley students into Sausalito's Richardson Bay School was not without its problems. For example, after the arrival of the five Mill Valley classes early in the fall of 1965, it became obvious that the decision to keep these students together in classes with their own district's teachers was unwise. In light of the desegregated nature of the Sausalito classes, the Mill Valley group stood out in isolation. Neither the Mill Valley teachers nor the students were happy with their segregated status at

Richardson Bay School. Sausalito students displayed dissatisfaction, too, at the highly visible exclusive nature of the Mill Valley classes. This problem of isolation was partially solved when the Mill Valley teachers secured parental and Board approval to allow some of their students to exchange places in academic classes with Sausalito students. Thus, while not all Mill Valley students were involved, a further form of desegregation took place.

During the winter of 1966, the Mill Valley and Sausalito Boards of Trustees appointed a joint committee to explore the possibility of continuing the transfer program for another year. After study and deliberation, this special inter-district committee suggested continuation of the program for another year in the following form:

1. Only volunteers should be permitted to engage in the program.
2. Participating Mill Valley students should be dispersed throughout the regular Sausalito District classes.
3. Mill Valley teachers assigned to the program should receive regular assignments as a part of the Richardson Bay School staff.
4. The holiday and vacation calendars of the two school districts should be synchronized.
5. The Mill Valley School District should continue to rent space from the Sausalito School District and pay cash for related expenses.

SUMMARY AND PROSPECTS

This paper has discussed two educational programs by which communities sought solutions to the problem of *de facto* school segregation. Both solutions are examples of creative responses to a social problem. Sausalito's dilemma was solved through the school board's willingness to abandon the tradition of the neighborhood school by distributing grade-level assignments among four school plants. The limited solution achieved in the case of the Mill Valley perplexity was unique. A means was found—voluntary transfer of students and teachers—to provide a desegregated educational experience where no legal provisions or precedents had existed. Because of these accommodations the horizon beyond is brighter.

As of September, 1967, the Sausalito School District continues to operate as a desegregated school system. Concern for racial balance has led to the institution of a placement policy which prevents any classroom from being dominated by one ethnic group. This practice supplements the cluster ability-grouping program initiated with the termination of *de facto* segregation in 1965. The inter-district transfer program with the Mill Valley School District is entering its third year. The project has grown to include some 125 white Mill Valley students enrolled in grades five through eight at Sausalito's Richardson Bay School. Mill Valley students are now integrated throughout the classes of the school. Further, the transfer teachers assigned to Richardson Bay teach classes no longer comprised only of Mill Valley students.

part **III** ....

The

Educational Challenge

RESIDENTIAL SEGREGATION OF SOCIAL CLASSES AND ASPIRATIONS OF HIGH SCHOOL BOYS

9

ALAN B. WILSON

Associate Professor of Education and Associate Research Educationalist, Survey Research Center, University of California, Berkeley

Dr. Wilson is Associate Professor of Education on the Berkeley campus of the University of California. He is also Associate Research Educationalist, Survey Research Center, on the same campus. He is presently the Principal Investigator in the Richmond Youth and Community Development Project. Following his survey with Edwards of correlates of attitudes and academic success, he directed an investigation of the administration of public school systems. This investigation was financed by the Russell Sage Foundation.

This article has been reprinted many times and listed In countless bibliographies. Its importance derives partly from the tightness of the research design, rendering its conclusions largely irrefutable; and

Reprinted by permission of the American Sociological Association from *American Sociological Review*, 24, No. 6 (December 1959), 836–845.

partly from the light it sheds concerning peer and school influence upon level of aspiration. The report analyzes the vocational aspirations of boys in the high schools of several distinctive Bay Area communities.

....

Consistent and strong evidence has been accumulated showing that members of different socio-economic strata, as groups, adhere to differing values which reinforce their respective statuses.[1] Members of the working class tend to devalue education and to aspire to modest but secure occupations and income levels. Through familial socialization and divergent perceptions of their opportunities these aspirations are transmitted to the younger generation. The social inheritance of such values and attitudes tends to inhibit social mobility.

Many investigations have shown the relevance of individual personality characteristics to aspirations. These aspects of personality have been linked in turn to such variations in the familial socialization of children as direct exhortation and positive valuation of education and status, early independence training, the level of adult-child contact indicated by the size of family or the child's position in the order of siblings, and matriarchal *versus* patriarchal authority structure within the family.[2] Since the familial characteristics which are conducive to a high level of aspirations are more typical of the middle class than of the working class, these variates can be viewed, at least in part, as intervening between the parent's social class and his children's aspirations.

While the association between youths' educational and occupational aspirations and their parents' class position is strong, regardless of what dimension of social stratification is employed, there is considerable variation in aspirations among youths within a single class. This study is concerned with a related matter: the derivation of values from the immediate social milieu—the climate of the school society.*

A variety of experimental and descriptive investigations have demonstrated the influence of social context upon judgments, attitudes, and aspirations.[3] Berenda, using the technique developed by

_____

* The research reported herein was performed pursuant to a contract with the United States Office of Education, Department of Health, Education, and Welfare. The writer is indebted to T. Bentley Edwards, director of this research program, for permission to analyze and report this aspect of the problem; and to Seymour M. Lipset, Martin Trow, and T. Bentley Edwards, for their suggestions and criticisms.

Solomon Asch, found that when a child is confronted with classmates giving unanimous, incorrect judgments, only seven percent of the younger children (ages 7 to 10) and 20 percent of the older children (ages 10 to 13) remained independent.[1] A series of studies have shown the homogenization of certain social and political attitudes at college.[5] Herbert Hyman also has suggested that a current reference group, such as one's current co-workers, may provide a systematic factor accounting for differences in values among individuals with common class-origins.[6]

Because of the sifting of like social types into specific zones within an urbanized area, school districting tends to segregate youths of different social strata. Consequently school populations have modally different attitudes toward educational achievement and aspirations for a college education. The proposition that the aspirations of the bulk of the students in a high school district provide a significant normative reference influencing the educational aspirations of boys from varying strata is investigated in this paper by comparing the aspirations of students with similar social origins who attend schools characterized by different climates of aspiration. Concretely, are the sons of manual workers more likely to adhere to middle-class values and have high educational aspirations if they attend a predominantly middle-class school, and, conversely, are the aspirations of the sons of professionals more modest if they attend a predominantly working-class school?

PROCEDURE

The data for this study are provided by a survey of students' interests as related to their success in school and their decisions about educational and occupational specialization. This survey gathered information on students in thirteen high schools in and around the San Francisco-Oakland Bay area.[7] Five of these schools, located in cities and places outside the urbanized area, are excluded from the present analysis; and the study is confined to boys, since the educational and occupational aspirations of girls are more homogeneous and are conditioned by different factors.

A high degree of concordance ($W = .92$) is found among the several rank orders of occupational and educational stratification obtained from the census data describing the populations from which the student bodies were recruited, and the data from the observed sample of students at the seven public schools.[8] The entire population of a

TABLE 1. CENSUS AND SAMPLE DISTRIBUTIONS OF EDUCATIONAL AND OCCUPATIONAL VARIATES BY SCHOOLS

Schools	1950 Census			High School Sample			
				College Graduates		Fathers' Occupation	
	Median Years of Schooling	Professional	Laborers	Fathers	Mothers	Professional	Manual
Group A: Upper white collar							
1. Private boys' school	*	*	*	65%	53%	30%	6%
2. Residential	13.3	26%	2%	51	35	22	2
3. Sub-urban	12.3	13	8	28	23	14	22
Group B: Lower white collar							
4. Metropolitan	12.0	13	5	27	21	8	32
5. Metropolitan	11.1	11	9	21	17	13	38
Group C: Industrial							
6. Predominantly Catholic	10.7	5	10	11	5	1	53
7. Heterogeneous	9.6	4	12	2	2	4	56
8. Predominantly Negro	8.7	2	32	9	7	6	72

* The private school's population is drawn from scattered tracts.

private boys' school, the students of which are not recruited from continuous tracts, was sampled. The sample distributions obtained clearly place this school in the first rank (group A) in Table 1. The schools are grouped, for this study, on the basis of these rank orders, as well as congruent distinctions not reflected in the statistics—

TABLE 2. DISTRIBUTIONS OF SELECTED VARIATES BY SCHOOL GROUPS

Variate Category	School Group		
	A	B	C
Fathers' occupation			
Professional	22%	8%	2%
White collar	42	29	25
Self employed	17	20	8
Manual	10	30	49
Not available	9	12	15
Fathers' education			
Some college or more	65	35	14
High school graduate	20	29	26
Some high school or less	14	32	54
Not available	2	3	6
Mothers' education			
Some college or more	56	31	12
High school graduate	34	41	39
Some high school or less	9	25	45
Not available	1	3	4
Residence in California			
Over 25 years	58	48	32
Race			
White	98	78	66
Religion			
Catholic	21	27	38
Number of cases	(418)	(480)	(457)

impressions of the school "atmospheres" obtained while observing students in the classrooms, halls, and playgrounds. Because of the high concordance between the various dimensions of stratification, the grouping would be the same whichever combination one might choose to emphasize.[9]

Detailed contrasts between the three groups of schools (designated A, B, and C, respectively) in the distribution of several dimensions of stratification are shown in Table 2. The distributions show the gross correlation between these various dimensions of stratification, and reflect the extent of segregation between strata due to school districting along lines of social concentration. While only 10 percent of the students in the group A schools are children of manual workers, one-half of the boys in the group C schools are manual workers' sons; and while 65 percent of the fathers in the group A schools have at least some college education, only 14 percent of the fathers of students at the group C schools have any college training. Other comparisons show similar contrasts. (It is interesting to note that the families of the students in the group A schools have resided in California longer than those in the group C schools. This reflects the predominantly working-class origins of the recent large-scale immigration into California and the upward mobility of the established urban residents.)

FINDINGS

It was found, as anticipated, that there is a great divergence between the schools in the proportions of students aspiring to a college education.[10] Eighty percent of the students in the A schools, 57 percent in the B schools, and only 38 percent in the C schools want to go to college. (See the bottom row of Table 3.) This difference is due to a great extent, of course, to attributes of the parents who serve as reference individuals for the students. This is seen by making vertical comparisons in Table 3: many more children of professionals have collegiate aspirations than children of manual workers in each school group. But *within* occupational strata, reading across the table, we see that attributes of the reference group—the norms of the school society—symmetrically modify attitudes: while 93 percent of the sons of professionals in the group A schools want to go to college, less than two-thirds of the sons of professionals in the group C schools wish to do so; whereas only one-third of the sons of manual workers wish to go to college if they attend a predominantly working-class school, more than one-half of such sons so wish in the middle-class schools. This isotropic relationship provides *prima facie* confirmation of the cumulative effects of the primary and contextual variates—the boys' own class origins and the dominant class character of the high schools' student body.

It is possible, however, that these differences between schools reflect uncontrolled systematic variation in the attributes of the parents. Within each of these broad occupational strata there is considerable variation of occupational status, income, education, habits of consumption, and the like, each of which makes a cumulative impact upon values. The more successful and better educated professionals tend to move to more exclusive residential areas, send their children to private schools, or both; among the "white collar" occupations more prosperous executives reside in the group A school districts, clerks in

TABLE 3. PERCENTAGES ASPIRING TO GO TO COLLEGE BY SCHOOL GROUPS AND FATHERS' OCCUPATIONS

Fathers' Occupation	School Group		
	A	B	C
Professional	93%	77%	64%
	(92)	(39)	(11)
White collar	79	59	46
	(174)	(138)	(111)
Self employed	79	66	35
	(68)	(90)	(37)
Manual	59	44	33
	(39)	(140)	(221)
Weighted mean of percents	80	57	38
Total	(373)*	(407)*	(380)*

* The total number of cases on which these percentages are based is less than the totals shown in Table 2 because cases for which data were unavailable for either the control or dependent variates are not shown. Variation in the total number of cases in the succeeding tables is for the same reason unless otherwise noted.

the group C districts, and so on. Differences of this kind between schools within roughly defined occupational strata are shown in Table 4.

If the apparent effects of the school climate were in fact due to such uncontrolled variation along several dimensions of familial status, then one would expect the differences between the aspirations of the students at the different schools to diminish as the control categories are progressively refined—that is, as the students are compared within more homogeneous background categories. The refinement of any one or a few dimensions of stratification will result in groups which one may reasonably assume are also somewhat more homogeneous with respect to uncontrolled correlated dimensions.

This question is considered in Table 5, which is designed to show the impact of school norms upon students from more homogeneous occupational strata. This table is not, of course, "independent" of Table 3, which can be reproduced by recombining the sub-strata shown in Table 5. But it indicates that the refinement—the homogeni-

TABLE 4. PERCENTAGES WITHIN EACH OCCUPATIONAL CATE-
GORY WITH HIGH STATUS JOBS AND HIGH EDUCATION BY SCHOOL
GROUPS

Occupational Stratum Sub-stratum and Education	School Group		
	A	B	C
Professional			
"Free" (self employed)	59%	55%	27%
Some college or more	96	98	73
Number of cases	(92)	(40)	(11)
White collar			
"Executive"	42	14	3
Some college or more	65	47	20
Number of cases	(177)	(141)	(113)
Self employed			
Merchants (e.g., retail)	51	41	30
Some college or more	62	36	14
Number of cases	(71)	(95)	(38)
Manual			
Skilled	60	52	43
Some college or more	21	14	9
Number of cases	(40)	(144)	(225)

zation, so to speak—of the control categories, does not systematically modify the effect of the school society upon aspirations. For example, three-fourths of the children of self-employed artisans and skilled manual workers aspire to go to college at the group A schools, while considerably fewer than one-half of them do so at the group C schools.[11]

The education of the parents is likewise known to have a strong independent effect upon students' aspirations. Fathers' and mothers' educations are controlled in Tables 6 and 7, respectively. The effect of

TABLE 5. PERCENTAGES WITHIN OCCUPATIONAL SUB-STRATA ASPIRING TO GO TO COLLEGE BY SCHOOL GROUPS

Fathers' Occupation	School Group		
	A	B	C
"Free" professional	94%	67%	...
	(54)	(21)	(3)
Salaried professional	92	89	...
	(38)	(18)	(8)
Executive	88	79	...
	(75)	(19)	(3)
Upper white collar	79	59	55
	(68)	(64)	(40)
Lower white collar	55	53	40
	(31)	(55)	(68)
Self employed: merchants	88	77	18
	(33)	(35)	(11)
Self employed: artisans	73	60	44
	(33)	(53)	(25)
Manual: skilled	75	46	40
	(24)	(74)	(93)
Manual: semi- and unskilled	33	42	29
	(15)	(66)	(128)

TABLE 6. PERCENTAGES ASPIRING TO GO TO COLLEGE BY SCHOOL GROUPS AND FATHERS' EDUCATION

Fathers' Education	School Group		
	A	B	C
College graduate	88%	73%	73%
	(207)	(109)	(30)
Some college	79	68	58
	(61)	(56)	(33)
High school graduate	74	51	35
	(81)	(138)	(115)
Some high school	63	39	30
	(32)	(74)	(109)
Grammar school or less	32	29	33
	(22)	(76)	(131)

the school society upon aspirations is still found to be operative and strong when holding constant the influence of either parent's education. A comparison of these two tables does not substantiate the notion that the mother's education is more influential than the father's upon the high school boy's educational aspirations. Hyman suggests the importance of the woman's role in the transmission of educational values on the basis of the fact that youths and adult women both *recommended* college more frequently than adult men.[12] Perhaps women directly exhort educational values more frequently, independently of their own educational background. But these data do not

TABLE 7. PERCENTAGES ASPIRING TO GO TO COLLEGE BY SCHOOL
GROUPS AND MOTHERS' EDUCATION

	School Group		
Mothers' Education	A	B	C
College graduate	87%	77%	67%
	(64)	(88)	(24)
Some college	87	54	53
	(67)	(57)	(30)
High school graduate	74	54	35
	(140)	(191)	(170)
Some high school	50	35	39
	(20)	(69)	(120)
Grammar school or less	44	34	24
	(16)	(47)	(83)

suggest that the mother's role is more significant than the father's with respect to the more subtle and indirect effects of the parents' own education.

Looking more closely at the effect on educational aspirations of the interaction between the education of the two parents, it can be seen, in Table 8, that each makes an independent and cumulative impact of about the same degree. The only asymmetrical effect lies in the extreme combinations: if the father has not completed high school it makes little difference whether the mother has gone to college or not, but it makes considerable difference whether or not the father has gone to college even though the mother has not completed high school. Since these extreme combinations are the rarest, however, their effects are the least reliable.

The possibilities of holding several variates constant simultaneously are limited in tabular analysis, due to the rapid reduction of the number of cases which can be matched. The homogenization of categories is carried as far as is feasible within the limitations of the size of our sample in Table 9. In this table the educational and occupational attributes of the parents are simultaneously held constant while comparisons are made between the educational aspirations

TABLE 8. PERCENTAGES ASPIRING TO GO TO COLLEGE BY FATHERS' AND MOTHERS' EDUCATION

	Mothers' Education			
Fathers' Education	Col.	H.S.	Less than H.S.	Total*
Some college or more	85%	72%	53%	79%
	(309)	(149)	(36)	(495)
High school graduate	71	50	37	51
	(65)	(191)	(75)	(334)
Some high school or less	40	38	31	35
	(50)	(154)	(239)	(445)
Total*	77	53	35	56
	(430)	(501)	(355)	(1311)

* Marginal totals include those cases for which information is unavailable on the respective control variates.

of students in different groups of schools. While the reduced numbers of cases makes these percentages less reliable, of the nine comparisons available,[13] seven clearly substantiate the hypothesis, while the two reversals are small. The average percentile differences between adjacent schools are as great within these homogeneous groups as in the coarser groupings of Tables 3, 6, and 7, where the fathers' occupations and parents' education are controlled separately. The only comparison available for all three school groups is among the sons of manual workers both of whose parents have a high school education. Among these boys, 60 percent in the A schools, 54 percent in the B schools, and 32 percent in the C schools seek to go to college.

TABLE 9. PERCENTAGES ASPIRING TO GO TO COLLEGE BY SCHOOL GROUPS WITHIN EDUCATIONAL AND OCCUPATIONAL STRATA

	Mothers' Education							
	College Graduate		High School Graduate			Less than High School		
	School Group		School Group			School Group		
Fathers' Education / Father's Occupation	A	B	A	B	C	A	B	C
College graduate								
Professional	92% (52)	78% (18)						
Upper white collar	86 (57)	94 (17)	83% (24)	62% (13)				
High school graduate								
Upper white collar			85 (20)	65 (20)	20% (15)			
Lower white collar				50 (10)	32 (25)			
Manual			60 (10)	54 (26)	27 (15)		32% (25)	35% (48)
Less than high school								
Lower white collar				60 (10)				
Manual							36 (45)	26 (86)

ACHIEVEMENT AND EDUCATIONAL VALUES

Educational values and achievement interact and reinforce one another. On the one hand, those who devalue education are poorly motivated to achieve; on the other, those who have been poor achievers will defensively devalue education, and perhaps realistically, modify their educational aspirations. A much higher proportion of students in the middle-class schools obtain "A's" and "B's" than do those in the working-class schools. In addition to the influence of the family and school norms upon achievement, with which hitherto we have been

TABLE 10. PERCENTAGES ATTAINING HIGH ("A" OR "B") ME-DIAN GRADES BY SCHOOL GROUPS AND FATHERS' OCCUPATIONS

| | School Group | | |
Fathers' Occupation	A	B	C
Professional	66%	50%	18%
	(91)	(40)	(11)
White collar	50	28	18
	(176)	(138)	(111)
Self employed	51	35	11
	(71)	(95)	(37)
Manual	35	13	11
	(40)	(141)	(221)
Weighted mean of percents	52	27	13
	(378)	(414)	(380)

concerned, there is the possibility that teachers grade more liberally at the middle-class schools—either for entirely extraneous reasons or, more plausibly, because the parents' expectations and the students' aspirations place pressure on them to raise the grading curve.

If the latter interpretation is sound, then the students who are high achievers at the group C schools will be higher achievers, on an absolute basis, than those at the group A schools. But, holding grades constant and reading across the rows in Table 11, we see that even under these conditions more students receiving the same grade in the middle-class schools want to go to college.[14] Virtually all of those who receive "A's" at the group A schools want to go to college, but only three-fourths of the "A" students at the group C schools want to go to college.[15]

TABLE 11. PERCENTAGES ASPIRING TO GO TO COLLEGE BY
SCHOOL GROUPS AND GRADES

Median Academic Grade	School Group		
	A	B	C
"A"	98%	96%	78%
	(60)	(24)	(9)
"B"	90	89	72
	(152)	(90)	(46)
"C"	72	55	41
	(145)	(207)	(184)
"D"	43	21	25
	(47)	(120)	(169)

Using IQ scores as an index of achievement which is standardized
across school lines, and thus eliminating the possibility of systematic
differences between school grading policies, we see in Table 12 that
high achievers are less likely to wish to go to college if they attend a
working-class school and, conversely, that low achievers are more apt
to want to go to college if they attend a middle-class school.[16] Almost
all of the students with IQ scores over 120 at the group A schools hope
to go to college, whereas only one third of those with such scores at
the group C schools want to do so. Those who adhere to the interpretation of intelligence test scores as more or less valid measures of
innate capacity will see the "waste" of talent implicit in the horizontal

TABLE 12. PERCENTAGES ASPIRING TO GO TO COLLEGE
BY SCHOOL GROUPS AND IQ SCORS

IQ Score	School Group		
	A	B	C
120 +	96%	83%	33%
	(100)	(81)	(18)
110–119	93	72	51
	(128)	(108)	(53)
100–109	76	52	41
	(87)	(89)	(82)
90–99	47	24	35
	(30)	(63)	(68)
89–	25	29	25
	(12)	(69)	(111)

contrasts in Table 12, from the stance of the prevalent concern with the conservation of talent.

Comparing the effect of the school climate upon grades and upon educational aspirations in Tables 10 and 3, we can see that the devaluation of education in the working-class schools affects academic achievement as much as it is reflected in educational aspirations. In fact, it adversely affects the achievement of the sons of professional and white-collar workers more than it does their aspirations.

TANGENTIAL CONFIRMATION

The imputation of the variation in educational aspirations and behavior between schools to the "moral force" of the normative values within the school society is of course inferential.[17] This interpretation has been argued, up to this point, by holding constant other factors known to affect educational attitudes and attributing the residual difference to the hypothetical factor. The hypothesis, moreover, is theoretically congruent with a considerable accumulation of research on small groups, studies of peer-group influences, and of the differential effects of contrasting community structures: it has been shown that the perception of the opportunity for upward mobility by lower-strata youth is facilitated by the economic and occupational heterogeneity of the community.[18] Yet, if Occam's razor is to be scrupulously applied against the contextual hypothesis, it might be argued that, however homogeneous the students' familial backgrounds may be in terms of all available external indices, those working-class families living in predominantly middle-class districts are showing "anticipatory socialization" in their values and are inculcating them in their children.

While the latter interpretation is reasonable, it is not so persuasive to argue the corollary that middle-class families would act to depress the aspirations of their children if they live in a predominantly working-class neighborhood. ". . . inherent in the very existence of a stratification order, of higher and lower valuations of social positions, is the motivation to move up in the social structure if one's position is low, or to retain one's position if it is high."[19] It is plausible to assume that middle-class youth, even when living in a predominantly working-class neighborhood, will be stimulated by their families toward educational diligence and to aspire to high-status occupations. The fact that the aspiration of these children is depressed when they attend a

TABLE 13. DISTRIBUTION OF PEER-GROUP OFFICES
AMONG OCCUPATIONAL STRATA BY SCHOOLS

	School Group		
Fathers' Occupation	A	B	C
Professional	25%	9%	3%
White collar	49	38	40
Self employed	18	29	7
Manual	8	24	50
Number of cases*	154	160	92

* Percentages are based on the number of students
who have held some peer-group office—either within the
school, such as team captain, student council member or
class president, or outside of school, as an officer of "De
Molay," "Teen-age Club," or similar group.

working-class school is more compelling evidence for the effect of the
school milieu and peer-group norms than is the fact of the upward
mobility of working-class youths in middle-class schools.

It has been reported frequently that students from middle-class
families are generally over-selected for peer-group leadership positions. But "in order to become a *leader* . . . one must share prevailing
opinions and attitudes."[20] This view has led to a presumption of the
universality of upward aspirations. It was found in the present study,
however, that one-half of those who had held peer-group offices in the
group *C* schools were children of manual workers, while only eight
percent of those in the group *A* schools were the sons of manual
workers (see Table 13). The distribution of peer-group offices among
occupational strata is very close to that of the student bodies at large
at each school group (as can be seen by comparing Table 13 with the
first distribution in Table 2). But, consequently, the leaders who
reflect, express, and mold the attitudes of the school society reinforce
and extend the pre-existing differences in group characteristics.

THE IMPACT OF SCHOOL NORMS UPON OTHER VALUES

Sociologists concerned with inter-generational mobility and the
formation of social attitudes might well direct more attention to the
investigation of contextual variables—attributes of membership
groups which serve as references during the adolescent period of
socialization—particularly to the society of the school. While the

importance of both the family and the peer-group in the development
of the economic and political values of the adolescent have been
pointed out, most investigations have concentrated upon the influence
of the family.[21] That the influence of the school climate is not confined
to educational aspirations is shown by brief explorations, presented in
Tables 14 and 15, into the differences between schools in occupational

TABLE 14. PERCENTAGES ASPIRING TO PROFESSIONAL OCCUPA-
TIONS BY SCHOOL GROUPS AND FATHERS' OCCUPATIONS

	School Group		
Fathers' Occupation	A	B	C
Professional	78%	60%	60%
	(81)	(35)	(10)
White collar	61	37	35
	(160)	(120)	(31)
Self employed	44	47	23
	(62)	(79)	(106)
Manual	44	31	27
	(36)	(121)	(198)
Weighted mean of percents	60	39	30
	(339)	(355)	(345)

TABLE 15. PERCENTAGES EXPRESSING PREFERENCE FOR THE
REPUBLICAN PARTY BY SCHOOL GROUPS AND FATHERS' OCCU-
PATIONS

	School Group		
Fathers' Occupation	A	B	C
Professional	81%	71%	33%
	(73)	(31)	(9)
White collar	72	64	36
	(120)	(98)	(72)
Self employed	80	62	39
	(56)	(68)	(23)
Manual	50	32	24
	(26)	(107)	(161)
Weighted mean of percents	74	53	29
	(275)*	(304)*	(265)*

* Percentages are based on the number of students expressing
preference for the Republican or Democratic party, omitting those
who indicated "other," "none," or failed to respond.

aspirations and in political preferences. These tables provide *prima facie* evidence, comparable to that of Table 3, suggesting that the dominant climate of opinion within a school makes a significant impact upon students' occupational goals and their political party preferences.

CONCLUSION

Whether the modification of attitudes by the normative climate of the school society persists or a reversion toward familial norms in later life takes place cannot be determined on the basis of static comparisons. But certainly the student's high school achievement and his decision for or against college entrance have irreversible consequences in channeling him into the stream of economic and social life, and in biasing the probability of future intimate contact with countervailing reference groups.

The Supreme Court has found that, even though the "tangible" provisions of schools are the same, schools segregated along racial lines are inherently unequal. The "sense of inferiority affects the motivation of the child to learn." The *de facto* segregation brought about by concentrations of social classes in cities results in schools with unequal moral climates which likewise affect the motivation of the child, not necessarily by inculcating a sense of inferiority, but rather by providing a different ethos in which to perceive values.

part **IV**

The Greater
New York Experience

10 | THE MANHASSET REACTION TO ELEMENTARY SCHOOL INTEGRATION

TERRY FUNKHOUSER

*Former Member of the Citizens Advisory Committee on Publications,
Union Free School District Number 6, Manhasset, Long Island*

Mrs. Paul Funkhouser lives within the boundaries of the Manhasset School District. Her husband is president of a New York City firm dealing in computer-oriented data files. Their four children have attended the Manhasset schools at various times at three different levels—kindergarten, elementary school, and junior high. She served as a member of the Citizens Advisory Committee on Publications after the Manhasset School District was confronted by a lawsuit on behalf of twelve pupils whose parents charged *de facto* segregation.

The two strands, carefully designed data collection and intimate personal association, are discerned in this article. Although Manhasset is primarily a suburb of homes for the well-to-do, it has had a less well-to-do group since the early days of the Long Island Railroad, when immigrant labor was brought in to work on the railroad. This group has long since moved out, and their housing has been occupied for a number of years by families of Negroes, many of whom serve as domestics in other homes. The situation is not common, but still has many interesting facets.

Manhasset was one of the first communities to be charged in the courts with *de facto* segregation. The case of "12 Minors v. Manhasset Board of Education" was brought by the NAACP, but this forceful action was preceded by complaints from the teachers at an "All-School Council." A decision by the School Board to comply with the court order to close the Valley School and bus the children to other schools in the district was put squarely to the voters when two seats on the Board were sought by candidates pledged to contest the ruling.

Although the compliance of the Board was upheld by a narrow margin in the community, many citizens complained about lack of communication from the School Board, despite the existence of a Citizens Committee.

Most of the article describes the results of an opinion survey held a year after the closing of the Valley School. The author voices the hope that "the views held . . . the assembled pros and cons will evoke an understanding of this community's response to legally initiated elementary school integration and will provide a meaningful basis for comparison with other communities, where applicable." Some of the major findings are worth emphasizing:

1. Although three quarters of the parents were in favor of bringing all the children together, only one third thought that present educational standards would be maintained.
2. Most of the people in the community agreed that the School Board had complied with their role expectations, that "they did what they should."
3. Some people gave evidence of being racially prejudiced, but the examples were isolated.
4. Race and social-class influences upon learning were not generally distinguished by those interviewed.
5. Most people were willing to rely on "tracking" to take care of differences in learning rates.
6. A few referred to the importance of integration as part of the experience of white children.
7. A few people, other than Negroes, were willing to examine the Negro feeling of identity.
8. Several referred to official New York State policy on integration.
9. Comparatively few inter-home visits were reported.
10. The closed school was used as a center for community enrichment.

11. The thrust of integration seemed necessary to prod both white and Negro parents about the need for compensatory education.
12. There was a feeling that schools ought not be left to do the full job of integration by themselves. Housing and job integration might follow school integration or they might not. And they might be slow in following.
13. A need for tax money to build a new school seemed to reopen the entire question.

■■

INTEGRATION IN 1964

Parents escorting their starchy children to the first day of school in September of 1964 delayed a moment to watch Bus 11 unload. The other buses discharged their regular riders without attracting curious attention. However, Bus 11 brought the first load of children from the legally abandoned Valley School to one of the two remaining public grammar schools in the commuter town of Manhasset, New York. To the watching parents these Negro children descending the steps of the bus represented reality. Twenty-two months of controversy and litigation had culminated in the Board of Education's compliance with U.S. District Court Chief Judge Joseph C. Zavatt's order on January 24, 1964, to present a proposal to the Court to desegregate the schools. The Negro children approaching the school were, then, the brothers, sisters, neighbors, and friends of the twelve minors in whose behalf the suit "12 Minors v. Manhasset Board of Education"[1] had been instigated; they were the actualities of *de jure* integration, the result of the voters' narrow decision not to appeal the Court's ruling, but, instead, to support Board members who proposed closing the Valley School. It was a small margin of victory these children carried with them up the stairs and through the open door.

The Community Described

The Manhasset community is a combination of several residential villages and unincorporated areas* located on the North Shore of

---

* Incorporated villages of Flower Hill, Munsey Park, Plandome, Plandome Manor, Plandome Heights, North Hills; large unincorporated areas of the Town of North Hempstead.

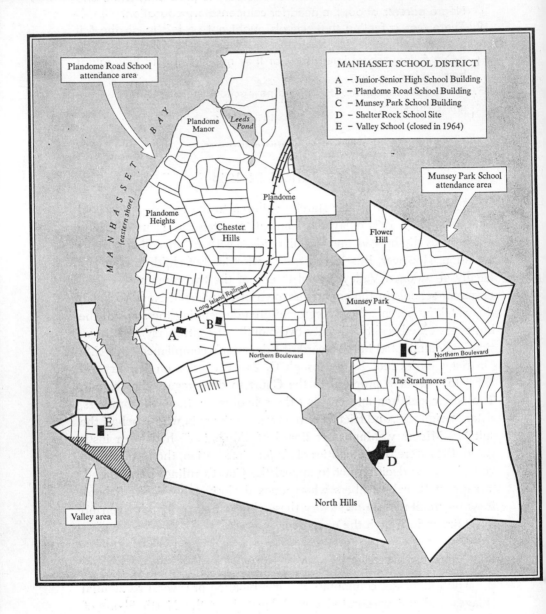

Plandome Road School attendance area

MANHASSET BAY (eastern shore)

Plandome Manor

Leeds Pond

MANHASSET SCHOOL DISTRICT
A — Junior-Senior High School Building
B — Plandome Road School Building
C — Munsey Park School Building
D — Shelter Rock School Site
E — Valley School (closed in 1964)

Plandome

Munsey Park School attendance area

Plandome Heights

Chester Hills

Flower Hill

Long Island Railroad

Munsey Park

A

B

Northern Boulevard

C

Northern Boulevard

The Strathmores

E

D

Valley area

North Hills

Long Island, adjacent to Manhasset Bay and Long Island Sound (see map). Low rolling hills and woodlands have attracted a relatively homogeneous group of residents, over fifty percent of whom commute by rail or car the thirty-five-minute distance of seventeen miles to Manhattan. This is a prosperous community of approximately 17,000 people—the average income of $30,000 far exceeds the national average—composed of a predominantly upper-middle-to-high socio-economic class of professionals and executives (Table 1); a substantial

TABLE 1. OCCUPATIONS OF FATHERS OF CHILDREN ATTENDING MANHASSET PUBLIC SCHOOLS, GRADES K-6—JUNE 1963

	Total No. of Returns	
	From Other Elementary Schools 1140	From the Valley School 141
Professional	30%	1%
Owner-executive	34	3
Misc. "white collar"	26	10
Skilled and semi-skilled	3	13
Unskilled	1	39
Information not available	3	31
Not identifiable	3	3

stratum of merchants and white-collar workers; and, concentrated in a small district commonly known as the "Valley area," a segment of about 1,500 people, mostly Negro semi-skilled and manual laborers with a median annual income of $4,700.

The Previous School Policy

As far back as 1922, the Board of Education of the Manhasset Union Free School District Number 6 established boundaries for three elementary school districts based upon the neighborhood-school concept: Plandome Road School, Munsey Park School, and the Valley School. Until 1964 those lines and that policy had remained unchanged. The Valley area, a hollow of little land value, was populated in 1922 primarily by immigrant and other white low-income families, skilled and semi-skilled. In the intervening years the socio-economic composition and real-estate desirability of the Valley area have remained fairly constant while homesites in the adjoining areas have continued to increase in their exceptionally high property value. The

white Valley area inhabitants of two generations ago have melted into
the metropolitan complex as their skills and their orientation to the
American social system have improved. Their houses are now occupied by other manual laborers, predominantly Negro, who were originally attracted from the South by job opportunities associated with the
building of a huge trestle for the Long Island Railroad. Low-income
housing developments with a total of 150 dwelling units for approximately 500 people have more recently attracted other Negroes to the
Valley. The result has been *de facto* segregation of the neighborhood
Valley School, segregation in fact if not by design. In the 1963–64
school year, all of the 150 Negro public elementary school students
attended the Valley School; only white students were enrolled at the
two other elementary schools. Altogether, there were 1340 grade-
school students in the Manhasset public school district: 166 attending
the Valley School; 600 attending Plandome Road School; 576 attending Munsey Park School. An additional 1115 attended St. Mary's
parochial elementary school and a small number were enrolled at
various private schools.

The Legal Action

Growing concern over the implications of racial segregation
within the school system brought expressions from teacher representatives at the "All-School Council." During meetings called between
1957 and 1960, the membership discussed the neighborhood-school
policy and the adverse educational environment created by distinct
patterns of residency. They proposed to the School Board that "each
elementary school should have a student body which is culturally,
socially, and economically heterogeneous as opposed to the homogeneity that is produced by a neighborhood school policy." The Board
took no action. In the spring of 1962, at the urging of local NAACP
representatives, the Board appointed a Citizens Committee to study
the situation. The Committee study was subsequently held in abey-
ance to await the outcome of a formal suit filed by the NAACP in
March, 1962—a court action implementing a statement made by Roy
Wilkins, Executive Secretary, that the NAACP would start an all-out
campaign against segregation in northern schools. After preliminary
hearings, the case of "12 Minors v. Manhasset School Board" began in
November, 1963, with the plaintiffs contending violation of constitutional right because students were assigned to schools on the basis of

segregated housing patterns. The defendants countered that "racial imbalance is due solely to patterns of housing in the District for which they are not responsible, and, therefore, they are not obligated to change attendance rules or areas."

The case is particularly noteworthy for two reasons: First, while legal decisions had been made involving de jure, or intentional, segregation, no legal opinions on de facto segregation existed as yet. Second, both plaintiffs and defendants agreed that school policy operated equally in each attendance area, an uncommon situation in many previous cases of this nature.

On January 24, 1964, the Court ruled, in short, "The question is not whether the State has an affirmative duty to balance the races, but, rather, whether it is to be enjoined from countenancing and thereby perpetuating, a system of virtually separate elementary schools for Negro and white children." In the judgment of the Court, the responsibility of the School Board was to prevent a school from becoming segregated and to act to integrate such a school.

Election after the Court Decision: "No Appeal" Wins

Within seventy-two hours after the decision was handed down and prior to the regularly scheduled Board meeting, the School Board announced it would not appeal the case. Public clamor was widespread. The most telling community reaction came with the filing of opposition candidates for the two vacancies on the School Board—in the May 6 annual election of the Board of Education of Union Free School District Number 6 of the Town of North Hempstead, Nassau County, New York. The election was based almost exclusively on the issue of "appeal" or "no appeal." The turnout of registered voters on election day was exceptionally high, with a record 3257 votes cast compared with the previous year's total of 216, when no issues were at stake. The cause of the "appeal" candidates, opposing the School Board, was strengthened by the news a few days before the election that in the Gary, Indiana, case the Supreme Court[2] had upheld rulings by the lower courts affirming the right of the Gary School Board to assign pupils to neighborhood schools. This news encouraged those who supported an appeal. On the other hand, the ranks of those supporting the School Board's decision and the "no appeal" candidates were swelled by a most dramatic combined effort on the part of thirteen ministers, priests, and rabbis—both from the pulpit and in

published statements—emphasizing the moral aspects and reminding
people of their religious duty. The two "no appeal" candidates ("for
education, not litigation") won 53 percent of the total vote against 47
percent for the two "appeal" candidates ("protect Manhasset's right to
run its own schools"), with a small but decisive victory margin of 204
votes. Manhasset's court-ordered integration was ready for implementation.

The Citizens Committee was reactivated, this time to determine
the most satisfactory method of compliance with the Court order.
After reviewing the Committee's recommendations, the School Board
chose to close the Valley School and distribute those children evenly
between the remaining two, formerly 100 percent white, schools. In
the school year 1964–65, Plandome Road School had an enrollment of
709 students, Munsey Park School an enrollment of 643 students. On
the first day of school in September, 1964, as buses from the Valley
arrived at the two schools, parents, teachers, and students witnessed
the first living elements of Manhasset's elementary school integration.

REACTIONS AFTER A YEAR OF INTEGRATION

To ascertain Manhasset's reaction nearly one full academic year
after the closing of the Valley School, over fifty leaders of religious,
political, and parent groups were interviewed. Respondents were chosen to reflect the various ethnic, religious, social, and age factors
within the community. Since the aim was to determine the reaction of
the community itself, the School Board and the teaching staff were not
included. All those interviewed replied to the same questionnaire
(Appendix A) to insure uniformity and objectivity in eliciting replies.[3]

What follows does not purport to be a scientific analysis that can
be mathematically projected. It is, instead, a thoughtful study of the
issues and concerns prevalent in the community during early spring of
1965 after the implementation of the Court order. It is hoped that the
thoughts voiced, the views held, the assembled pros and cons will
evoke an understanding of this community's response to legally initiated elementary school integration and will provide a meaningful
basis for comparison with other communities, where applicable.

The School Board: Lack of Communication

In the middle was the School Board. "During the case, the School
Board was battered by the pro-integration group to integrate immedi-

ately. But the Board couldn't take any steps until the case was finished. After the decision was handed down, the pro-integration group ceased battering the Board and the anti-integration group began. "I feel the politeness with which the School Board reacted while they were being badgered from all directions was impressive and they remained consistent in their firmness," stated the minister of a large congregation. The director of one organization said, "Those who were vicious towards the Board roused those who supported it, thereby galvanizing public opinion." A parent commented, "With so many conflicting points of view ranging about in the community, nothing the School Board did during this incident was destined to please everyone."

At the present time, it is generally felt by both sides that the single persistent error committed by the School Board was its nearly total lack of communication with the community.

A white leader: "People felt the Board did not take into consideration the feelings of the community."

A Negro father: "The Negro community was upset the Board did not talk. After they decided not to appeal, the Negro community was glad and felt there was hope."

A leader of the School Community Association: "As citizens, the public did not have the facts and was not given the time to discuss it."

A Chamber of Commerce member: "People are still talking. They had hoped the Board would get the community's opinion. The fault of the Board was lack of communication."

One of the first to break the silence that bound the community was a prominent white clergyman who explained from his pulpit in March of 1963: "For some months now the lawyers for the Manhasset School Board, in the case 'State NAACP versus School Board' on behalf of twelve Manhasset Negro children, have kept discussion under wraps. School Board personnel in particular are forbidden by their lawyers to discuss the case or anything that may be construed as related to it. The Community Citizens Committee, set up by the School Board some months ago to study the problem and to bring recommendations, has been held in limbo since the suit began, and, in general, the community has been requested to say little or nothing lest we prejudice the case in some way. Now, however, . . . it seems to me that the time has come for Manhasset citizens to speak out or to forever forego the right to responsible citizenship." The fact that the local weekly newspaper, the *Manhasset Mail,* when reporting current developments in the April 16, 1964, issue could only say "Thus far, the Board has made no indication that . . ." and "At Monday evening's School Board meeting, the Board did not reveal what definite steps it would take . . ." serves to illustrate the frustration experienced by the community at that time.

Except for the bitter criticism of the Board for its failure to communicate with the community, reaction toward this body by the large majority of the people who were interviewed showed that the Board was held in especially high esteem. "They did what they should according to their position in the town and handled it with dignity," said one woman. Another commented, "The strong, middle-of-the-road leaders feel the School Board deported itself very well and has the confidence of most of the people." A Negro parent said, "I really feel the way they have done it is right and had to be. It is my personal feeling that our school system will handle any situation that should arise."

The Negro Attitude

The Court action that did arise was, as pointed out earlier, in large part instigated by the national body of the NAACP because the situation in Manhasset was so well suited to a test case on *de facto* segregation. However, immediately prior to that time "only fifteen or twenty percent of the Valley people wished for a change in the segregated pattern," a Negro leader estimates. "The rest were not activated to that end." With a suit filed and a case in the court the whole situation became spotlighted for the Negro. There were meetings. Led by their ministers and the NAACP leaders, the Valley parents were educated to take an interest and most of them did. Because the School Board chose to pursue the case rather than rectify the *de facto* situation immediately, a representative of the Negro community recalled: "Tremendous bitterness and resentment existed in the Valley during the court case. Last year the Valley was very angry. Now, however, there is a marvelous change from the apathy and bitterness in the Valley during the court case to one of hopefulness." As another Negro said, "It is my impression that the Negroes are extremely pleased with the arrangement. It has gone remarkably smoothly."

The White Hard Core

One segment of the white community did not concur. It was noted above that 1502 of the total 3257 votes cast in the School Board election of May 1964 were for the opposition candidates. Of that number, "those who were totally and adamantly against the elementary school integration are still opposed," a father said. "They would prefer that children of different races did not go to school together," stated a clubwoman. A homeowner told of "two families I know who met the situation by transferring their children to private schools and one family who moved to another area." "Two Girl Scout troop leaders refused to take Negro girls into their respective troops," volunteered a woman active in scouting. While these are isolated incidents, they serve to illustrate the intensity with which the hard-core opposition had reacted. Of the opposition vote, "those who were afraid of the influence of the Negro element on their children, afraid of the possibility of increased taxes, reluctant to overburden existing facilities and resentful toward the School Board's handling of the situation—the middle group and by far and away the larger group—are now far less strongly opposed," the head of one organization said.

The Middle Group

The complete range of reaction within this middle group is, of course, great. However, for the most part, the fact that "everything has quieted down," that they "are not being led," that "they've seen it in operation for six months without serious effect and with only isolated incidents to note" has lessened the antipathy that these people felt. Answered a lawyer, "I would say that the middle group, where there is least leadership, tends to forget the issues with time, and I think tempers have gone down on this thing." And a layman spoke in educator terms: "The elements that tended to threaten their values and arouse their fears have for the most part been lessened or abated. The large percentage of last year's opposition group have accepted the situation now that tensions and tempers—and the unknown—have passed over." A Negro leader admitted, "There is a minority who feel separate schools are better, but most of Manhasset is not against integration so much as they have had fears about what would happen to their own individual child in an integrated school."

Effect on the Education Level

The effect on the level of education—that is the area where the community evidences most concern. When asked "Do you think the community feels it's good to have children of different races go to school together or would they prefer separate schools?" seventy-five percent answered in favor of "school together," albeit occasionally grudgingly. When asked "How do you think the mixing of races in elementary schools affects the educational level?" only one-third of the responses suggested that the present level would be maintained.

One mother said, "The Negro children are slower because of their home environment. Slower children bring down the pace of the class." A businessman thought "the mixing of races in the lower grades does affect the educational level. . . . Some of the Valley children are not able to keep up with the work." On the other hand, a parent-leader felt that "if there had been more Negroes, the mixing would have affected the educational level drastically. Here the number of Negro students per white student is so small that the effect is negligible."

Socio-economic factors and not the race issue were emphasized by many. A Jewish mother said, "It's not the race, but the difference in social strata. Because of their background, the Negro children come to school lacking the will to succeed." Economic considerations were stressed by a member of the parent-teacher council: "The mixing of races might not affect the educational level in some communities, but it does here because of economic disparities. Environment and economics are the problems, really, not the race."

Local educational policy was credited by some with lessening or eliminating any consequential impact integration might have on the educational level: "Mixing does not affect the high level of education in our community one bit because ninety percent of the children are college bound and because of our fast, medium, and slow system. I feel this system is geared for and works for each individual child," said one respondent. (See Table 2.) And said another: "The way the public school is set up, I don't imagine it affects the educational level at all. Several of the Negro children with extremely low I.Q.'s were removed to a special school. For the rest, we already have reading levels in the classes."

Social education was stressed by one white parent: "It's a two-way deal. Our boys will know how to deal with Negroes later if they go to school with them now—and more Negroes will be in business by the time our boys are." And another: "If they are not prepared they cannot cope with life outside a one-stratum group—as in the military service. . . ." Having been educated during the Court case to the social advantages Negro children would derive from being in a classroom with children of various backgrounds and achievement levels, a Valley mother asserted: "Valley parents are happy their children have

TABLE 2. DISTRIBUTION OF MANHASSET HIGH SCHOOL GRADUATES
OF 1961 THROUGH 1964*

	1961	1962	1963	1964
Total number of graduates	178	185	174	227
Number attending four-year colleges	124	120	124	173
Number attending junior colleges	19	29	25	20
Number attending secretarial schools	4	5	2	1
Number attending hospital school of nursing	1	3	2	4
Number attending technical schools	5	4	3	3
Number working and unaccounted for	25	24	18	26

* 87 percent went on to further education.

the opportunity to broaden their lives—above and beyond their pleasure in integration for integration's sake itself."

The Psychological Aspect

One comment by a Valley woman gives insight into the Negro point of view. She said, "There is a lack of self-identity among the Negro children. They act and react as a group. Even if one tries to do something by himself, he is teased or jeered at and forced back into the group. It may have to do with the fact they all live so closely together and play constantly together. We are trying to encourage individuality, and maybe when they are more with the white children they will see and learn how to break away from this group complex." The Negro in Manhasset knows that he is not integrated in the full and moral sense of America's prevailing code concerning man's duty to his fellow. And he recognizes that the economic factors in this community preclude immediate integration in other than a mendacious sense. At this point in time, however, he feels that meaningful progress has been made for his own young children and that, as far as the elementary school situation goes, "everything is working out extremely well."

A statement by a Catholic man who does not have children, "You cannot deny minority groups equal opportunity, and it starts with the children," is an apt summary of comments by a local minister in a sermon to his white congregation: "It is well to keep in mind the fact that the official policy of the State of New York, recommended to the public school boards and administrations, is essentially one of endorsement of the position of the NAACP on *de facto* segregation. This official policy of the State is still in effect. Through the Board of Regents, the State says:

Modern psychological knowledge indicates that schools enrolling students largely of a homogeneous ethnic origin may damage the personality of minority group children. Such schools decrease their motivation and thus impair their ability to learn. Public education in such a setting is socially unrealistic, blocks the attainment of the goals of democratic education, and is wasteful of manpower and talent, whether this situation occurs by law or by fact.

Another way of putting it is to say that the emotionalized attitudes of children begin early, and that if we expect to influence the person toward understanding and tolerance, as opposed to prejudice, it must begin when it can be most effective.

The elementary school children themselves are the ones who are directly affected. "The children are the ones who have to live with it," said an active citizen. "It is their education, their 'broadening,' their day-to-day responses that are actually and ultimately involved. Theirs is the generation that will guide the integration movement in the future." As one minister said, "Let the people of the church accept our responsibility to lead in the community and set examples for our children. What greater heritage can we give them as they prepare for tomorrow's world than an example of people of all races and religious groups living together in peace and justice?"

The Children's View

How do the white children in the lower grades react to one or two or three Negro students in the classroom? Time and again parents, whether they themselves were for or violently against integration, have said, "Our children do not make a point of the fact that another child is Negro. Children do not share the emotional background of

their parents at these early ages and traditionally are the easiest ones
to deal with in this respect." All the problems of adjustment, of
working within the group, exist as usual, but "the children are not
concerned with the makeup of the group itself." One mother of four
said: "Children are more natural. I accompanied two classes on field
trips. The children did not show any difference about the Negro
children at all. The children do not overcompensate." Another parent
remarked: "In my own case, my children didn't even mention it the
first day. Now they mention a classmate who has created a disturbance, and nine times out of ten that child is a Negro. But the children
don't make a point of its being a Negro." A commuter father supported these views with the comment: "My children have never mentioned that there was a Negro in the class. It's the parents who have
done the panicking and worrying. It is too bad some children had to
hear all that. But, from my view, the children themselves have accepted it in a very natural way."

How do the Negro children in the lower grades react to twenty or
twenty-two or twenty-five white students in the classrooms?

A mother: "The children are very happy in general."
A mother: "There were no great upsets for the children. It is just like
    going to school any place else. The children have been delighted."
Others: "The Negro children are early at the bus stops, actually eager
    to go to school."
"Their remarks about school and tales brought home from school
    in almost every instance are repeated with a sense of pleasure."

One Negro mother added: "They have been visiting back and
forth. But the visits that have been are few." In this more personal
area, outside the scope of School Board action and court restraints, the
Negro community feels that the friendships which can now be made
by the children at school are a great advantage. The ideal of integrationists is that classmates at school become playmates outside. In what
degree of speed or intensity this ideal will be reached, the Negro
community is unanimous in saying: "It is too soon to know."

The Girl Scout program, formerly set up on a neighborhood basis,
has been affected by the closing of the Valley School. Now interested
Valley girls join either the Plandome Road or the Munsey Park troops,
depending on what school they attend. But one troop leader observed:
"Most of the Valley girls have dropped out. Transportation is the main

problem—getting them home after the meetings; additional leaders are another."

A white respondent voiced the situation in these words: "It is here in the extracurricular sphere that the situation divides between the naturalness of the child making up the birthday party list or the child responding to an invitation and the inhibitions of the parent who edits the list or the parent who influences the response." On the whole, neither the Negro children nor the white children in the lower grades emphasize race differences or economic disparities and have gone directly on with the far more complicated business of comprehending "new math."

THE COMMUNITY LOOKS AHEAD

"While there is widespread hope in the community that the eventual effect of transferring the children will be beneficial to the entire community, no one suggests there won't be transitional problems. If the Valley children are to receive the maximum benefit from early integration with children from all of Manhasset, they must receive every help the community can extend to them."[4] To this end, a number of programs within the community are extending their horizons, and other programs are being initiated to create an atmosphere of social and cultural enrichment in order to enable the Valley children to better perceive, and thereby adjust to, the new learning situations in the integrated grammar schools. As one journalist has written,

No one pretends that the problems of the children of the Valley are solved. The fact remains that there is a gap between two segments of the population. Manhasset answered to a legal dilemma and is now working to solve the harder problem, a question of personal and social values. Pride in this community is high. There are today in Manhasset the beginnings of comprehensive, diversified and creative programs to deal with its problems. In July the School Board passed a resolution permitting the North Hempstead Housing Authority to lease the [Valley] school building and grounds for the coming year. As a result of the cooperation between the School Board, New York State, and the North Hempstead Housing Authorities and the Board of Supervisors of the Town of North Hempstead, the Valley School was no longer deadwood, but was opened for use by the general community. Space in the school was made available to all non-profit, non-political and non-religious groups in the town of North Hempstead. The most enthusiastic responses to this offer came from groups that have been formed to answer the needs of the Valley itself.[5]

Community Service Center, Inc.

The Community Service Center, Incorporated, is a case in point. Originally a servicemen's lounge during World War II, the Center later turned its attention to the needs of the Valley children. The Center has enlarged its scope to "launch a massive intervention effort aimed at remaking the cultural milieu in which Valley children mature and take their place in adult society." In essence, the Center would try to make up for inadequate homes in which many Valley children experience cultural undernourishment.[6]

In the summer of 1964, the Center submitted plans for its enlarged program to the Nassau Health and Welfare Council. The program was approved by the County, which allocated $9,877.50 of County and $18,755 of State funds, thus leaving an additional $12,518 to be raised from private sources to meet the estimate requested by the Center. The School Community Association (Manhasset's form of the usual P.T.A.) gave $1,000 and pledged to raise another $4,000 locally. The Board of Education agreed to take steps to incorporate the program in their budget after the pilot project is successfully completed.

The quest for public funds for this and other projects has uncovered some latent opposition. An activity-oriented resident related the following incident: "An organization in town was approached on the matter of making a contribution to the 'Community Service Center.' Members of the organization's Board of Directors voted down giving the money. I was surprised at some of the statements made. There was a definite carry-over from last year—that the need and expense of this program now was a direct result of the integration; that the need and expense wouldn't be necessary if the case had been appealed and, presumably, won." On the other hand, "The majority of organizations that opposed integration last year," reported a woman involved with raising funds, "are now actively aiding the Community Service Center's new program by contributing funds. I feel this definitely reflects an improved outlook."

The aim is golden. But real concern exists among both white and Negro, as the following comments indicate:

White: "To make the Negro child strongly motivated is hard on the child. I've talked to the teachers; some of the Negro children are doing fine, but others are going to take a good deal of the teachers' time. Remedial help is important and that is why we are working on the various programs now. I think most of the community feels the larger issue of integrating was more important than the immediate and transitory troubles we will have for awhile with learning."

Negro: "There would be no measurable effect on the white children, but ultimately it would be of help to the Negro children." This same man was concerned that until time and effort had gone into preparing the Negro child more adequately, until he was "put up against tougher competition, the less advanced child may even fall back farther."

Maintaining School Standards—Community Participation

Pride in the standard of education that Manhasset has traditionally maintained and a new awareness of the gap that exists between Valley children and others (Appendixes B and C) brought about by publicity connected with the integration move, appear to be the primary motivations prompting community support for these programs, even from strong anti-integrationists. Comments from the questionnaires indicate a reaffirmation of concern for education, awareness of the problem, and a willingness to participate in proposed solutions.

A Jewish lawyer: "It is interesting that some of the strongest opposition has actively supported the pre-school program. It doesn't mean they've changed their minds about Negroes, but they do want to see quality education kept up."

A School Community Association member: "People want quality education. It really is a primary concern."

A club president: "There is a real community desire, now that the [integration] fact is accomplished, to make the whole thing good with enrichment, etc."

A Catholic father: "I think people have been made so much more aware of the problem that they are ready to do the things they are told might help, such as preparation of the Valley children."

A senior citizen: "The community wasn't aware until the Court case of the gap in the level of the Valley children and other children.

Now, we are more aware of the Negro's problems, of what we must do and what they must do to help themselves."

The Negro has responded affirmatively to these outgrowths of elementary school integration. More and more Negro parent participation and interest can be seen. The Contract Document reports: "It has been found that although many adults in low-income groups have been discouraged about the chances to better themselves, they are motivated to help their children."[7] Examples gleaned from interview responses confirm increased participation by Valley parents.

White chairman: "The fact that the Valley women are also raising money needed for the new program has impressed many. The point is, things are not just being handed to them. They are showing a lot of cooperation, too."

Negro leader: "Through the various community programs, last year's anger has been channeled into a more positive attitude and they [the Negroes] are definitely taking more interest. Many more Negro parents are attending meetings and becoming more active in general."

Contract Document: "This year for the first time we have been able to recruit Valley fathers for our Boy Scout program, formerly run by our own staff."

Negro father: "The Negro teenagers realize if they really work, scholarships will be available to them and this is a completely new development and approach for them."

Enthusiasm and support for the programs was further verified by suggestions for action in areas that have not yet received attention. "I would suggest the School Board help the children who are already in school, and therefore most immediately affected, with a program similar to the Pre-School one," stated a Negro leader concerned with the adjustment of the 166 children who were suddenly thrust into a new school environment. "To be totally successful in any community where this [integration] has taken place, there should be a workshop available for interested persons to discuss integration problems and to learn to understand, especially in a sociological way. Both Negro and white should attend, perhaps under the auspices of an Adult Education course," suggested a former member of the School Board.

"It is said that in Manhasset parents are ambitious for their children and generally have the economic resources to send their children to college.* Ninety percent of the young people from this background attend four-year colleges after graduation from high school, and another five percent continue in Junior College or enter technical or trade schools. With facts and figures such as these in mind," a Protestant minister reflected, "when I am told that a very high percentage of the Valley pupils will not be going to college it seems to me to follow that there must needs also be some radical change, perhaps addition, to the present curriculum emphasis. . . . In the school system we recommend and encourage the authorities appointed to represent us to set into motion plans to provide for the adequate training of children, both Negro and white, 'to better fit the subsequent employment of the pupil.' " (See Table 2.)

In her report for the year 1963, the President of the Community Service Center said:

We know we have just begun to move in the right direction. In view of the dynamic times in which we live, we know we must continue to grow and broaden the type of program offered here. We must involve the adults as well as the children. We must do more to broaden the horizons of these children and get them more involved in the surrounding community. We must help them to get the most out of the schools and other cultural facilities.[8]

Possible Aftermaths: Integration in Housing and Jobs

The educational programs have community pride and a new awareness of what needs to be done to encourage their creation and advancement. The trend toward further integration in housing and jobs does not have this advantage. Here the economic picture in Manhasset acts as a major deterrent to significant advancement.

Federal law as stated in the U.S. Code decrees that

---

* "Many of these well-to-do families who some years ago would have sent their children to private schools now find the costs prohibitive and admission difficult because of increasing selectivity at the better-known schools. Consequently, they look to the public schools to provide the same degree of academic excellence and the same assurance of college admission that the top prep schools traditionally have provided. The result is that the public high schools in these heavily college-oriented communities have reverted to the sole function that most high schools had at the turn of the century; namely, that of preparing youth for college." James B. Conant, *Slums and Suburbs*, New York: McGraw-Hill Book Co., 1961, pp. 82–83.

All citizens of the United States shall have the right as is enjoyed by white citizens thereof to inherit, purchase, lease, sell, hold and convey real and personal property.

New York State law, too, prohibits discrimination in housing—as well as in employment—on the basis of race, color, or creed. Legal sanctions for the segregated housing and job patterns in Manhasset do not exist. Economic sanctions do, in the fullest sense, and have been nearly one hundred percent effective. "Integration in housing is here by law, but in Manhasset I don't think this will help the Negro because of the financial situation," said a white respondent. When asked "Is there a prevalent belief in the Negro community that integration in housing and jobs will follow the elementary school integration?" each of the Negro respondents answered, "Yes, definitely." On the whole, the white community does not seem to share their confidence.

Those opposed to integration of any sort are afraid that school integration is an entering wedge. The large majority of the Manhasset populace, however, believe that elementary school integration "is a beginning of sorts, but that integration in housing and jobs will follow only to the degree that it progresses as a social trend in the rest of the country." "It will not speed up in Manhasset simply because of the school situation." One lawyer said, "At this time, people are resigned to the fact that Negroes will have more jobs because it is becoming more common in general. As far as moving in next door, I don't know. It will take time." A housewife was more personal: "I believe it will happen in jobs, but not in housing in this community because the people care too much about their neighbors."

Even with a significant national trend toward further integration in housing and jobs, most Manhasset residents feel the housing picture, especially, will be very slow to change because of economic factors. One of those interviewed said, "The Negro cannot afford Manhasset housing. As the Valley people increase their resources and standard of living, they move to other communities where housing is more available to them financially. It takes too much money to buy a house here. It will take time before they [the Negroes] can afford the housing." An attorney summed it up this way: "Integration in housing and jobs will not come about because we have integrated our schools, but it is a trend and will happen. While the issue in Manhasset has many prejudices, it is still more economic than racial."

A prophecy that improvement in the elementary school balance will increase the number of low-income housing units,[9] and therefore encourage an influx of low-income families seeking improved education for their children, cannot be accurately assessed at this time. "There is some fear the housing projects will spread and spread. But I don't see a tremendous possibility of this here. Even before the recent gains in integration here, the high quality of the former Valley School, the long-integrated high school, and the large parochial school had already made Manhasset attractive to low-income groups," commented a local realtor. Also, the wisdom of crowding more low-income housing units into the Valley area is questionable to many. One minister said, "To add to the burden of an already depressed area, an area of concentrated poverty, is, to say the least, illogical and ill-advised." And, finally, the lack of inexpensive land in the rest of the community on which to build such housing caused those who were interviewed to view public elementary school integration as an "additional, but by no means a dynamic, impetus to future low-income developments."

COMMUNITY DEVELOPMENTS TRIGGERED BY SCHOOL INTEGRATION

Construction began in 1967 on the new 800-pupil Shelter Rock Elementary School (D) located in the southern, sparsely populated residential area of the Manhasset School District (see map at beginning of chapter). The building is expected to be completed by September, 1968, at which time the Plandome Road Elementary School (B)—situated in the most populous area—will be closed. The children from the southernmost section of the Valley area (shown by the shaded area on the map), who attend the Plandome Road School, will transfer to the new school; the remaining Valley area children will continue to attend the Munsey Park School (C). This realization has not arrived without hazard.

Initially, widespread opposition to the new school had to do with site selection. Nobody wanted it in his own back yard. One faction wished to place it near the Junior and Senior High School (A), thus forming an Educational Park close to the commercial district of the town of Manhasset; another, upon the recommendation of the Citizens Advisory Committee on Site Selection and a private consulting firm, advocated a site near the heavier student population in the northern residential district. However, after two bond elections, the Shelter Rock site was finally selected. Cost, tax rate, and, to some degree, design were the secondary issues of the bond elections. Conservative elements and some individuals who did not have children in public school, as well as an apathetic overconfident support force, defeated the first bond issue in June, 1966, by a vote of 1772 to 1603, a margin of 169 votes. The School Board, which had worked very closely with the community to select a site acceptable to all without extended litigation, went back to work with the diverse elements. The "Fors" organized to counteract the "Againsts." A second bond issue was presented in November, 1966, which sacrificed 13,000 square feet of floor space at a saving of $400,000. The new proposal was approved by a vote of 2534 to 1908—a margin of 626 votes—the additional turnout of 1077 voters deciding the sentiment "For."

Integration as a contributing factor in the need for a new school, while surely a matter of personal consideration for some, was never mentioned in any of the many public meetings, in fliers distributed by the various groups, nor in the newspaper accounts.

Establishment of the Economic Opportunity Council as part of the Federal Poverty Program about three years before had become more of a community action program than was true at its inception. Abandonment of the relatively new Valley School in favor of integration within the other attendance areas seemed to have triggered the action needed to bring solace to a varied community in ferment three years ago.

The pre-kindergarten program for children of culturally deprived families—begun with Federal, State, County, and local funds, under the auspices of the Community Service Center (located in the abandoned Valley School)—proved so successful that the Manhasset School Board took it over after only two years. The pre-kindergarten program will be housed in the new Shelter Rock School upon its completion. Two improvements of benefit to the entire community can be traced to the closing of the Valley School.

Working with suggestions from representatives of the Manhasset Community Relations Council, the Community Service Center, and the physical-education departments of the Manhasset and adjoining Great Neck School Districts, Nassau County officers have developed a 23-acre recreation center southwest of the Long Island Railroad trestle. The half-million-dollar park, with its tennis, handball, stoopball, and basketball courts, its parking and picnic facilities, and its ice skating and model boating on the 7-acre Whitney Pond, attracts people from all parts of Manhasset as well as from the more thickly populated Great Neck district.

Urban renewal, under a Town of North Hempstead plan, is being designed to include a widening of Northern Boulevard as it runs through the Valley area on its way to Manhattan, 17 miles distant. The subsequent removal of many of the substandard structures in that area seems unlikely to be followed by a widescale development of low-income housing.

More community involvement is still needed, but as an instrument to develop leadership among the poor and as a vehicle for all to express a voice, the Economic Opportunity Council is an important force in stimulating good community relations.

APPENDIX A. QUESTIONNAIRE

1. As you know, in the School Board election last May a huge turnout of voters gave Carmichael and Wahlert a slim 204 vote win over Wiemann and Hartung. What do you feel were the real issues of that election?

    a. "social" legislation
    b. reaction against School Board
    c. fear of increased taxes
    d. wish to clear Manhasset's name
    e. integration—elementary education only a beginning (housing, jobs, to follow)
    f. against integration
    g. for integration
    h. classroom crowding
    i. busing
    j. Negroes for integration
    k. Negroes against new distance children would have to go
    l. other

2. Do you think there has been much reaction towards the School Board and the way they handled the situation; that is, their silence during the case and their decision not to appeal?

    a. Why do you say that?

3. Does the subject of increased taxes for schools enter in here?

        Yes _____
        No _____

If *yes*, with what segment of the community?

    a. parochial school parents
    b. older people, no children
    c. majority of people
    d. some people

    e. few people
    f. other

4. How do you think the people in the Valley feel about the new arrangement?

    a. sorry school not in neighborhood
    b. against busing
    c. in favor of busing
    d. pleased with arrangement
    e. other

5. Is there a belief prevalent in the (Negro) community that the elementary school integration is just a beginning and that integration in housing and jobs will follow?

6. What about crowding of classrooms? What have you heard on that?

7. Do you think the community feels it's good to have children of different races go to school together or would they prefer separate schools?

8. How do you think the mixing of races in elementary schools affects the educational level?

9. Do you think (and this is important) that those opposed to integration of the elementary schools feel somewhat less strongly opposed now that the fact is accomplished?

10. In your opinion, is there much support for the view that "it's too soon to know"?

11. To sum up, are there any other areas of insight into Manhasset's reaction to elementary school integration that you can think of?

12. What alternatives, suggestions or changes would you recommend?

APPENDIX B. MANHASSET PUBLIC SCHOOLS: THE READING PROGNOSIS TEST,* GRADE 1—OCTOBER 1963

	Language Scores			Perceptual Discrimination Scores			Total Scores	
	No. of Pupils			No. of Pupils			No. of Pupils	
Score	Munsey Park School	Valley School	Score	Munsey Park School	Valley School	Score	Munsey Park School	Valley School
21–22	3		31–33	11		75–80	1	
19–20	6		28–30	8	1	70–74	7	
17–18	15		25–27	18		65–69	2	
15–16	9		22–24	13	1	60–64	10	1
13–14	10		19–21	10	6	55–59	8	
11–12	4	2	16–18	2	1	50–54	8	
9–10	3		13–15		6	45–49	13	
7–8	6	1	10–12		5	40–44	6	2
5–6	4	2	7–9		2	35–39	6	2
3–4	1	5	4–6		3	30–34	1	6
1–2	1	7				25–29		3
0		7				20–24		4
						15–19		2
						10–14		4
						5–9		
Median	15.2	1.8	Median	25.3	13.5	Median	53.03	27.5

* *The Reading Prognosis Test* by S. Feldmann and I. M. Mahler is a two-part test of language and perceptual discrimination, which yields both part scores and a total score. It was administered individually to all **first** grade students in the Valley and Munsey Park Elementary Schools under the direction of the staff of the Institute for Developmental Studies, Department of Psychiatry, New York Medical College.

APPENDIX C. MANHASSET PUBLIC SCHOOLS: STANFORD ACHIEVEMENT TEST PUBLIC SCHOOL NORMS, GRADES 5 AND 6—DECEMBER, 1963

Sub Tests	Other Manhasset Elementary Schools Median	Valley School Median
Grade 5:		
Paragraph Meaning	76	25
Word Meaning	78	30
Spelling	75	30
Language	78	—
Arithmetic Reasoning	60	28
Arithmetic Computation	40	23
Grade 6:		
Paragraph Meaning	72	23
Word Meaning	82	14
Spelling	82	35
Language	73	22
Arithmetic Reasoning	63	13
Arithmetic Computation	30	10

11 | THE ENGLEWOOD–TEANECK, NEW JERSEY, EXPERIENCE

DAVID SPENGLER

Editorial Writer, The Record, *Hackensack, New Jersey*

Mr. Spengler edited much of the reportage on the Englewood school-desegregation struggle while serving as an editor on the city desk of *The Record*, a daily published in the Bergen County seat. He also contributed editorials on Englewood and became full-time editorial-page assistant and writer in the midst of the Teaneck controversy. A resident of Englewood since 1959, he is a graduate of the University of Michigan and has a master's degree in music education from Teachers College, Columbia University.

Events, as we live through them, are often confusing. So many characters appear on the scene, often operating from varying frames of reference, that the unschooled observer is bewildered by what he sees. This case history, written by an experienced journalist, is an accurate account of events as they happened—and for that reason may be confusing to the reader who is unfamiliar with the developments in Englewood or in similar situations. (Events in Teaneck, which followed, were much less complicated.) As an aid to the reader, the full cast of characters is offered by the editors, together with a synopsis and a calendar of events.

Cast of Major Characters in Englewood

Hughes, Richard, Governor of New Jersey

Kiss, William, President of School Board at the start

Perry, John, President of School Board after May, 1962

Shedd, Mark, Superintendent of Schools after June 2, 1962

Spruill, Deborah, Secretary, local NAACP (and husband, John, President of Board of Health)

Stearns, Harry, Superintendent of Schools, 1944–1962

Tibbs, Vincente, Councilman for Ward Four

Vaughn, Carmen and Leroy, and daughter, Laurie, Lincoln School parents and pupil

Volk, Austin, Mayor of Englewood

Zuber, Paul, lawyer for the "Englewood Movement"

Cast of Minor Characters in Englewood

Baer, Anne and Byron, CORE leaders who had been jailed in Mississippi

Banks, Calvin, national director, NAACP

Batchelor, Willie Mae, member of CORE

Breslin, John, attorney for the City

Breslin, William, attorney for the Save Our Neighborhood Schools committee (SONS)

Brogan, Thomas J., former Chief Justice, attorney for School Board in 1954

Brown, Arnold, civil-rights attorney and later State Assemblyman

Brown, Gordon, Bergen County Judge

Derner, The Rev. George, chairman of conciliation committee, Ministerial Association

Dodson, Dan W., Professor of Education, New York University, consultant to Superintendent Stearns

Elliott, Sally, President of Bergen CORE

Gamrin, Mr. and Mrs. Alfred, white opponents of SONS

Garrity, Francis, Assistant Superintendent of Schools

Graham, Harold, Chairman of Englewood P.-T.A. Council

Greenberg, Emanuel, attorney for 18 parents

Greenberg, Sandra and Robert, Liberty School parents and Freedom School workers

Groezinger, Eric, State Assistant Commissioner of Education for Controversies and Disputes

Gutman, Robert, Professor of Sociology, Rutgers University, consultant to Superintendent Stearns

Harrison, Augustus, President, local NAACP

Henriksen, Thorlief, Principal of Cleveland School

Huckin, LeRoy, City Attorney

Jones, Helen, teacher in Freedom School

Kay, Barbara, housewife who had been jailed in Mississippi (wife of composer Ulysses Kay)

Kuntsler, Robert, attorney for the Spruills

Lacey, Mrs., member of CORE

Lawless, John, Police Director of Englewood

Lebson, Abram, attorney for the School Board

Major, Russell, leader of the Prometheans

Maniscalco, Fred, Supervisor of Buildings and Grounds for the School Board

McLinn, Angela, teacher in Freedom School

Miller, The Rev. Robert I., President of Human Relations Council

Morris, Barbara, attorney for NAACP

Nealy, Maggie, Lincoln School parent

Ozzard, William E., Acting Governor while Hughes was in Florida

Pickering, Jack, member of Urban League and later President, Cleveland P.-T.A.

Platoff, Robert, attorney for 12 parents

Pugach, Louis, Chairman of Save Our Neighborhood Schools committee (SONS)

Raubinger, Frederick, State Commissioner of Education

Shohan, Leo, economist and Urban League member

Slauson, Sidney, President, Bergen Urban League

Smith, Jeanne, temporary chairman of local CORE

Tate, Herbert, attorney for NAACP

Taylor, The Rev. Walter, Pastor of Galilee Methodist Church

Van Alstyne, David, Jr., former State Senator

Wilson, Virginia, parent who sent a telegram to the Governor

Wood, Robert C., Professor of Political Science, M.I.T., consultant to Superintendent Stearns

Wright, Mr. and Mrs. Benjamin, Liberty School parents (professionally Dr. Virginia Wright was a psychiatrist)

Synopsis of Action in Englewood

The action takes place in Englewood, New Jersey, a suburb of New York. Most of the inhabitants enjoy a comfortable social position.

Englewood is divided into four wards. The boundaries were determined when the town was bisected first by a line running east and west (Palisade Avenue) between the Second and Fourth Wards, to the south, and the First and Third Wards, to the north; then by a line running north and south, called Engle Street between the First and Third Wards and Grand Avenue between the Second and Fourth. Two names for the same street or avenue imply that the roadway changes character. Indeed it does, for most of the Negroes in town live off Grand Avenue in Ward Four, and many of them travel from their homes to work in the houses of those citizens in the other wards who can afford to engage their services. All the children of Englewood attended neighborhood schools when the story begins. Hence students of some of the schools were likely to be white, and students of others were likely to be black. No school had more Negro children than Lincoln, a fact that paid unworthy tribute to the President after whom the school is named.

No court decision was aimed particularly at the Englewood School Board, but several organizations, including the Urban League, the NAACP, and the Lincoln PTA had expressed severe dissatisfaction with the segregation of Negro school children and the kind of education provided for them as early as 1954. In this year spokesmen for the dissenters lodged a complaint with the New Jersey Commissioner of Education in Trenton. But action against segregation at the elementary level did not take place until October 28, 1963. On this date a compulsory fifth-grade central school was opened, and Lincoln School was turned into an administrative and special-education center.

Calendar of Events

Original protest in 1954; closing of Lincoln Junior High ordered.

June, 1961, protests by Mrs. Spruill and Urban League of Bergen County against *de facto* segregation at Lincoln Elementary School.

August 23, school board offered to meet with persons concerned.

September 5, meeting where superintendent's study was promised.

October 10, Superintendent Stearns acknowledged Lincoln School problem.

January 15, 1962, budget recommended with no money for desegregation.

January, 1962, integrationists demanded Stearns report before budget.

February 1, peaceful demonstration after hearing where budget was passed.

February 16, eleven demonstrators acquitted.

March 12, Stearns report: one warning and five options.

May 15, board plan to refurbish Engle School as open-enrollment demonstration school; adopted without superintendent's approval.

June 27, plan dropped when criticized as tokenism.

July 12, new proposal, compulsory citywide fifth-grade central school.

July 26, Save Our Neighborhood Schools committee (SONS) formed.

July 31, Board of School Estimate refused $35,000 cost of central school.

August, Englewood Movement launched—rallies, picketing, and unsuccessful attempt to boycott merchants.

September, half of Lincoln students absent for three days.

September, parents' petition to State Commissioner of Education—six-man team appointed.

October, report of team—called a whitewash by integrationists.

November, referendum—majority in favor of neighborhood schools.

January, 1963, sit-ins at State House for 48 hours.

February 26, second boycott of Lincoln School—half of students away; "Freedom School" organized for boycotting pupils.

March, more picketing in Englewood and Trenton.

April 1–17, hearings on parents' complaints to State Commissioner.

April 23, 18 Lincoln School parents tried to register their children at Cleveland School.

April 24, same attempt at Quarles School.

April 25, same attempt at Roosevelt School.

May 7, thirty-two unauthorized children entered Cleveland School.

June, Ministerial Association conciliation committee formed.

July 2, Commissioner Raubinger ordered reduction of Negro enrollment at Lincoln School.

October 28, 1963, central school opened for all fifth graders in the city; Lincoln School closed and made into administrative center.

■■■■■■■■■■■■■■■■■■■■■■■■■■■■■■■■■■■■■■■

ENGLEWOOD

Laurie Vaughn, 9 years old and pretty, stood hand in hand with two companions at the closed door of Cleveland Elementary School, Englewood, N.J. The date was May 7, 1963, an unusual date for children to report to a new school, but Laurie was one among 32 children who were caught up in an unusual circumstance.

They were unauthorized visitors to Cleveland School, their status having been defined for them by a school board that was reluctant to shut them out from integrated education but had not yet found a way to let them in. The school to which Laurie had been assigned, Lincoln School in Englewood's Fourth Ward, was attended almost exclusively by Negroes. Laurie's father and mother, Leroy and Carmen Vaughn, were among those parents who had been fighting hard for some time against a school system in Englewood that had been racially imbalanced. They had approved of a plan designed by the school board a year earlier to alleviate imbalance. They had seen the plan frustrated by the city's administration. For them time and patience had run out.

Laurie, a fourth grader, was reporting to Cleveland School on the second day of a sit-in. On the other side of the door a graying man shook his head as Laurie pulled at the handle. She would later come to know Thorlief Henriksen, Cleveland principal. To her now he was a stranger. He was no threatening stranger, however. He stepped out and said, "I'm sorry; you can't come in."

Children assigned to Cleveland School, some with their parents, were just beginning to arrive. A woman near Laurie pointed to them. "If we don't get in," she said, "they don't get in." The visitors sat on the steps. Henriksen opened the door. "Come in, children," he said, and stepped aside. He was following a directive from Dr. Mark Shedd, a youthful man completing his first hard-pressed year as Englewood school superintendent. Shedd had remarked: "Principals have been cautioned to avoid any incident or activity which would be disruptive to the school program or which might harm any child, whether that child is enrolled or not." As she had been told to do, Laurie entered the first classroom she saw, and sat down. From May 7 until school closed on June 20 she and the other visitors would continue to do so.

Englewood (population in 1960: 26,057), once the home of Dwight Morrow, banker, diplomat, father of Mrs. Anne Morrow Lindbergh, was nationally known as a wealthy community largely owing to the wooded estates along winding roads in the First and Second Wards on the East Hill. Englewood has two names for one major north-south thoroughfare, Engle Street–Grand Avenue. Across Engle Street from the First Ward lies the Third Ward, middle-class, predominantly white, characterized to great extent by Tudor, Dutch colonial, and Spanish villa houses that had been built in so many communities during the 1920's. In lowlands west of Grand Avenue lay the Fourth Ward, which before World War II had been the residential enclave for Negro domestic servants for whom a mile walk up Palisade Avenue—Englewood's major east-west thoroughfare and major retail street—took them directly along the northern margin of their ward, across Engle Street, up the hill to the estates. Although in the years between the end of World War II and 1963 a few Negroes— professionals, successful entertainers—had moved into the First Ward as well as Englewood's other predominantly Caucasian wards, most of the Negroes, managers and professionals as well as clerks and laborers, who continued to arrive moved into the Fourth Ward.

The uninvited visit to Cleveland School in 1963 was the active expression of a sense of hurt which nine years earlier had been put into words at a hearing in the state capital at Trenton. Before New Jersey Education Commissioner Frederick Raubinger was a complaint that the Englewood Board of Education had drawn district lines designed to keep Lincoln School segregated. A part of that school was being used as the smaller of Englewood's two junior high schools, the other being a building on Engle Street. A school nearby, Liberty School on Palisade Avenue, had both Negro and white students (in 1961 Liberty would be 61 percent Negro); Cleveland in the Third Ward and Roosevelt in the Second were almost exclusively white.

In 1954 the school board's argument was that Englewood's neighborhood schools simply reflected the nature of Englewood's neighborhoods, for which the school board was not accountable. The board was represented by a former New Jersey chief justice, Thomas J. Brogan. In the year in which the United States Supreme Court's redefinition of segregation had yet to be clarified in experience, Justice Brogan submitted his argument in Trenton: "There is no statute or case which requires the board to foster integration in schools." The president of the school board added: "I didn't know that it (integration) was a binding part of the new (state) constitution."

Due process of law set the tenor of the hearing, but the tenor of what was in store for Englewood a decade later lay in a statement by the education committee of the Urban League in Bergen County, the county in which Englewood is located and of which Hackensack is the county seat. The League's statement read: "When parents and children and their future are involved in a situation which produces a sense of hurt and anger, the result affects the entire community, and not simply those in the forefront of the controversy."

As a result of the 1954 hearing the Education Commissioner found no evidence of a school-districting gerrymander, but he ordered Englewood immediately to close its segregated Lincoln Junior High

School. Locked in its ghetto, however, Lincoln Elementary School continued to teach Negro children.

Young and recently married, Leroy and Carmen Vaughn moved into Englewood in 1951. Leroy Vaughn was a plant engineer—he would commute daily to East Brunswick, New Jersey—and Carmen Vaughn was a psychiatric social worker who had been awarded an A.B. degree by Hunter College and an M.A. degree by Columbia University.

Across the George Washington Bridge a ten-minute bus ride carried Carmen Vaughn from an uptown Manhattan subway station to her home in the Fourth Ward on a tree-lined street bordering McKay Park, an expansive stretch of woods and green. She had a choice of bus routes. One route followed the top of the Palisades, which thrust abruptly up from the Hudson River, a few miles north to Palisade Avenue, then down the Seven Sister Hills through the leafy First Ward into town. The other route followed a highway sloping west from the bridge, intersecting Grand Avenue, then turned north into town.

Not yet the parents of school children, the Vaughns had a resident's interest in the 1954 hearing. In the quiet years following the hearing, they would watch the construction of a spacious auditorium, Academic Hall, on the campus of Dwight Morrow High School, and a new integrated junior high school next to the auditorium. They would visit a new all-white elementary school, the Donald Quarles School, built like a miniature college on a campus in the First Ward.

The Vaughns' acquaintanceship in Englewood at first was not wide, but it would grow. They would get to know Gus Harrison, who worked for the New York Transit Authority and was a leader in the local NAACP; Russell Major, who had been an athlete at Dwight Morrow High School and an officer in the Prometheans—a Negro society dedicated to improvement in Englewood—and later would be a leader in the Englewood Movement; Mrs. Deborah Spruill, for awhile secretary of the NAACP, and her husband, John, who had been a power engineer in the New York subway system and would become president of the Englewood Board of Health and manager of the Spruill Insurance Agency.

The Vaughns would confront John Perry, a teacher in a Harlem school, who would be the first Negro to preside over the Englewood school board. With Mrs. Sandra Greenberg, who lived in an integrated neighborhood in the Third Ward, Carmen Vaughn would seek sponsors and plan the first workshop that led to the Englewood Human Relations Council, an organization later led by the Reverend Robert I. Miller, on the staff of Union Theological Seminary. With the Urban League and Parent-Teacher Associations, the Council would be a major arena for exchange of opinion and recognition of the increasing depth of emotion in Englewood.

There would be Arnold Brown, a young attorney with political aspirations, and his wife, Lydia. There would be many others, those who supported the position of the Vaughns—integration, now—and those who would fight it as hard as they knew how. And the Vaughns would learn that, although organizations would be identifiable in the impending confrontation, the fight for integration could be carried only by individuals, Negro and white, working without letup against dissent and, even more frustrating, against apathy.

On June 12, 1961, Mrs. John Spruill, whose husband then was a member of the Board of Health and later would become its president, asked the president of the Englewood Board of Education for his attention. Then to the five-member board she read a statement: for seven years the board had taken no action on a problem it had been discussing, that of racial imbalance at Lincoln School in the Fourth Ward. If segregated neighborhoods forced segregated education, Mrs. Spruill said, then the idea of the neighborhood school must be sacrificed. William Kiss, president of the school board, accepted the petition. He made no comment.

Mrs. Spruill had said she represented residents of the Fourth Ward, the Lincoln School P.-T.A., and the National Association for the Advancement of Colored People. Two weeks after Mrs. Spruill's protest, directors of the Bergen County Urban League sent a resolution to the Englewood school board: "Recent events indicate that the community is more aware of the situation at Lincoln School than formerly, and may actively through protest create a furor. It is unthinkable that the Board of Education will not make all possible efforts to integrate the Lincoln School." The resolution urged on the board a reassuringly deliberate way to make haste: that the board make a statement affirming positive educational values in ethnic integration; that it appoint a committee to study means toward integration at Lincoln School; that it study educational standards, motivation, and the recruitment and assignment of teachers throughout the system. The board published no response.

During a quiet July Laurie Vaughn's mother was asked by a new neighbor how she might enroll her daughter in a kindergarten other than that in Lincoln School. Mrs. Vaughn reached for her phone book to look up the local chapter of the National Association for the Advancement of Colored People. It wasn't listed. Augustus Harrison of Englewood was president of the Bergen County chapter, and when Mrs. Vaughn telephoned him at his home he invited her to the chapter's next meeting. At that meeting she asked what her neighbor might do; when the meeting ended, Mrs. Vaughn was the chapter's education chairman.

August 23, 1961, the school board broke its silence, issuing a statement to the press that it would meet with civic leaders to discuss Mrs. Spruill's protest. It made no mention of the Urban League's resolution nor of a statement by Calvin Banks, national NAACP director, that he would ask the board whether Lincoln School had been deliberately segregated nor of Augustus Harrison's reiteration of Mrs. Spruill's thesis that the neighborhood-school system is not sacrosanct when one school is segregated. The school board's statement was cautious:

> At its last public meeting in June the Board of Education received a communication relating to the concentration of one racial group in Lincoln School. Although this is the first time such an inquiry has been made, the board is aware that the problems associated with patterns of enrollment in the public schools can be very complex and can affect the entire community.
>
> Accordingly, the board has invited to a series of informal, private meetings certain members of the community who have expressed opinions and interest in the matter. The first meeting will take place early in September.
>
> In this way it is hoped to obtain a clearer understanding of exactly what is being sought from the board in order to help the board arrive at a solution.

The informal private meeting proved to be first in a series of one. In the Dwight Morrow High School library September 5, Mrs. Vaughn greeted Arnold Brown, a young Englewood attorney who had preceded Harrison as Bergen NAACP president and who was a member of the Urban League. She nodded also to Sidney Slauson, president of the Bergen Urban League, and to Banks, Harrison, and Mrs. Spruill. As had most residents in Englewood, Mrs. Vaughn had learned of Mrs. Spruill's protest only when she read reports of it in the newspapers. Now she was listening to Dr. Harry Stearns, who had been Englewood's school superintendent since 1944, report that the school board had asked him to submit a study in depth of Englewood's school-enrollment problems. Dr. Stearns was saying he would welcome help from the NAACP, the Urban League, and others at the meeting, and he added that he would enlist the aid of outstanding authorities in education and allied fields. To Mrs. Vaughn the characterizing phrase was "in depth." She believed that central in Dr. Stearns's report would be racial imbalance at Lincoln School and a plan to put an end to it.

A month later, October 10, Dr. Stearns at a routine school board meeting proffered a kind of work-in-progress report. One of the problems: Lincoln School. The report followed a spate of activity in the Fourth Ward. Four candidates for election as Fourth Ward councilman had called for school integration. Among them was Democratic candidate Vincente Tibbs, who said that he'd had faith in the school board since 1954, at which time Lincoln Junior High School had been closed. Tibbs joined the other candidates in asserting that he would not press for school integration unless most of the Fourth Ward residents demanded it. From Augustus Harrison of the NAACP came a dissent to which Mrs. Vaughn was to become implacably committed: "We are demanding that the basic rights of a minority be fully extended to all citizens, rights which are theirs even if a real or hypothetical majority does not wish to recognize this fact."

Some days later Harrison spoke out again, pointing out that the New York State Education Commissioner had just announced a policy of ending *de facto* segregation in all schools. Harrison suggested that the Bergen NAACP should take more positive action. "Recent meetings with the (Englewood) Board of Education and school officials have somewhat disillusioned the (Bergen Chapter, NAACP) with the prospect of the (Stearns) study," he said.

Dr. Stearns's work in progress was mentioned again October 13, when Harrison said that irrespective of recommendations in the report the NAACP chapter had set a deadline for total integration in Englewood: September 1962. On the same day he announced the appointment of legal counsel, Paul Zuber, a resident of Croton, New York, who had won a ruling from federal judge Irving R. Kaufman that Lincoln School in New Rochelle, New York, had been deliberately maintained as a segregated Negro institution, a ruling that was affirmed by the United States Supreme Court in December, 1961.

What some Englewood residents would look for in Dr. Stearns's report was further defined in an announcement from Dr. Harold Graham, chairman of the Englewood P.-T.A. Council. The council supported the Stearns study, which in part it interpreted as a search for a practical solution to racial imbalance at Lincoln.

The Stearns report was mentioned yet again January 15, only two weeks before Dr. Stearns had said the result of his study would be made available. On that evening the school board announced a $2,499,516 budget, open then to discussion, to be adopted early in February. Arnold Brown was in the audience. President Kiss earlier had received a telegram from the NAACP asking the school board to approve no budget until it knew what recommendations Dr. Stearns might make. Now Brown got to his feet to ask why he had just listened to the presentation of a budget in which there was no provision for desegregating the schools. The school board, Kiss answered, was bound by law to adopt a tentative budget before February. "There are certain deadlines that must be met," Kiss said, and Brown replied: "Then the study should have been concluded first."

The following day Harrison of the NAACP remarked: "It certainly appears that the Board of Education is attempting to block any desegregation in Englewood for at least another year." A week later the Bergen NAACP, together with the Bergen chapter of the Congress of Racial Equality, of which Dr. Jeanne Smith of Englewood was then temporary chairman, released a statement: "Any attempt to rush the budget through before consideration of the study can only be viewed as a tactic to obstruct school desegregation and an act of bad faith."

Englewood's Board of School Estimate made its appearance now in a calendar of deadlines on which in part Dr. Smith based her charge of bad faith. In the Englewood scheme of school financing the Board of School Estimate has a nearly incontestable power of veto; although the budget is drafted by the Board of Education, it is inoperative until it is approved through a simple majority vote by the Board of School Estimate. The latter board is composed of two members of the school board and three members of the city government—the mayor and two councilmen. Harrison charged: "This year the public hearing was announced for February 2, then changed to the even earlier date of February 1, . . . two full weeks before the 1962–63 budget must be adopted by the Board of School Estimate. If no budgetary allowance is made for implementing recommendations of the (Stearns) study, there can be no change in the racial complex of the City's schools for at least another year."

In addition to the sense of frustration that gripped many Fourth Ward residents following the public hearing of the budget, resentment from an attempt in January 1962 to make way for construction of an apartment building in a Fourth Ward residential area still rankled. Before the Englewood Board of Adjustment, attorney Paul Zuber had argued against a request by a resident in the Third Ward for permission to build units that would rent for about $35 dollars a room a month in a neighborhood of attractive houses. At that hearing were more than a hundred residents of the Fourth Ward. Ironic laughter followed every suggestion that an apartment house would improve the neighborhood that needed no improving: it was plain that the audience felt it was witnessing an opportunistic attempt to blight a neighborhood. A few weeks later the Board of Adjustment rejected the application, but resentment was not dispelled.

Now the Vaughns sought out Paul Zuber, and on February 1 he accompanied them, together with Laurie, eight other children, and five other parents to the Donald Quarles School. Zuber had announced that he expected rejection, at the school as well as from Dr. Stearns. He would follow the rejection, he added, with a suit. Two of the children who were applying attended Liberty School. Their father was Benjamin Wright of *Ebony* magazine, their mother, Dr. Virginia Wright, a psychiatrist. The parents told newsmen they were acting independently of the Bergen NAACP, whose president, Harrison, had said it would adhere to its commitment to await the outcome of the Stearns report. After Zuber and the parents conferred with Dr. Stearns, the children returned to Lincoln and Liberty Schools.

On the evening of that February 1, Carmen Vaughn walked to the Municipal Building on Palisade Avenue. Here the Board of School Estimate would approve—she had no doubt—the controversial budget. On the steps at the entrance of the building, in the lobby, at the staircases circling to the right and left up the wide well to the second floor were residents of the Third and Fourth Wards, white and

Negro. She recognized many of them, of course, friends and acquaintances she had made in the past several years. There was Mrs. Barbara Kay (listed as "housewife" on the police docket the following morning), who had spent 40 days in a Mississippi jail during an interrupted freedom ride the preceding summer; Byron Baer, CORE leader and film and television technician, who also knew the inside of a Mississippi jail; Mrs. Angela McLinn, who would a year later help administer a freedom school in Englewood. The word was out: this would be an all-night sit-in.

Announcement came that the crowd was too large to be seated in the Municipal Building chamber, and the Board of School Estimate recessed to call a meeting in the spacious Academic Hall. As time wore on, those who stayed at the Municipal Building sang and spoke extemporaneously on the harm in segregation. Some went out to bring back coffee and sandwiches for others, passing them through the windows when police locked the door.

To no one's surprise that night the budget was passed. Carmen Vaughn could stay with the protesters no longer than midnight; she had left Laurie and a younger sister with a baby-sitter. The following morning, however, eleven persons, seven of whom were white, remained and were confronted with a choice—leave or be arrested. All but one woman—who explained that her 10-month-old baby was ill—refused to post $10 bail. Reporter Frank Sherry, an Englewood resident, followed the woman out of the building. He wrote later: "Outside the City Hall, Mrs. Bernard Brightman burst into tears and said, 'Segregation has no place in a democracy!' A Negro woman standing by put her arm around the distraught housewife, and comforted her, 'Come on, baby,' she said. 'You've had it. I'll take you home.'"

Byron Baer's wife, Anne, and Mrs. Kay were the last to leave the municipal jail a few days later. At a hearing on February 16 before a County Court judge in Hackensack, to whom Arnold Brown introduced Paul Zuber, a courtesy required in New Jersey for a lawyer out of the state, the eleven were acquitted.

Dr. Stearns submitted his report at a regular meeting of the school board on March 12, 1962. The title page lists Dr. Stearns as coordinator, and, as consultants, Dr. Dan W. Dodson, professor of education, New York University; Dr. Robert Gutman, professor of sociology, Rutgers University; and Dr. Robert C. Wood, professor of political science, Massachusetts Institute of Technology. The report, "Englewood, Its People and Its Schools," contained 158 pages of text, tables, and charts. Its press run was 100 copies, and President Kiss told members of an audience of about 100 persons that each copy was available on a ten-day loan to responsible organizations. In a letter of transmittal bound into the report, Dr. Stearns said that he had been directed in April 1961 to make the study and that, having been relieved of all school administrative detail by the assistant superintendent of schools, he had devoted his full time to the report.

The report offered six alternatives—or, more accurately, one warning and five options. The warning was that a policy of drift, adhering to the neighborhood school, at least until a federal court ordered otherwise, would not meet the requirement of a conscious effort to correct imbalance. The remaining alternatives were:

1. Neighborhood renewal and a higher-horizons program: that is, improving the poor housing encysting Lincoln School and proffering a program similar to New York City's effort to work through school and social-service agencies to improve the incentive of children from underprivileged families and environments. The authors pointed out that this did nothing to correct the imbalance at Lincoln, warning that it was certain to prolong the tension among Englewood citizens.

2. An open-enrollment program: a plan to let parents from Lincoln seek enrollment for their children in schools outside their neighborhood where classrooms had room for additional pupils. The authors listed reasons why this plan would be disadvantageous in Englewood.

3. The Princeton Plan: a program patterned after a pairing of schools in Princeton, N.J., which in Englewood would distribute grades among the five elementary schools and bus many children across neighborhood lines.

4. A plan to close Lincoln School: abandonment of that building and adding wings to Englewood's other schools.

5. Extensive neighborhood renewal plus a central intermediate school: taking advantage of an Englewood master plan for renewal of the Fourth Ward, Lincoln could become a central intermediate school when its environment had been made desirable.

Although the authors selected none of the proposals to recommend to the board, they stated that racial imbalance existed in a tense city, that it was harmful, and that doing nothing about it would make matters worse. The implication was that some variation of a central intermediate school plan (a solution independently urged by the Urban League) would be among the most workable solutions to the problem, and they pointed out that some step toward integration should be taken by the opening of the 1962–63 term. Dr. Stearns had said that the report would be his last major act as superintendent, from which position he would then resign. As authoritative as the report was, as detailed in its presentation, and as sensitive in insight as it proved to be, "Englewood, Its People and Its Schools" had no great immediate impact in the city, primarily because of the caution with which it was received by the school board.

Kiss had said the Stearns report was a report to the school board, not by the board. Abruptly the distinction was to be made clear. Even while the Stearns report had been holding stage center, the school board had been working at its own plan, an integrated demonstration school. On May 15, to about 200 persons in Academic Hall John Perry, board vice president, a teacher in New York City and the only Negro on a Bergen County school board, read a six-page announcement. Mrs. Vaughn followed it closely. The school board planned to refurbish the Engle Street school building—recently a junior high school, closed when a new building was completed—for use in an open-enrollment program. Parents from any part of Englewood could apply. Grades from kindergarten through sixth would offer team teaching, expanded audio-visual programs, the most modern educational concepts. The plan, Perry said, had been proposed by a member of the school board, whom he did not name. Mrs. Vaughn felt the sting of anger as she listened: "Because of the obvious excellence of the suggestion," Perry was saying, "the board was immediately impressed by its advantages, and in April the plan was discussed with Dr. Robert Wood of the Massachusetts Institute of Technology, one of the consultants of the depth study." Mrs. Vaughn heard no report of Dr. Wood's reaction, but she was to remember a remark by Dr. Stearns after Perry had finished reading. The superintendent said he had not been consulted on the plan until after the school board had decided to act on it. Perry, rather than the school board president, had read the demonstration-school proposal that night for a surprising reason: William Kiss had resigned.

Response to the demonstration-school plan came quickly. Gus Harrison called it token integration. Councilman Vincente Tibbs said it misplaced the emphasis. Arnold Brown, now president of the Bergen Urban League, said the plan would leave Lincoln School even more impoverished. Jack Pickering, education chairman of the Urban League, later president of the Cleveland P.-T.A., said that without transportation, which the school board said it could not provide, the plan would result in socio-economic discrimination in addition to racial discrimination. Within a month the demonstration school had been disapproved by CORE, by the Cleveland School and Liberty School P.-T.A.'s, by the Englewood Democratic Club, by the League of Women Voters, and, apparently, by most Englewood parents, indifferent as they were to an opinion survey by the school board.

In the Fourth Ward Mrs. Vaughn dialed the telephone and rang doorbells to help defeat the board's plan. Addressing an audience that packed the auditorium of Bethany Presbyterian Church on Palisade Avenue, Paul Zuber scathingly characterized the plan as notification from the plantation owners on the Hill to liberals that they now would have a place where they could send their kids to school with the Mau Mau. In any case, Zuber said, liberals when the going got rough could be expected to cut and run. To those Negroes whom he had accused of subservience, Zuber had come prepared for a gesture. From his pocket he whipped a red bandanna; then, his voice rich with scorn, he shouted: "If it fits . . ." The audience thundered back: "Wear it!"

On June 27, 1962, the school board announced it had dropped the demonstration-school plan and would prepare an alternative by July 12. On that evening in Academic Hall Mrs. Vaughn was one among 400 Englewood residents gathered to hear the new proposal. She ignored a petition being circulated in the audience. The petitioners, about 1400 of them, according to the resident who had initiated it, urged resistance to any change in the neighborhood-school system, and it sought a referendum, a technique that school board attorney Abram Lebson said the board had no authority to initiate. Lebson warned the audience that disorder would close the meeting to the public; then Perry announced the plan. The school board would operate a compulsory central fifth grade, to begin in September, as a first step toward integrating the entire system of five elementary schools. Mrs. Vaughn listened closely for any word about closing Lincoln School. No word came.

Support of the central school, qualified as merely a first step toward integrated education, came at once from the Urban League, the League of Women Voters, the Ministerial Association, the Cleveland School P.-T.A., and the Junior High School Parent-Teacher Organization. Dr. A. Harry Passow, Professor of Education at Columbia Teachers College, stood at the microphone to address the board. "I'm sure in the long run Englewood will be served by taking this step," he said.

From the audience Fourth Ward Councilman Vincente Tibbs made a statement: "I will do everything I can to support it, but I hope it will be just a first step in eliminating the evil of segregation in our schools. I'm not satisfied, and never will be as long as Lincoln School stands as it does." Mrs. Vaughn agreed with Augustus Harrison of the NAACP, who was saying: "The plan is just another in a long string of delaying tactics to avoid facing the real issue of *de facto* segregation in our elementary schools."

Within two weeks was formed the organization that was to become Englewood's major voice of opposition to the school board's plans, then and later, albeit for reasons diametrically opposed to Mrs. Vaughn's. The Save Our Neighborhood Schools committee (SONS), of which Louis Pugach, a resident of the Second Ward, was chairman, announced that it had the support of 500 residents, many of whom had sent telegrams to Governor Hughes. "We are not opposed to integration," Pugach said, "but we feel that there are better ways to accomplish it, without taking children out of schools near their homes."

Governor Hughes later announced that he had received about 50 telegrams, identically worded: "Strongly protest action Englewood School Board. Suggest this not in accordance with your stated policy of adaptability of neighborhood school to *de facto* segregation situation. Action forces 10-year-olds from neighborhood school, compelling them to travel by public carrier, constitutes serious threats to safety and well-being. Urgently request aid your office and Education Commissioner halting this injustice."

As he said he would do, Dr. Stearns retired after he submitted his report. On June 2 had appeared a newspaper announcement of the appointment of Dr. Mark Shedd as superintendent of schools. Shedd had been supervisor of elementary education at Auburn, Maine, and superintendent of schools in Westbrook, Conn. He had directed a curriculum study in Auburn, and supervised special education. He had begun an extensive public-relations program, also a workshop program in education of the gifted child, and had expanded other supervisory programs. On July 1 he became Englewood's superintendent. He immediately announced the policy to which he adhered throughout every crisis that would confront him. He would do what was best for the education of Englewood's children.

Since the beginning of July 1962 Fred Maniscalco, supervisor of buildings and grounds, had been directing work at the Engle Street school. The library had been renovated and toilet facilities had been refurbished. Maniscalco's crews were at work on the cafeteria, the gym, corridors, and classrooms. Shedd had made a date to speak at Quarles School with parents whose children would enter fifth grade in September. A formality remained: it was necessary that the Board of School Estimate approve a $35,000 expenditure for the refurbishing under way. On July 31 in a heat-quiet town the Board of School Estimate met and rejected the appropriation. The two school board members voted for it; the three representatives of the common council, including Mayor Austin Volk, voted against it.

The August following this stunning rejection was a month of wide activity. There was an immediate response from Mrs. Sally Elliott, now president of Bergen CORE: "The apparent conclusion now seems to be that those entrusted with power in Englewood never intended to try to alleviate racial imbalance in the elementary schools." The mood of the Bergen NAACP, Harrison said, was one of disgust. "Now we know that the City is hiding behind every dodge and is looking for any way out."

On August 2 the school board met for more than five hours, then announced it would seek another meeting with the Board of School Estimate. The call never came, however, and a year later John Perry would recall the reason: as a pioneering step, such a meeting summons would doubtless have required court action, and the school board's attorney thought resolution would require at least two years.

A statement, signed as individuals, was released by Harrison, Russell Major, Leon Smith, and Barbara Kay: "The Negro community of Englewood announces an all-out battle in calling in attorney Paul B. Zuber to coordinate pending action in Englewood. This move is necessitated to save the Negro community from the Committee to Save Our Neighborhood Schools and other segregationist organizations. Our actions will be boycotts, pickets, and actions that are necessary to ward off the tyranny of economic and political pressure used against the Negro in the City of Englewood." From Paul Zuber came the assertion: "The situation in Englewood has degenerated into a white versus black struggle." Zuber said that within ten days there would be a huge rally on a city street. Negro leaders throughout the country would be invited to launch the Englewood Movement.

One goal of this first Englewood Movement rally was a boycott of merchants whose shops were on Palisade Avenue. This boycott was disapproved by the ministers of two of the Fourth Ward's larger congregations, Walter Taylor of the Galilee Methodist Church and Isaiah Goodman of the First Baptist Church. Among leaders whom Zuber had invited to the rally was Malcolm X, then Black Muslim leader in New York City, and Taylor asserted: "I respect Paul Zuber as a lawyer, but I don't approve of the line he's following here." From Goodman came the assertion that the board of education would do a good job, and that the tactics planned by Zuber and Malcolm X would fail. Harrison was supportive: "This movement is the anguished cry of many a maid, butler, and other domestic; of the white-collar worker, the minister, and the public servant who know they dare not speak out about the hurt in their hearts." Said Zuber of his invitation to Malcolm X: "I personally have a divergent point of view from Malcolm X, but we want to give the people of Englewood the opportunity of hearing all shades of Negro opinion." He added: "You're not always going to be able to deal only with those people you want to deal with."

On August 19 about 400 people gathered in Mackay Park, green acres in the Fourth Ward a block from Lincoln School. Malcolm X was missing; he had announced that opposition to his appearance made it undesirable for him to be there. Louis Lomax spoke, as did Zuber. Along Palisade Avenue a block to the north, Englewood shoppers, white and Negro, were scarcely aware of the activity, and this reflected the characteristic tone of Englewood rallies. Those who attended were deliberative demonstrators. The emotion that drove Englewood civil-rights leadership was not of the sort which suggests the tension of the mob, the explosive charge waiting to be touched off. When anger ran high it invariably led directly to the heart of the matter—school integration, now. The impassioned single-mindedness of Englewood in 1962 would never be better illustrated than in the rejection of the summons to a boycott of the merchants. Englewood rallies were inflexibly nonviolent; they were as characteristically purposeful as litigation.

Two weeks before the opening of the 1962 fall term Mayor Volk visited Governor Hughes in Trenton. "I have a guess that some changes will be made in the Negro population of the Lincoln School, but I'm not sure it will be made by the time school opens on September 5," Hughes said following that visit. Newsmen asked Volk whether a change in Lincoln School assignments would occur by September, but they received no direct response. On that day Shedd announced that fifth-grade students would report to their neighborhood schools. The day before school opened, Englewood's civic and religious leaders released a statement to Mayor Volk, which asserted in part:

We believe you exceeded your proper authority in blocking the school board on a matter of school policy. Even more serious, however, is the fact that your action halted progress on this problem at a crucial hour and left us without a plan for the coming year.

For that reason your action caused many citizens to believe that your administration is pursuing a policy of deliberate obstruction, and this has generated explosive resentment. This must be set right or Englewood is in trouble. . . . You must do this immediately, before schools open, because we cannot expect children to learn in a climate of hate, tension, and disruption.

Represented in that statement were the Englewood Human Relations Council, the Ministerial Association, the P.-T.A. Council, the Democratic Club, Fourth Ward residents through Councilman Tibbs, and the Urban League. Activists in these and other civic-reform groups—consisting mostly of liberal Democrats but with influential Republican allies—kept constant pressure on the Mayor and City Council before, during, and after the school-desegregation struggle. The thrust of the reformers was toward extending the advantages (cultural, recreational, and socio-economic) of Englewood's privileged three quarters to its less privileged quarter, which was disproportionately but by no means exclusively Negro. Formidable expertise was available to the reform movement in the city's large contingent of Columbia and N.Y.U. professors as well as foundation and national church headquarters staff members. The sparkplug of the civic reformers was the Rev. Robert I. Miller, assistant to the president of Union Theological Seminary (president of the Human Relations Council, director of the Urban League, and nearly successful Democratic candidate for city councilman-at-large), and a typical activist was Leo Shohan, economist for the National Industrial Conference Board (a leader in the Urban League and the Cleveland School P.-T.A.).

When school opened on September 5, 1962, more than half of Lincoln School's 540 pupils stayed away. On the hot concrete paving of Englewood Avenue stood clusters of spectators, stretching from the empty, unpainted frame church past barber shop, employment agency, and beauty salon to the auto-body yard. Among the pickets— including parents, sympathizers white and Negro, and the clergy— reporters and photographers spotted Fourth Ward Councilman Vincente Tibbs. School board attorney Abram Lebson was also there, and he told reporters that the board had no objection to picketing if it remained orderly and that it would bring no charge of truancy against the children until they were absent for five days. This was the first day of a three-day boycott that Leroy and Carmen Vaughn had helped plan. Leroy Vaughn had argued against the three-day limitation, asserting that a city government that had frustrated the school board would scarcely be swayed by a limited protest. He had been voted down, however.

At the school a bus pulled to the curb. About thirty of the fifth and sixth graders boarded it for a trip to Manhattan's Museum of Natural History. Younger pupils were grouped in classes in houses in the Fourth Ward. For three days, with minor variations, this was the scene at Lincoln School, and on the third day of the boycott, Liberty School, an integrated school located only a few blocks from Lincoln, reported the absence of nearly a third of its pupils. The first day of the boycott a group of parents, about half of them white, left a statement at Mayor Volk's office, protesting the city's failure to implement a central-school plan. The parents included a number from the city's remaining three elementary schools—Cleveland, Quarles, and Roosevelt—one of whom said she would like to have seen a one-day demonstration at Cleveland.

The third day of the boycott fell on the date of a routine council meeting. Into the corridors of the Municipal Building were crowded 250 persons; the councilmen moved the meeting to Academic Hall. Before the meeting Councilman Tibbs had remarked: "I don't know what is going to happen, but I just have a feeling it's going to be a whopper." But at the meeting the council president imposed a rule— residents would be permitted to speak for three minutes each; officials would answer no questions. Harrison, now of both the Englewood Movement and the Bergen NAACP, responded: "It shows why we need demonstrations like the one at Lincoln School." The council president closed the meeting at 10:45 P.M. It was, he remarked, getting late. The boycott ended after the third day. When the children returned to school on Monday, however, Laurie Vaughn was not among them.

Neither John Spruill, who was then vice-president of the Englewood Board of Health, who had made the original protest to the school board, and who was a member of the Lincoln School P.-T.A., nor Mrs. Spruill approved the three-day boycott. They now made a move which Zuber criticized as taking the school board off the hook. With the cooperation of the national office of the NAACP the Spruills petitioned the State Commissioner of Education to end imbalance at Lincoln. School board attorney Lebson approved: "We have held all along that orderly process should be followed, and the matter should be taken to the commissioner." The Englewood Movement itself, Zuber asserted, had been placed in an untenable position. His usefulness had been compromised.

Now at a restaurant in Princeton members of the Englewood school board met with the State Education Commissioner, Dr. Frederick Raubinger; they would discuss the city's problems at a moment when Mayor Volk had just released the results of a poll he had commissioned a private organization to make. Of 8000 questionnaires mailed to Englewood residents, 3600 had been returned, with a majority favoring retention of neighborhood schools.

Following the meeting Commissioner Raubinger named a six-member team to conduct a study and submit recommendations on Englewood within a month. The team included two county superintendents, the state director of elementary education, and a field representative of the state division on civil rights. While the team made its survey from headquarters in the unpopulated Engle Street school building, other forces in Englewood continued in motion. Superintendent Shedd reiterated that changes planned for the Engle Street school were well within the limits of the budget. A rabbi asserted: "I can respect (at least as honorable) persons who have taken a stand in this matter, even if it is opposed to right. But I cannot respect the silence of some clergymen and community leaders who ran and continue to run from their moral responsibility." He added that the State's intervention was a tragedy; that the only duty in the city was to judge between the stand taken by the Board of Education and the Board of School Estimate.

Now another polling of opinion was initiated. Midway in September 1962 four of the five councilmen, over the opposition of Vincente Tibbs, voted to place a question on the November general-election ballot. The question: "Are you in favor of transferring certain elementary school grades from their present schools into a single school for such grades?" Several days later the viewpoint of SONS was given its first full expression by the SONS chairman at a Human Relations Council forum: "The board looked to solve the problems not by addressing itself to the real cause, but sought to placate the forces pressuring them by engaging in social engineering and trying to hide it behind better education."

He asserted that in the Supreme Court's 1954 ruling the important phrase is "segregated solely by race," that this applied to the South but not to northern communities where *de facto* segregation is the result of housing patterns, not the premeditated consequence of official sanction. He decried a thesis: "The argument of underachievement caused by a stigma to an all-Negro enrollment is to my mind a tenuous one, and certainly should not be the cause for which we would make radical changes in our schools." SONS recommended a crash educational program for Lincoln School pupils, coupled with a higher-horizons program. "We should attack underachievement frontally, with more teachers, plus specialists in reading and writing skills, and modern teaching equipment, and not hope that underachievement will disappear through some pedagogical osmosis incidental to sitting next to some child of a different color." The chairman added: "We must not disregard the rights of others when requesting advantages for some."

As the state's fact-finding team continued its investigation, Dr. Raubinger received two petitions in addition to that from the Spruills. One, from ten Englewood parents, reflected the SONS' position, protesting any deviation from the neighborhood-school system. The other, on behalf of 24 parents, who would come to be identified as Ancrum *et al.*, represented by Arnold Brown, not only charged the school board with failure to correct segregation, but asserted that the city council and the Board of School Estimate had blocked corrective action.

Thus, confronting Raubinger were three petitions from Englewood on the day in October that the team presented its report to the Englewood school board. The recommendations pleased no one, although Governor Hughes said mildly that the plan listened well. They included construction of a $1-million school in McKay Park, a block west of Lincoln School, on Englewood Avenue, and abandonment of Lincoln as an elementary school. SONS denigrated the plan for a new school, and Zuber said flatly the report was a whitewash. Harrison said the Englewood Movement had sent a telegram to Zuber to pull out all the stops. The Urban League asserted that, rather than reduce the concentration of Negroes in the Lincoln School, the proposals would tend to perpetuate racial imbalance. John Perry, now school board president, agreed. The school board rejected the state team's suggestions and reasserted its faith in its own central-school plan.

The report disquieted Leroy and Carmen Vaughn, as it did many of their friends, primarily because it found no pattern of deliberate segregation. By now the Vaughns were convinced that the city administration was doing its best to maintain segregation. Mayor Volk's informal survey had done nothing to dissuade them, nor had the council's decision to place the question on the ballot in November, nor had the assertion by Bergen County Judge Gordon Brown when he denied a request by Mr. and Mrs. Alfred Gamrin of Englewood to have the question on schools removed from the ballot: "The courts should favor every effort by those responsible for government to canvass sentiment of the electorate where public policy is concerned." Clear-cut in the Vaughns' memory were assertions by United States Supreme Court Justices William Douglas and Hugo Black that only the courts can protect the rights of minorities against majority opinion.

In the November 1962 election, which returned in full strength the political establishment against which the Englewood Movement was directed, the vote was overwhelmingly (5825 to 1549) negative in response to the question as the council had propounded it: "Are you in favor of transferring certain elementary school grades from their present schools into a single school for such grades?" SONS once again urged its plan of voluntary open enrollment, and Mayor Volk said that the vote revealed that a large majority of the residents opposed the central school. He added that the matter now was in the hands of the school board, making no reference to the Board of School Estimate's frustration of the school board's plan nor to Arnold Brown's charge that the common council had blocked corrective action. Said Paul Zuber: "It's becoming more and more obvious that the courts will have to compel the city to grant Negroes their constitutional rights."

In Magistrate's Court in Englewood a few days later appeared Leroy and Carmen Vaughn, together with their daughter Laurie. For about a half hour before court opened, some fifteen persons, including CORE members, picketed to support the Vaughns. An attendance officer testified that she had visited Mrs. Vaughn to ask why Laurie wasn't in school. What had Mrs. Vaughn said? That she would not allow her daughter to attend a segregated school. The magistrate found the Vaughns guilty of being disorderly persons under a State truancy law, and fined them $5, suspending collection until the Vaughns could appeal to a higher court. At the meeting in which the school board had rejected the plan proffered by the State Commissioner's team, a SONS representative had made a suggestion: let the school board abandon all attempts to deal with a racial imbalance stemming from socio-economic conditions and thus beyond the province of the board. Warren Lewis, a board member, responded: if racial imbalance results in unequal opportunity for students, the board is bound to act. School board president Perry added: "We didn't open up Pandora's box; it was brought to us already open." Carmen Vaughn was fully committed to her own answer to socio-economic reasons for imbalance—Laurie would return only to an integrated school.

As he drove to Trenton January 25, 1963, Arnold Brown was well aware of Leroy and Carmen Vaughn's commitment. Brown was satisfied with the prescription of the hearings in which he would take part before Eric Groczinger, Assistant Commissioner of Education for Controversies and Disputes. The hearing would encompass three petitions: that of the Spruills, to be represented by Barbara Morris and Herbert Tate, attorneys from the national office of the NAACP; that of 12 parents (Ancrum *et al.*), to be represented by Brown and Robert Platoff of Englewood; and that of SONS, to be represented by William Breslin of Englewood, a former president of the Bergen County Bar Association. The school board would be represented by its attorney, Abram Lebson, and the city by John Breslin and LeRoy Huckin. In Trenton the attorneys agreed on one session, in April.

But a leisurely hearing of the Englewood problem was a procedure disquieting to many who felt that the problem had long ago been stated. Some Lincoln School parents, together with members of CORE, Bergen NAACP, and the Englewood Movement, argued that the State had an obligation not merely to hold hearings but to act, since the City refused to do so. A few weeks after Arnold Brown had been in Trenton, Byron Baer and Mrs. Willie Mae Batchelor of CORE, Augustus Harrison of Bergen NAACP, and Mrs. Maggie Nealy, mother of a child at Lincoln, visited Commissioner Raubinger in Trenton. They were discouraged to hear him say that, although the Governor's statement of statewide policy carried great weight, it had not been translated into the formal policy of the Education Department. (In June Democratic Governor Hughes had written Democratic Councilman Tibbs: "While preservation of the neighborhood school policy is essential, when it collides with the concept of equality in education, its adaptation to circumstances to prevent *de facto* segregation is not only necessary, but normally feasible.") The Commissioner's visitors released a statement intended for Governor Hughes: that the problem was developing too rapidly for delay, that feeling was running high as Negroes faced another school term under segregated conditions.

Governor Hughes was on vacation in Florida, and six parents, including Carmen and Leroy Vaughn, announced they would remain in the State House until they saw him. Acting Governor William E. Ozzard, Republican Senate President, delivered a brief lecture on legal morality which convinced none of its listeners: "What you are asking is that the laws be set aside," Ozzard said. "But we all have time enough to protect the sovereignty and dignity of the state." A parent responded, "It's not your time." The sit-in at the State House lasted 48 hours. Governor Hughes sent a message: "I think the people of New Jersey do not expect me to be a political coward. I do not expect to return from these few days of vacation with my wife and family to satisfy an obvious publicity bid by these unannounced visitors." In Trenton, CORE chairman Mrs. Elliott offered a rebuttal: "It is obvious that they acted out of desperation and concern for their children's future. To term them publicity seekers is to blind oneself to the fact that a real issue exists; and, after years of waiting, Negro parents will accept no more delay."

When the parents left the State House, Mrs. Batchelor released a statement which in part read:

The Governor has termed us "publicity seekers" and said we all have enough time. What is enough time when watching the capacities and potential of your child wasted steadily, term after term, the result of a segregated and inferior education?

We made this appeal with the greatest sincerity, and we are not interested in futile gestures. We are in dead earnest.

Our purpose in returning to Englewood is to join with other Negro parents to end segregation in Lincoln and other schools in our own way, as parents. We are contacting other parents now with a school boycott as a definite possibility.

During the Trenton sit-in SONS restated its position: "The assignment of children to schools should not be made on a racial basis. The State of New Jersey should not have any policy which directs that a child should be assigned to a school on a predetermined racial ratio. Racism, whether used to exclude or include, is illegal and immoral."

On February 26, when Englewood schools opened for the second semester, nearly half of Lincoln School's 498 pupils failed to appear. Rather, seven pickets led by Fourth Ward Councilman Vincente Tibbs arrived in subzero weather, and they walked for an hour. The children boarded a bus, to be taken to the Bergen County Ethical Culture Society Building in neighboring Teaneck and to homes in the Fourth Ward that had been prepared as "freedom schools." Said Tibbs: "This is it. This is no dry run. This is the boycott." On that day Mrs. Virginia Wilson sent a telegram to the Governor: "What we ask is simple. We are not asking you to interfere with the privately initiated litigation which individuals may choose to prolong for years. We only ask that the State set and implement its own policy, which [it has] every right to do." At a press conference in Newark two days later Attorney General Robert Kennedy said the controversy was being watched by the Justice Department but he hoped the matter could be settled locally. Governor Hughes had earlier said he would rather not comment on whether the boycott was intemperate, adding that he would not want any statement by him to make the situation worse.

The Spruills, who a year and a half earlier had made the original complaint against segregation, disapproved the boycott. They issued a statement which said in part: "Hearings have been scheduled for the first week in April, and until Mr. Raubinger renders his decision (which we and the national NAACP believe must be favorable) countersuits will not alter the already established decision and changing trend, nor will boycotts, pickets, sit-in demonstrations, or what-have-you alter this legal procedure of law."

On March 2 at Lincoln School auditorium James Farmer, national director of CORE, appeared with Paul Zuber to support the boycott. Zuber then announced that the House Subcommittee on Education, of which Adam Clayton Powell (D., N.Y.) was chairman, would be asked to conduct a hearing on Englewood segregation. At that rally a statewide mass meeting on the steps of the Governor's mansion in Trenton was announced, planned for March 17. In Paterson, Arthur Holloway of the Passaic County NAACP said commitments had been made by groups from Newark, Orange, New Brunswick, Passaic, and Paterson. Hughes announced that on March 17 he would be in Newark for a St. Patrick's Day parade. The mass meeting, identified as support for Englewood Mobilization, was then postponed for a week, until March 24.

For the first seven days of the boycott, picketing had been confined to Lincoln School, and, doggedly, Vincente Tibbs had appeared each day before he went on to his own job, sometimes wearing his Navy Reserve parka against the biting cold. Then, on March 6, Carmen Vaughn and four others appeared outside Cleveland School, a mile north of Lincoln, and there picketed to protest that Cleveland School had only one Negro child enrolled. A day earlier a statement had been released by CORE, the Englewood Movement, and Bergen NAACP: "So often when the fight for equality becomes heated, Negro leaders hide behind the famous line 'No comment' or take vacations or lecture tours to Africa to show off American Democracy." (Speaking in a neighboring town the Reverend Walter Taylor, pastor of Galilee Methodist Church in Englewood, had said the boycott was not adequately prepared and would be short-lived. He added that the Negro in Englewood was further along in his bid for equality than in any other city in America. John Perry, president of the school board, was criticized by Zuber for planning a trip to Africa in a summer in which he would be needed in Englewood.) The statement went on: "We call upon all Negro leaders, local or otherwise, to stop paying lip service to ideals and join Vincente K. Tibbs by backing up their fancy words with action."

On March 11 the term "hard core" entered the Englewood vocabulary, when Tibbs was quoted as saying that a hard core of about 50 students would stay out of Lincoln indefinitely, this on a day following the ninth day of the boycott, by which time all but 46 of the students had returned to Lincoln School. "Hard core" became useful in reports on Englewood, and, indeed, developed into a synonym for "Englewood Movement." At the core of the hard core were those few who, like Leroy and Carmen Vaughn, held implacably to one goal that Carmen Vaughn compressed into two words for anyone—and there were many—who asked what she really wanted: "Integration, now."

On March 15 Holloway of the Passaic County NAACP wired Hughes: "You will be interested to know that in addition to this delegation will be a large number of citizens assembled from all over the State to express their support for the fight of the parents of Englewood and other New Jersey communities to desegregate their schools." Hughes responded that he would be willing to meet with representatives of any group, but not with picketing demonstrators. "While I don't criticize the demonstration, I don't care to join it," he said.

In the third week of March 1963, direct action in both Englewood and Trenton reached an interrelated climax. As the weekend approached, nine parents and 10 children waited in the school board offices at Engle Street. The group said it would stay there until its demand was met: immediate school reassignments from Superintendent Mark Shedd. Among those who stayed the night were Leroy and Carmen Vaughn. An impasse was resolved when Paul Zuber announced that the motive was to be served summons for failure to send children to school, and that the parents would leave now that Abram Lebson had presented the names of 24 parents for processing by municipal court because of the absence for 16 schooldays of their 33 children.

As the weekend approached the Governor again declined an invitation to see the demonstrators. On Saturday, Joseph Katz, an aide to the Governor, told newsmen Hughes had become increasingly concerned with overcrowding in the reformatories and would be visiting Bordentown, N.J., at the time the demonstration was planned. On Sunday pickets marched at the State House, from which the Governor was absent. One reporter guessed that there were about 250 demonstrators there, dressed as though for church. In addition to representatives of CORE and NAACP, pickets included members of the Teamsters and of the United Auto Workers unions.

By March 26 Commissioner Raubinger had ruled out the Englewood Council and the Board of School Estimate as defendants at the hearing after he reviewed a brief from the City's attorney, John Breslin. Pickets at Lincoln School now carried signs for Hughes to intervene. Two days later Roy Wilkins, then national executive secretary of the NAACP, announced withdrawal of the NAACP attorneys from the Spruill petition. Wilkins's statement said in part: "Our attorneys are now appearing as co-counsel with Arnold Brown and other attorneys in the suit filed in behalf of Kenneth Ancrum *et al.*, which protests segregation in the Englewood schools." Mrs. Spruill responded: "We hesitate to engage in any open controversy. However, in view of the many people who have expressed approval and preference to the language and plea of our position, we strongly suggest everyone interested demand an investigation of the withdrawal at the last minute from a petition that they [NAACP attorneys Robert Carter and Herbert Tate] alone drew and filed and have now abandoned." She added that she had approached another attorney.

Representing the Spruills, attorney Robert Kunstler, of New York City, made the opening statement on April 1 in the county seat at Hackensack, at the first session of a hearing which would continue through eight additional sessions until April 17. To Eric Groezinger, State Assistant Commissioner for Controversies and Disputes, presiding at the hearing, Kunstler said that in Englewood there was a racial imbalance in enrollment, harmful to pupils. He added: "The only issue is a remedy." Arnold Brown, representing the Ancrums and others, concurred. From William Breslin, representing SONS, came the countering argument: "The only real solution is to give the children the concentrated help they need."

As Brown, together with Platoff and Barbara Morris and Herbert Tate, attorneys with the national NAACP, developed their argument, it became apparent that the credentials of Dr. Stearns and the report "Englewood, Its People and Its Schools" would play an important part. Were Groezinger to reject these credentials, arguments at the hearing could have been hopelessly dispersed in the labyrinths of every man's or any man's penny edition of educational and sociological premises. On the second day of the hearing, Dr. Stearns's qualification as expert witness was questioned, and John Perry was permitted to say that he had read the report but was not allowed to say what he saw in it or whether the report mentioned racial imbalance.

Success for Brown came on the second day of the hearing. Groezinger accepted the Stearns report and said: "Full weight will be given to the factual material presented by Dr. Stearns." The report said imbalance existed in Englewood, that it was harmful, and that doing nothing about it would increase tension, and it suggested five alternatives, one of which, with a variation and development by Dr. Shedd, the school board had approved. Thus were the remaining days of the hearing given direction, and although Dr. Stearns would be closely questioned by the SONS attorney, as would some of the school board members and Dr. Shedd, the Englewood problem had at the outset been stated.

At the close of the hearing, Groezinger defined the issues on which Commissioner Raubinger would rule:

1. Is the Board deliberately maintaining a racially segregated school system?
2. When a school's enrollment consists predominantly of Negroes, is the Board required to take affirmative action to reduce the imbalance?
3. If the answer to Question 2 is affirmative, to what degree must this action give way to other factors and considerations in order to mitigate the problem?

Said Groezinger: "I assure you that in deciding the issue the Commissioner will not address himself to any specific plan or proposal should the petitioners prevail. The Commissioner has consistently taken the view that his judgment should not be substituted for that of local officials. . . ."

Carmen Vaughn had been following the hearing closely, of course, but with little faith that it would lead to what she felt was vital to the well-being of the children at Lincoln: integration, at once. She shared with many others the feeling that the hearing was merely the beginning of a series of actions that could continue indefinitely through the courts; that the Governor's commitment at the end of the hearing to press for a ruling by the Commissioner before September promised a great deal less than Fourth Ward parents were looking for.

On April 23, 18 parents of children who had been kept from classes in Lincoln School attempted to register them at Cleveland. The principal, Thorlief Henriksen, greeted them courteously, told them he couldn't accept their applications, but offered them registration blanks. One of the parents, expressing disappointment in the State hearing, said that they wanted their children to return to school, but not to a segregated school. "Since the State will not impose desegregation, we feel it is up to the local board. We do not intend to wait. We are going to continue our fight." The following day the parents applied at Quarles School, and Councilman Vincente Tibbs had this to say: "It has been brought home to us, viciously clear, that the Board of Education, the

Council, the Board of School Estimate, and other civic leaders are determined that the status quo in education will continue, and, as American citizens we are just as determined it will not remain, and this is part of what we intend to do to carry on the fight." A day later, the parents, again accompanied by Tibbs, appeared at Roosevelt School.

Superintendent Mark Shedd had said that all applications would be processed through his office but that none would be accepted if school zone lines would be crossed. On April 26 Tibbs led the parents to Shedd's office to ask about the applications. Shedd met them in the corridor, reminded the group that he had no choice but to carry out the school board's policy, and reminded them also that a ruling was awaited from Raubinger. He added: "My disagreement with you folks is that you do not seem ready to await orderly process of law." Tibbs said the parents would schedule additional meetings, but not that day because they were due in court in the afternoon. And that afternoon the parents were fined $5 each for failure to send their children to school on February 26. The magistrate delayed imposing the fine, however, until the argument of their attorney, Emanuel Greenberg of Jersey City, had opportunity for appeal. Greenberg's argument: law requiring attendance refers to a legally constituted school, thus was not applicable to a racially segregated school. The magistrate had not permitted testimony about segregation.

During the boycott television turned its eye on Englewood, and Carmen Vaughn saw on the screen a brief interview with her friend Helen Jones. Mrs. Jones, a teacher on leave from the New York City system, was principal of a freedom school for boycotting children. Among those who worked hard organizing daily the curricula and the trips to classes in the basement recreation rooms of homes in the Fourth Ward was Mrs. Angela McLinn, wife of a Negro dentist in the Third Ward. The faculty was various: parents sympathetic to the move-ment—including a number whose children were in schools other than Lincoln—served as teachers, as did professional teachers from Paterson, from Newark, from New York, as well as from Hunter College and Yeshiva and Fairleigh Dickinson Universities. The free-dom school had held its first classes in Teaneck, at the Ethical Culture Society Building, and had moved to the homes when they were told that under Teaneck's building code the site was inadequate.

At the freedom school the children used materials selected by

Mrs. Jones, supplied by private schools in New York, and transported by parents like the Vaughns, whose living rooms became school warehouses as books and materials were shuttled to the children. In the freedom-school classrooms, the pupils also received an unusual orientation program; here was their opportunity to complain that their friends who were not boycotting Lincoln teased them. "You know you're not going to pass," was a usual remark. As part of the orientation, Dr. Virginia Wright met with some of the children in sessions at her home in which they could ventilate their anxiety. And there was orientation toward the day that the boycott children would visit Cleveland. Mrs. Jones has since said, "We'd tell them, 'If the children in Birmingham can go to jail for what's right, you can stand for a few names.'" Incidentally, the names were not to materialize. Said Mrs. Jones: "But I can truthfully say there wasn't any need for that orientation. None of that came to pass. The Cleveland children were just wonderful."

For Carmen Vaughn, one in a vast audience, television's eye in this period was also turned on former State Senator David Van Alstyne, Jr. Interviewed in front of his lawn on the Hill, the aging Senator outlined all that Englewood had done for its Fourth Ward in the long past. In his eyes, blinking directly at Carmen Vaughn through the hot screen, was honest bafflement. What, he asked, do "they" want?

Carmen Vaughn and others had replied that nothing would suit them except integration, now. On May 6 nine boycott children entered the side door of Cleveland School, found classrooms, and sat down. At the school were Englewood's police director, John Lawless, and the assistant superintendent of schools, Francis Garrity. Lawless asked the parents not to go above the first floor of the school; Garrity told the children that, since school was in half-session only that day, they could remain. As it turned out, tension was greater among television crewmen, news reporters, and other observers than it was inside the school. Laurie Vaughn had not gone to Cleveland School that day; the parents had sent only the older children, those in sixth grade, until the nature of their reception would be known.

On the second day, however, Laurie Vaughn, as she had not done since September, got dressed to go to school rather than to meet her tutor. With her mother and other children and parents, she arrived early at school, well before the doors were opened to the pupils. She and a friend, hand in hand, chose a door and waited. Through the glass she could see Principal Henriksen, whom of course she didn't know. After a while he came out to speak to her mother and the others. Her mother then told her to stand fast, and together with the others sat at the steps of the four main entrances to Cleveland. Laurie heard someone say, "If we don't get in, they don't get in." Soon Mr. Henriksen returned to the door and opened it. "Come in, children," he said, and stood aside. Laurie, as she had been instructed to do, entered the first classroom she could find, and sat down. A teacher told her that the place belonged to another child, and Laurie went to the back of the room. A man she hadn't seen before entered the classroom, and the teacher told him there was no seat for Laurie. He looked at Laurie—Laurie thought he was quite nice—and then left the room and returned with a chair. Later, telling her mother about her day, Laurie said that the children were friendly. Yes, she had joined in the games at recess. No, the teacher never called on her.

Through the weeks of the sit-in, the Englewood school administration, teachers, and pupils found a way to live with the unusual. The administration, through the teachers, told the children they were uninvited visitors and would not take part in classwork. The teachers, however, were free to make the classrooms as comfortable as possible for the visitors, and those who shared crayons and called on the visitors heard no word of reprimand from the superintendent. Carmen Vaughn and two others had asked for a list of textbooks, and had been refused, but with a month only left in the semester, the parents didn't press that point.

Responses from residents in the Cleveland School zone were varied, but they remained verbal. Knots of white and colored parents appeared at school in the morning during the first few days, but very soon the children were again walking unaccompanied to school. There was a great deal more drama in what was being said about the sit-in than there was at Cleveland School, which began to look like any other school on any usual school day. One Cleveland School mother told a reporter she was delighted with the friendly way the Cleveland kids greeted the newcomers. On the other hand, another said that her first- and third-grade children had come home for lunch disturbed and confused. She added: "I'm not anti anything except, perhaps, anti-school bus. If these children from Lincoln lived in this area they would have the right to be here and would be welcome." A Council member of the Board of School Estimate said: "The governing body is a law-abiding group, and we are going to follow procedures through the proper channels to their proper conclusion. No amount of threats and blackmail is going to deter us from this position." He was answered by Mrs. Lacey of CORE: "The children are crying out now, and it is inconceivable that Englewood can refuse to listen to them. Answer your Negro children. You cannot ignore them." The Englewood Movement fortified the sit-ins with weekly marches, moving in general from Lincoln School in a swing past the Municipal Building to Cleveland.

In Trenton, Commissioner Raubinger was assessing the results of the Hackensack hearing against a deadline suggested by Governor Hughes. In Englewood, it was almost as though the hearing was considered inconsequential; action in Englewood focused on two centers. The Englewood Movement had moved into Cleveland School and supported the move in a series of rallies and marches, invitations to which were being accepted by men of national reputation. Political steps, concurrently, were being taken by Mayor Volk, apparently to state the problem and to find a solution within the framework of the statement.

At an Englewood Movement rally in Mackay Park, Representative Adam Clayton Powell, chairman of the House Subcommittee on Education, characterized Englewood as an appropriate city for hearings on educational segregation in the North. Later school board president John Perry was to affirm that he had received a letter from Powell saying: "Although local hearings have been concluded, we have been advised that it will take 11 weeks for a decision to be rendered. A cancerous condition such as this cannot be allowed to continue." Perry answered: "There are no federal funds involved in any part of our activity with respect to the hearings which have just been concluded. Therefore we fail to see where this becomes a problem for your committee at this time." As it turned out the hearings failed to materialize, but no one in Englewood shrugged off the threat.

Roy Wilkins, then national secretary of NAACP, on the steps in front of the Municipal Building, asserted: "Englewood is carrying on a courageous fight. If you haven't accomplished everything you would like, you have called attention to conditions in a city which had been thought just a little this side of heaven for Negroes."

Others in Englewood—would they be called moderates in a later political year?—were active in the crisis, of course. The Englewood Ministerial Association created a conciliation committee to which they invited representatives from the Englewood Movement and from SONS, as well as the Citizens Advisory Committee, the League of Women Voters, the Health and Welfare Council of Bergen County, and of course the city administration. The committee was led by the Reverend George Derner, pastor of St. John's Evangelical Lutheran Church, and it was to meet without interruption until a settlement had been reached. It came perhaps a year too late. The parents whose children were visiting Cleveland mistrusted it, and although the mayor during a committee meeting appointed a quasi-official group to negotiate, there was no one sufficiently representative of the entire Englewood Movement with whom to talk.

On the last day of school, June 20, with the visitors still in attendance, Governor Hughes said that he expected a decision from Commissioner Raubinger in a week. On July 2 the decision came. The Commissioner ordered the Englewood Board of Education to reduce the concentration of Negroes in Lincoln School by September. He reserved the right to issue further orders to assure an amelioration of segregation, saying: "Continuation will damage the pupils not only of [Lincoln] school but all others in the community. Hence the entire community has a stake in a solution which will make it possible for the school staff to devote its undivided attention and effort to planning for better educational opportunities for all pupils."

Councilman Tibbs's response was immediate: "The hope of little people, it seems, will always be with the courts and state agencies. They work well but exceedingly slow. Let us now bring peace to our town." He added, however, that he thought opponents of integration would try to obstruct racial progress. "Just as such reaction caused this upheaval in the past it will cause much more in the future."

Resistance was not long in coming. The Board of School Estimate was still required to vote funds to implement the central-school plan it had blocked a year earlier. The focus of dissent in Englewood shifted from the Englewood Movement's resistance to segregation to a more diffuse resistance to the school board's planning to end it. As exemplified by the city's administration the resistance could be characterized not as malfeasance but as nonfeasance. Crucial in the school board's planning, for example, was the expansion of three of the five elementary schools. Yet when the school board requested the City to buy land across the street from one of these schools, Roosevelt, the City stood by while the property—known as the Edgewater Creche tract, named by the Protestant Episcopal Mission Society that had owned it—was sold as a home-building site to a corporation that had been created after the school board's request for it was made public.

SONS continued to fight. In August it was granted two court injunctions which the school board and the State had to take time to strike down. Although Mayor Volk reversed his vote in the Board of School Estimate to give the Board of Education five-to-three support for its desegregation plan, his action came too late to permit refurbishing the central school in time for the opening day in September. As a result Vincente Tibbs again found himself leading parents in protest against the operation of Lincoln School, to which pupils were assigned for the month it would take to prepare the central school for students.

For Carmen and Leroy Vaughn, for Arnold Brown, for Vincente Tibbs, as well as for CORE, the NAACP, the Urban League, and the Englewood Movement, the end of the 1963 crisis in Englewood can be dated October 28, 1963, the day the central school opened. Although SONS' challenge was to go on for some years, it failed to block the school board's plan; and for pupils beyond kindergarten, Lincoln School was closed.

Superintendent Shedd as educator still faced problems, of course; but at least they were administrative problems. At the close of the spring session the school board invited the parents of the Cleveland visitors to enroll them in summer session. Laurie Vaughn was among those who appeared for class. Of those who did not, evaluation in the fall placed them again into the system, and with few exceptions the visitors advanced normally. Shedd had insisted throughout the crisis that excellence of the schools and their constant improvement was the school board's primary responsibility, and he had steadfastly discussed integration within that framework. Among the challenges he faced now was to demonstrate the advantage of a central-school plan and to implement a program of excellence against the opposition not only of SONS and other dissenters but of skeptics within the city administration and, indeed, on the school board as members resigned and the administration appointed replacements.

Lincoln School had been criticized for being segregated; the building itself had never been belittled. Shedd made of it an educational nerve center. Into Lincoln he moved the school board's and superintendent's offices, together with the offices of administrators and planners. From the planning wing came programs that were to characterize Shedd's administration. The prekindergarten system in Lincoln School was in large measure a pilot for the federal Head Start program. Reaching into the community, an aide brought into the schools volunteer tutors to work with children who needed not only one-to-one help but a warm personal relationship. Funds outside the school budget, including federal and Ford Foundation grants, were applied toward hiring consultants and expanding special education. A day-school curriculum for adults was established, as were classes for pupils handicapped in educationally diagnosable categories. To accompany remedies for the result of segregated education—and concurrent with the growing vitality of the curriculum—a changed school plant was designed by Shedd and his advisers and accepted in outline by the school board.

The value of the central-school system is that racial balance can be maintained independently of whatever occurs in housing. On Palisade Avenue, Liberty School lay in the path of an expanding segregated neighborhood; a year after Lincoln School was closed, Negro pupils were in a heavy majority there. Englewood educators envisioned by 1970 the abandonment of both Liberty and the aging Engle Street schools, accompanied by the physical expansion of the three remaining elementary schools into education centers, prekindergarten through grade 4; a central intermediate school, grades 5 to 8; and a high school, grades 9 to 12. One measure of the city administration's good faith might have been purposeful support of the building program. But effective resistance in government and among the majority continued so that each step required the political pressuring traditionally required for a fresh appropriation, and although the Englewood educational system has forged ahead, the going has been hard.

As Liberty School became more racially imbalanced, it was converted to a second central intermediate school, children in some of its lower grades being sent to other schools. That step wasn't taken, however, until the Liberty P.-T.A. brought unusual pressure to bear, even picketing briefly in a recapitulation of the troubled years. After the desegregation plan was safely launched Superintendent Shedd accepted an appointment to head the Philadelphia school system; he was succeeded by Dr. Peter J. Dugan, who had administered a school-building program in Liverpool, an industrial suburban complex near Syracuse, New York.

By 1967 the scene in Englewood had shifted from school zoning to housing patterns. Integrationists were keenly aware that the city's children remained largely segregated in their extramural education: when classes were dismissed, most Negro pupils headed for the Fourth Ward while the others took buses, bikes, or sidewalks toward the other three wards. For six years civil-rights activists had demanded that the city's urban-renewal program take at least a first step toward breaking up the Negro ghetto, and U.S. officials had made federal funding contingent on the city's taking such a step.

Englewood's 1967 election turned on the housing question. The incumbent Republican administration advanced a plan to improve housing only within the Fourth Ward, relying solely on the city's borrowing power. The Democratic challengers pledged a program that would make a start in breaking down segregated neighborhoods, thereby qualifying for federal funds. A referendum on the ballot proffered both plans, as well as a third question on "scattered" low-cost housing. Election results were contradictory: citizens voted for a Democratic administration but supported the Republican plan for improving housing only within the Fourth Ward. Elected mayor by a slim margin was the Reverend Robert I. Miller, president of the Human Relations Council and director of the Urban League.

TEANECK

From the stage in the auditorium of Teaneck High School on May 13, 1964, Bernard Confer, executive secretary of Lutheran World Relief and president of Teaneck's nine-member school board, faced a large and unruly audience. Members of the Neighborhood School Association were there in force, as were members of other dissenting organizations, and Confer listened now as a fellow board member, Dr. Harry Warner, a vascular surgeon, strolled the stage. In a moment, Dr. Warner was saying, the school board would approve a plan that violated Teaneck's neighborhood-school tradition, and the school board was wrong.

Confer, an impeccable parliamentarian, urged members of the audience to maintain order, but he had no more success than would any chairman trying to gavel down an unruly demonstration at a political convention. Through the aisles strode petitioners soliciting signatures for a protest, circulating a statement demanding an election to recall seven of the school board members. Confer couldn't fail to notice that they were doing a brisk business. Yet, confronted by near-riotous dissent, Confer finished the announcement that Dr. Warner had begun. Teaneck, he said, would open a central sixth-grade school at Bryant in September. Bus transportation would be provided.

Teaneck is an affluent community of more than 42,000 residents in Bergen County, New Jersey. About four miles east of Teaneck the George Washington Bridge stretches across the Hudson River into upper Manhattan; along an eastern edge Teaneck is touched by Englewood. In 1949, when its population was 33,700, Teaneck was selected by the United States Army, training political advisers for occupied countries, as a model for municipal government. From time to time in letters to newspapers Teaneck residents refer to the Army designation, of which they are proud. Teaneck has no ghetto, but its Negro population is preponderantly in its northern reach in an integrated residential area. Here, a short suburban stroll along tree-lined streets from Englewood's Fourth Ward, is located Bryant School.

By April 1963, when the Englewood school boycott was under way, at least three organizations in Teaneck had expressed concern over the possibility of racial imbalance at two Teaneck elementary schools, in particular Bryant School. The organizations were the Council of P.-T.A.'s, the Fair Housing Committee, and Citizens for Public Schools. School board members had already said they wanted to prevent the crisis that had gripped Englewood, and they called inadequate the voluntary-enrollment plan they were trying. A report that school trustees were aware that imbalance could be a problem in Teaneck resulted in a letter from Protestant clergymen, commending them. In May 1963, a year before Confer's announcement, the school board voted to continue the open-enrollment plan, and now an additional organization, Teaneck Citizens for Improved Government, congratulated the school board's 1963 president, Dr. Harold Weinberger, professor of chemistry at Fairleigh Dickinson University, and Dr. Harvey Scribner, school superintendent since 1961.

By September 1963 only 19 pupils had applied from Bryant School to any of three other schools available to them. Dr. Scribner had estimated that a voluntary-enrollment plan could result in a reduction of at least 20 percent in the Negro enrollment at Bryant, which had been approaching 50 percent. Why had the number of applications been so meager? Dr. Archie Lacey, himself Negro, professor of science education at Hunter College, New York City, had conducted a survey among 800 Negro families in Teaneck. The study, he said, showed in part that Negro parents feared hostility toward their children from the white community. He listed additional reasons why Negro parents were wary of transfer:

1. A personal exhilaration stemming from the movement toward independence among African nations militated against transferring a child simply so he could be with whites. About 20 percent gave this response.
2. About 25 percent considered Bryant a good school, and saw no reason to leave it.
3. About 20 percent were influenced by the convenience of a neighborhood-school system.
4. About 10 percent were indifferent; and 5 percent, Dr. Lacey thought, lacked perspective.
5. About 20 percent adopted an attitude of "wait and see."

By October 1963 Trustee Lamar Jones, a public school teacher in the New York City system, among others said that it was time to step beyond open enrollment. The community learned in a report from the board's president, Dr. Weinberger, that the board was considering among other plans a central sixth grade, to be located in Bryant School. By December Dr. Scribner, as he spoke to diverse groups, found himself saying he was surprised by the negative reaction of some residents. At a P.-T.A. meeting at Benjamin Franklin Junior High School, he admonished: "The 1954 Supreme Court decision leaves no alternative but for the Board of Education to take seriously a school which has more than 50 percent Negro enrollment."

Teaneck school board elections occur each February, when three of nine seats become vacant. The issue of *de facto* segregation and what should be done about it sharpened as the 1964 campaigns got under way. The board was faced now by suggestions that a budget defeat would result if a request were made for funds for transportation, and two candidates were careful to point out that they were against segregation only if it were deliberate. Dr. Harry Warner led an attack on the central-school suggestion. Among his arguments were that a problem child is retarded by frequent transfers, that wasteful mass transportation becomes necessary as does the need for additional luncheon facilities. Dr. Warner's views were shared by a second candidate, F. Paul Margolis, an accountant and a major in the Air Force Reserve. Running for reelection to the board was Bernard Confer, who answered a question at a cottage party this way: "I am for the neighborhood school concept today. I am for it until somebody shows me a better one. But my mind is open, and I refuse to make that concept a sacred shibboleth."

As election day approached, Warner and Margolis made it clear that as board members they would oppose a budget which included an appropriation for school buses, that would, in short, provide for any school other than a neighborhood school. The school board had as yet proposed no single plan for integration; it was discussing three alternatives:

1. Continuation of the open-enrollment plan.
2. A modified Princeton plan, or pairing of racially imbalanced schools.
3. Use of Bryant School as a central school.

By attacking busing, Margolis and Warner attacked any proposal for desegregation other than an open-enrollment plan without mentioning the word "integration," a technique not unique in Teaneck, of course.

When Teaneck voters went to the polls they elected Warner and Margolis, in addition to Confer. Dr. Lacey, who had worked hard to get out the vote for Confer, as well as for the candidates defeated by Warner and Margolis, issued a pessimistic statement, in which he wrote in part: "The election . . . suggests once more that the possibility for the Negro's obtaining equal rights at the ballot box in this country is nil." The statement continued: "The election result was no different than the referenda that have been held in the South to determine whether schools shall be segregated or integrated."

Warner and Margolis were consistently to insist that their election meant that Teaneck desired, above all, a neighborhood-school system. Yet they were only two members on a school board of nine, and despite their election the board continued in its determination to measure the extent of imbalance and to do something about it. Confer faced the militant audience in the high school on May 13, 1964 with the result of that determination.

Five days after the central-school announcement, the Teaneck Neighborhood School Association, of which Mrs. Brenda Capasso was president and Mrs. Harry Warner was executive secretary, said that it would take action through its attorney, Milton T. Lasher of Teaneck. The Association joined the Lower Taxes League, a group whose chairman was Vincent Maher, Jr., in rejecting an invitation to a meeting called by the Teaneck Advisory Board on Human Relations. The Advisory Board had been created by Mayor Matthew Feldman, who headed a Township Council that as a group maintained rigorous neutrality in the conflict. The Board was led by Frank Burr, a former school board president and a vice president of Chase Manhattan Bank. With its rejection of the central school the Neighborhood School Association linked a commendation of Dr. Warner and Margolis: ". . . They have steadfastly opposed any system of racial quotas, regardless of the guise in which it was presented to the public. . . . The only way to eliminate or prevent racial tension is to treat all people simply as people, not as white or Negro. Quotas and other forms of racism in public facilities have no place in Teaneck or elsewhere."

The Neighborhood School Association's series of court actions began in June. In Hackensack, across the narrow Hackensack River from Teaneck, Superior Court Judge J. Wallace Leyden, following an application from attorney Lasher, ordered the school board to defend its central-school plan. The board retained Irving C. Evers, a Hackensack attorney. A few weeks later, before Superior Court Judge Theodore I. Botter, Lasher argued that the board's plan was unconstitutional because it was based on racial considerations and because it deprived children of a right to attend nearby schools. Judge Botter, citing among other decisions those reached in Englewood a year earlier, dismissed the suit because it failed to exhaust administrative remedies—failed, in short, to include a decision from State Education Commissioner Raubinger.

The Neighborhood School Association's executive vice president, Eugene Saypol, announced that Lasher had been authorized to determine the next step, and Lasher thereupon requested a hearing with Raubinger and announced a notice of appeal with the Appellate Division of Superior Court. Neither appeal was successful; on December 7, Judge Sidney Goldman handed down a 20-page opinion in which he said that the neighborhood-school system is not so immutable that it admits no exception, and on June 1, 1965, after the central

school had operated for a year, the State Supreme Court ruled in favor
of the board. The following November Commissioner Raubinger also
ruled for the board; by that time Teaneck parents had become so used
to the central school that the announcement of the Commissioner's
ruling created scarcely a stir.

Outside the courts, dissenting opinion was leading to direct action. As the September 1964 opening day of the Bryant central school
approached and as the Neighborhood School Association was an-
nouncing its legal course of action, a declaration came from a group of
parents of Hawthorne, Emerson, and Whittier Schools: when school
opened, they said, they would send their children not to the central
school but to their neighborhood schools. Direct action found additional expression when the Neighborhood School Association announced it would demonstrate in Atlantic City at the Democratic
national convention. Dr. Warner wired Governor Hughes, a Demo-
crat, and asked for a meeting which didn't materialize. The demonstration occurred, however; on August 24 about fifty Neighborhood
School Association members picketed Convention Hall. Among them
was Mrs. Warner.

Only a year earlier direct action still was playing a minor role in
Englewood; the Englewood Movement had not ended its boycott,
being mistrustful about the delayed refurbishing of Englewood's central-school building. Within a year, then, occurred a school boycott by
Englewood's Negro residents who criticized officials for doing too
little and a school boycott threatened by Teaneck's white residents
who criticized officials for doing too much. The Englewood threat
dissolved when a central school opened; the Teaneck boycott was not
realized.

In Teaneck school would open on a Wednesday, September 9.
The Township Council on September 2 approved a letter addressed to
the dissenting parents asking them to obey the law—to send their
children to the central school. The letter represented the Council's first
public stand. It was followed by a radio appeal from Mayor Feldman.
By opening day more than half of the sixty or so parents involved had
responded that they would comply. Dr. Warner also issued a statement, saying he would not condone any form of civil disobedience.
Central school opened as the board had planned; those of the 545
Bryant pupils who had been assigned to buses were waiting to board
them. A few parents appeared at Bryant School, stood by until the

incoming buses were unloaded, then left. Thereupon the Council sent a letter of commendation to the dissenting parents, who had followed the rules after all.

Now the Neighborhood School Association took a few hesitant steps toward grouping with kindred associations from other communities. On September 18 the Neighborhood School Association heard a speaker from Englewood, Mrs. Louis Pugach of the Save Our Neighborhood Schools committee, and a speaker from the Plainfield Neighborhood Schools Association, Glenn Gillette. In October at the Thomas Jefferson Junior High School, the Neighborhood School Association held its most heavily attended rally, when 450 persons heard talks by neighborhood-school proponents from New York and Philadelphia, among whom were Mrs. Rosemary Gunning, executive secretary of New York Parents and Taxpayers Association (P.A.T.), then picketing Gracie Mansion, Mayor Wagner's residence in Manhattan; John D'Amato, of Brooklyn P.A.T.; Barry Zoylan, president of Philadelphia P.A.T.; and Perry Gillery, chairman of the speakers bureau of the Joint Council for Better Education, New York. Rather than being a first step in a program of expansion, however, the meeting proved to be a climactic moment in the history of the Teaneck association's extramural rallies. In October was formed a new group, Mothers for Better Education, which concentrated on administrative flaws in the central-school plan's operation. In letters to newspapers and at cottage meetings, parents supplied data gathered from their children's observations: how much time a teacher might spend keeping order; how late a bus might run; how dry a cafeteria sandwich might be.

In the 1965 school board election, the number of members on the board (nine) and the elective system itself contrived to permit a decisive definition of the way Teaneck voters felt about the central school. Before that election the board had seven members who approved the plan and two, Warner and Margolis, who opposed it. In the election were six candidates for three seats. If Teaneck were to repudiate the central school, this was the opportunity; three candidates, George Kaplan, Mario Foah, and M. Richard Sampson, identified themselves with the dissent of the Neighborhood School Association, the Mothers for Better Education, and the Lower Taxes League. The issue in the election was thus clear-cut, for three candidates, Orville Sather, Joseph Coffee, Jr., and Jay Greenstone, identified themselves as proponents of the central school. During the campaign, incidentally, the latter three won the support of Eugene Saypol, Neighborhood School Association vice president, who had worked hard for the election of Warner and Margolis the preceding year.

Late in the campaign a 40-minute tape recording of a meeting of educators was circulated by unknown supporters of neighborhood-school candidates. Spliced into the tape was the recorded voice of a commentator who had not been at the meeting but who set for it a conspiratorial tone. The meeting had been an informal five-hour discussion in a motel selected because it was conveniently near the Newark airport. Present were Teaneck's superintendent, Dr. Harvey Scribner, and Dr. John O'Neill of the Fairleigh Dickinson University College of Education. Fairleigh Dickinson has a campus in Teaneck and the education school, in part through a grant from the Ford Foundation, had undertaken a co-operative venture with the Teaneck public school system, much like the co-operation between Harvard and the system of Newton, Mass. At the motel had been other educators, sometimes intense in their discussion, sometimes relaxed and free-swinging. Participants said that the edited 40-minute recording distorted the largely integrationist tone of the five-hour session.

The recording episode ended in failure. Sather, Coffee, and Greenstone were elected, although—to complicate the life of the political analyst—the budget proposal was defeated. (A year earlier, when Warner and Margolis were elected, the budget proposal was approved.) The central-school plan still faced challenges in the Supreme Court and before Commissioner Raubinger, but they were challenges about which the Englewood decisions a year earlier left little doubt. As it had before, Teaneck had reached a decision it could live with. The central school was established; whatever future Teaneck faced would be characteristic not of Teaneck alone but shared with the rest of the nation.

By 1967 the Teaneck central school had won endorsement from those whose opinion should matter most—the pupils. The children, who in large numbers reported at home that they liked what was happening, were formidable opponents to the dissenters. And the children's opinion had formal and effective support from a New York University team of observers who evaluated the central school at the invitation of the Board of Education. This team found that the school's strengths overrode its weaknesses, and indicated that the central-school technique should continue to be developed.

12 INTEGRATION IN THE MAJOR METROPOLIS

JACOB LANDERS

Assistant Superintendent of Integration Programs,
New York City Public Schools

Dr. Landers' role in the New York City Public Schools is undoubtedly the chief reason why segregated schools in New York run into less spectacular difficulties than those in some other northern cities, despite the undeniable fact that in general social problems seem more intense in New York than in other population centers. Landers is best known for his pioneering work on the higher-horizons program.

This article describes part of the response to the problem of segregation in New York City. Hundreds of articles have been written, either describing the problem or summarizing attempts to solve the problem politically and educationally. The task has been, therefore, one of selection and emphasis. Dr. Landers is in a most favorable position to perform this task.

Landers' description of the New York City response provides our most important case, for it not only describes the largest school district and the most difficult problem, it also describes the most enlightened response. Against the problem of ethnic segregation among a million pupils and fifty thousand teachers was marshaled every resource and every idea that has been thought of by anyone, anywhere. At the same time, all of the elements in our model of political decision making are clearly discernible.

Desegregation is emphasized in the description rather than the more difficult goal of integration. Provision of ethnic balance is difficult enough, for as whites move to suburbs or to private schools, fewer are left in the city and fewer fringe areas remain on which to site desegregated public schools. Other barriers to desegregation, financial, political, social, and educational, are explored, but with a fighting optimism. A measure of confidence derives from the city's long history of acculturation of immigrant groups. Controversy, much of it bitter, is expected to continue as the tiring climb from the pit of prejudice frustrates and angers those achieving a precarious foothold on its steep and slippery sides.

Six stages on the road to desegregation are distinguished: charges of segregation, an investigation of the charges, a policy statement, a suggested list of remedies, collection of additional data, and the production of a list of suggested remedies with steady testing and implementation. There is a wry comment that the Board of Education takes action only when the magnitude of the protest exceeds the magnitude of the problem.

Especially worth studying are the descriptions of the specific activities and the insights that Landers is able to provide. For example, with open enrollment, the group of students that moves is atypical for a variety of reasons. Principals of "sending" schools suffer a special kind of ambivalence. "Reverse" open enrollment works only if the magnetism of special programs is provided. Details of the operation of paired schools are provided to show that success comes only when special demographic characteristics are present. In line with Griffith's theory relating administration and change, comes the suggestion that fresh principals and a revised organization are needed for major modifications. Large schools with few grades are also calculated to provide the flexibility that desegregation of urban schools requires.

Perhaps the most important insight provided is that integration calls for planned development of the entire physical and social environment.

....

GENERAL CONSIDERATIONS AND BACKGROUND

Ethnic Balance and Integration

It is difficult to deal with New York City except in superlatives. The largest educational system in the world, with 1,076,000 pupils, its schools have been labeled by critics as among the best and the worst in the country. Its per pupil expenditure is by far the highest among the great cities, and its 51,000 teachers represent the largest instructional army. It has the greatest number of *de facto* segregated schools and the greatest number of well-integrated schools. It has made the earliest, the most consistent, and the most extensive efforts to eliminate *de facto* segregation, and the results have often appeared to be the most inadequate.

In short, New York City presents in macrocosm almost every problem of *de facto* segregation. It is somewhat like examining a specimen under a powerful microscope, so that the difficulties become at once both more apparent and more manageable, and the solutions more possible.

In this chapter, it is proposed to deal only with efforts at desegregation, that is, with efforts of the New York City Board of Education to improve ethnic balance in the schools. There is of course a vast difference between improved ethnic balance and integration. The former is often the necessary first step toward achieving the latter.

The mere juxtaposition of children to result in physical propinquity does not necessarily result in meaningful or improved educational experiences. Better ethnic balance may be achieved, but integration is a far broader concept involving the very essence of good education and the basic foundations of American democracy. As Rosen[1] has said, "What is now necessary is the beginning of a long process, extending over months and even years, of unlearning prejudices and establishing new democratic values through interaction in this newly desegregated environment."

It is not the purpose of this chapter, however, to deal with other aspects of the integration program of the New York City schools. It is intended to deal only with programs whose objective is to secure improved ethnic balance. This is not to minimize the importance of equalizing educational opportunity and of promoting sound programs of human relations. Without these facets, other efforts may be sterile or meaningless. However, at this time the sole sector of concern is the methodology for securing a desirable ethnic balance.

Definitions and Nomenclature

In assembling its statistical material, New York City has followed the classification system established in 1955 in a report of the Public Education Association:[2]

—A continental white school is defined as a school where the Negro and Puerto Rican population is 10% or less of the total school population at the elementary level, or less than 15% at the junior high school level, and is called a "Y" school.

—A Negro and Puerto Rican school is defined as a school in which the Negro and Puerto Rican population is 90% or more of the total school population at the elementary school level, or more than 85% at the junior high school level, and is called an "X" school.

In 1957, with the establishment of the Central Zoning Unit, it became the practice for the school system to conduct an ethnic census each year. Quite obviously it is impossible to take affirmative action in the direction of improved ethnic distribution unless basic data are available with reference to the current situation. It is then possible to ascertain the composition of each class, each grade, each district, each borough, and the school system as a whole. Except for the composition of individual classes, this information is available to interested groups.

Classroom teachers gather the basic data by inspection only or through existing records. No notation of any kind is permitted on any official record with reference to the ethnicity of an individual pupil.

In assembling its statistical material, New York City has followed the classification system established earlier in the report of the Public Education Association. All pupils other than those classified as Negro or Puerto Rican are placed under the general rubric of "Others." This term includes as well as whites all other ethnic groups—Chinese, Japanese, Cuban, Dominican, Indian, Polynesian, and others. For example, on the lower East Side of the borough of Manhattan there is an elementary school whose population is largely of Chinese descent.

There has been a general tendency to consider "X" schools as *de facto* segregated minority-group schools, and "Y" schools as *de facto* segregated white schools. It is apparent that this translation from a statistical fact to a sociological conclusion may contain the seeds of many errors and of many controversies. For example, the three categories noted above are treated as if they were mutually exclusive, while of course they are not. The category of "Others" is generally considered as consisting of mainland whites. In an individual school, it may be composed of non-English-speaking children from Cuba or Italy or Nationalist China. If at least one parent was born in Puerto Rico, a pupil is considered Puerto Rican for statistical purposes. The category "Negro" has tended to be applied to mainland-born children of mainland-born parents. If the method used to collect data were restricted to the visual only, then the great majority of pupils now classified as "Puerto Rican" would probably fall into the "Others" category.

The tendency toward convergence of social-class considerations and ethnic definitions often confuses matters even further. At the present time the Board of Education is seeking to develop a more satisfactory classification system which will be both more descriptive and more accurate. In the meantime, the statistical data should be interpreted with great care and only in the light of the definitions used.

Ethnic Changes and School Integration

By and large, programs of public school integration and indeed the possibilities for such programs are dependent upon four basic factors:

1. Total number of children of school age and their ethnic status.
2. Total number of children enrolled in the public schools and their ethnic status.
3. Geographic distribution in the city of children of different ethnic groups.
4. Administrative arrangements which place children in particular schools.

Of these four only the last is under the direct control of the school system. The quality of the public school program does of course in the long run influence both the total number of school children in a school district and the nature of the school population. It may even influence patterns of housing occupancy and of community development. However, the first three factors result most often from a complex of forces, many of them of an importance at least equal to that of

TABLE 1. POPULATION CHANGES: NET MIGRATION BY RACE AND ETHNIC GROUP, NEW YORK CITY, 1950–1960

| | Population | | Decade Change | | Natural | | Net Migration |
	April 1, 1960	1950	Number	Percent	Births	Deaths	Increase	1950–1960
New York City	7,781,984	7,891,957	−109,973	−1.4	1,520,824	773,811	747,013	−856,986
White	6,052,959	6,889,766	−836,807	−12.9	1,081,578	679,647	401,931	−1,238,738
Non-white	1,116,451	755,885	+360,566	+47.7	270,284	82,219	188,065	+172,501
Puerto Rican	612,574	246,306	+366,268	+148.7	168,962	11,945	157,017	+209,251

Source: Department of City Planning Newsletter, Oct. 1962. Based on 1950 Census of Population, 1960 Census of Population, and Department of Health data.

education—economic, social, psychological, and political. An examination of these three factors may indicate at least some of the problems faced by New York City over which it has little control.

1. *Number of School-Age Children*

For fifteen years or more there has been a consistent movement of Negroes and Puerto Ricans into New York City and a corresponding departure of continental whites. Between 1950 and 1960, for example, there was a net loss to the city of 1,238,738 whites who moved out of the city and a net gain of 172,501 non-whites and 209,261 Puerto Ricans who moved into the city. Taking into account the excess of births over deaths for all groups during this period, the total white population decreased by 836,807 or 12.9%, while the non-white population increased by 360,566 or 47.7% and the Puerto Rican population increased by 366,268 or 148.7% (see Table 1).

The proportion of children of school age to the total population within each ethnic group varies, being considerably higher for non-white and Puerto Rican groups than for the white group. Thus, in 1960, non-whites formed 14.3% of the total population, but 19.8% of the population between the ages of 5 and 9, and 16.2% of the population between the ages of 10 and 14.[3] In the group under 5 years of age the percentage of non-whites was 20.4, indicating a continuation of this statistical pattern. A somewhat similar trend exists with reference to the Puerto Rican child population.

In summary then, the total number of white children of school age in New York City has been declining steadily while the total number of non-white and Puerto Rican children has been increasing.

2. *Pupils Enrolled in Public Schools*

Between 1950 and 1960, the proportion of pupils enrolled in non-public schools increased from 25.4% of the total school enrollment to 29.3%. Since considerably more than 90% of the non-public school enrollment is white, it is evident that the percentage of other groups—non-white and Puerto Rican—in the public school population is higher than its percentage in the total school-age population.

This significant factor was emphasized in the Allen Committee Report[4] when it stated:

Residential segregation and a rapid thinning of whites is further
compounded by the fact that New York City parents have the option of
choice among public, private, and parochial schools. Because the latter are
overwhelmingly white in composition, and because the number of these
schools has grown substantially since 1950, the overall fraction of Negroes
and Puerto Ricans in the public schools far exceeds their representation in
the city population at large.

The trends in the ethnic composition of the entire population
of New York City and of the school-age population and in the
proportion of non-public schooling are reflected in the ethnic
composition of the public school population. Between 1958 and

TABLE 2. ETHNIC COMPOSITION OF SCHOOL REGISTER

Year	Puerto Rican		Negro		Others	
	No.	%	No.	%	No.	%
1964–65*	190,465	18.2	286,401	27.3	567,755	54.5
1963–64	179,223	17.1	267,344	25.6	598,987	57.3
1962–63	169,493	16.5	246,336	24.0	611,599	59.5
1961–62	162,235	16.1	228,592	22.8	613,438	61.1
1960–61	153,697	15.6	212,006	21.5	620,976	62.9
1959–60	146,432	15.0	197,517	20.2	633,582	64.8
1958–59	137,074	14.2	184,985	19.0	654,806	66.8

* Census taken January 15, 1965. For all other years, census taken
October 31.

1965, the number of "Other" pupils, mostly white, in the public
schools decreased by 87,051, from 654,806 to 567,755, or from
66.8% of the total to 54.5% (see Table 2). During the same
period of time, the number of Negro pupils increased from
184,985 to 286,401, or from 19.0% of the total to 27.3%, and the
number of Puerto Rican pupils increased from 137,074 to 190,465,
or from 14.2% of the total to 18.2%. Indeed, in January, 1965,
at the elementary level, "Others" formed less than half the total
number of pupils (see Table 3).

3. *Geographic Distribution*

The difficulties of securing proper ethnic balance within schools,
difficulties already increased as a result of changes in the total
public school population, are further magnified by patterns of

TABLE 3. ETHNIC COMPOSITION BY SCHOOL LEVEL—JANUARY 1965

City-Wide	Number of Pupils				Percentage of Total Register			
	Puerto Rican	Negro	Others	Total	Puerto Rican	Negro	Others	Total
Elementary	122,187	177,603	290,290	590,080	20.7	30.1	49.2	100.0
Junior High	39,472	58,942	112,344	210,758	18.7	28.0	53.3	100.0
Academic	17,613	36,185	144,926	198,724	8.9	18.2	72.9	100.0
Vocational	9,316	10,984	18,126	38,426	24.2	28.6	47.2	100.0
Special Schools	1,877	2,687	2,069	6,633	28.3	40.5	31.2	100.0
Total	290,465	286,401	567,755	1,044,621	18.2	27.3	54.5	100.0

housing occupancy and by local variations in non-public school attendance. For example, in one district in the Bronx, there are more pupils registered in non-public elementary schools than in public elementary schools. In some communities, the number of "Others" enrolled in non-public schools is greater than the number enrolled in the public schools.

The proportion of "Other" pupils in the public schools varies widely from borough to borough, from a high of 89.0% in Staten Island to a low of 29.4% in Manhattan (see Table 4). Moreover,

TABLE 4. ETHNIC COMPOSITION OF SCHOOLS, JANUARY 15, 1965—BOROUGH SUMMARY

Borough	Total No. of Pupils	Puerto Rican		Negro		Others	
		No.	%	No.	%	No.	%
Manhattan	177,169	56,807	32.0	68,469	38.6	51,893	29.4
Bronx	205,549	60,469	29.4	55,023	26.8	90,057	43.8
Brooklyn	392,433	64,981	16.5	115,662	29.5	211,790	54.0
Queens	242,403	5,626	2.3	46,382	19.2	190,395	78.5
Richmond	36,647	1,003	2.7	3,024	8.3	32,620	89.0
Total	1,054,201	188,886	17.9	288,560	27.4	576,955	54.7

the hardening and extension of patterns of minority-group housing concentration is evident within all boroughs. In Brooklyn, for example, there used to be many areas of Negro–Puerto Rican concentration separated from each other by areas of white population. This pattern, which is still characteristic to some extent of the borough of Queens, no longer exists in Brooklyn. There the areas of minority-group concentration have tended to merge and to form an almost continuous geographical extension. This huge area is separated from the areas of white-population concentration by a kind of ethnic frontier which is real although constantly shifting.

The net result of this process has been a gradual reduction in the number of fringe areas. This development, while most marked in Brooklyn, has also been apparent in the Bronx and in Manhattan, and to a lesser degree in Queens. Quite obviously the fewer the fringe areas, the greater will be the difficulties in securing an integrated student enrollment in the schools. At the present time, the great proportion of Negro and Puerto Rican population is concentrated in seven huge ghetto areas.

This problem has been further exacerbated by the development in areas of minority-group concentration of huge low-cost housing projects with large numbers of families. In some cases the projects have been so large that they have completely overwhelmed the neighborhoods in which they were constructed and have led to the creation of "satellite ghettoes" in their vicinity. In other cases their construction has intensified and accelerated processes of community change. In virtually all cases, the efforts of the school system to improve ethnic distribution in schools have been severely handicapped.

At the same time, high-rise middle-income housing has also increased greatly, tending to siphon off the whites living on the fringes of the ghetto and leaving a vacuum which is quickly filled by minority groups. When this middle-income housing is contiguous to an older, deteriorated area, it has generally supplied very few children to the nearby public schools.

For example, the largest cooperative-housing venture in the city is now under construction in the northeastern section of the Bronx near the city limits. It will include 15,500 families, of whom the great majority are likely to be white. It appears quite possible that these families will come in large numbers from areas in the western and central sections of the borough adjacent to present minority-group housing. The impact of the resultant changes upon the schools will be severe and extensive.

PRINCIPLES, POLICIES, AND PLANNING

Leadership Role of New York City

The Commission on School Integration of the National Association of Intergroup Relations Officers stated late in 1963:

Thus, considerable organized pressure from Negro citizens and their allies was brought to bear on the New York City Board of Education to move into its current program of school integration . . . As continuing . . . struggles over school segregation attest, New York City has by no means solved the problem; but school authorities are grappling with it, and with much more substantial measures than have yet been developed in any other big city.[5]

On November 17, 1963, Stanley H. Lowell, then Chairman of the New York City Commission on Human Rights, and one of the most articulate critics of the integration policies of the Board of Education, stated:

In the same fashion the Board of Education of the City of New York . . . a few years ago established as official policy the integration of our city's schools. Although the Board was not to blame for the many schools which contained only Negroes or Negroes and Puerto Ricans since this was based upon our segregated housing pattern, nevertheless the Board of Education rejected a color-blind approach to the schooling of our New York City children, and took a color-conscious approach seeking through various programs to achieve the integration of our schools.[6]

This leadership has been at least partly the consequence of the early acquaintance of the city with the problems of acculturation and integration. As the nation's leading gateway, New York City traditionally has had to provide much of the cultural orientation which immigrants require for adjusting to a different way of life. Long before other cities, the New York City educational system faced the complication of a vast in-migration of newcomers, many of them from the rural South, others faced with the necessity of learning English as a second language.

In the light of this generally acknowledged leadership position in securing improved ethnic balance, it may appear unusual that New York City should continue to be the scene of continuing conflict between the Board of Education and civil-rights groups. There have already been two massive boycotts and a third not quite so extensive but of longer duration and accompanied by greater violence. The relatively peaceful present appears more likely a temporary truce or a lull before the storm than an agreeable accommodation.

Part of the reason is inherent in the demographic changes which have taken place in the city during the past ten years and which make even the most extensive efforts appear puny and piddling. Another explanation may be the more liberal political and social climate of New York City and its traditions as a staging ground for the assimilation of newcomers. A third basis may well reside in the general thesis that a little progress is a dangerous thing, and that a taste of integration merely whets the appetite without satisfying it. As Handlin[7] has pointed out:

A rising level of expectations increases discontent and makes intolerable the grievances which the utterly hopeless accept as a matter of course. The black man is less willing to wait than before, because his goal has never before been so clearly visible.

It is quite likely that to some extent discontent with the pace of integration in New York City is a function of the progress which has taken place, just as in other cities quiescence (or acquiescence) may be a function of inertia or hopelessness.

Prerequisites for Action

De facto segregation is undoubtedly the greatest single problem facing all the largest cities and many smaller communities. However, the mere existence of a problem does not of itself offer any assurance that remedial action will follow.

First of all, the Board of Education and the Superintendent of Schools must be willing to accept the fact that the problem exists. Thus, for example, there is one great city which refuses to admit the existence of *de facto* segregation, as if by its refusing to say that ugly word the segregated schools would disappear overnight. A serious impediment to progress is the reluctance of school boards and school staffs to face the facts of injustice grown venerable with age.

Second, the school administration must recognize that segregation harms children, white as well as Negro. Three kinds of learning are impaired by segregation: growth of knowledge about oneself; skills and attitudes necessary to bridge differences between self and others; and, for minority-group children at least, growth in academic skills. Quite obviously, if this fact is either not acceptable or not accepted, the emphasis in the school system will be upon the equalization of separate resources and facilities. Indeed, with the present extension of compensatory programs, school systems often appear to be offering more-than-equal services in separate settings as a device to avoid tackling the problems of *de facto* segregation. What is implied here is, of course, recognition that the purposes of education in a democracy are broader than merely the acquisition of academic competence and skills. Pupils educated in a segregated classroom, be they white or Negro, are hampered by unrealistic experiences and views of the world. The role of the school to prepare children realistically for the future cannot be fulfilled under these conditions.

Third, the Board of Education and the Superintendent of Schools must be willing to create the kind of constructive controversy which alone can lead to fundamental change. This leadership will involve political, economic, social, and religious interests and will result almost inevitably in debates, disputes, and threats. A proper staging of the processes of change and a sensitivity to the art of the possible may minimize friction but not eliminate it. When the school leaders are dedicated to the maintenance of the status quo and the greatest enemy is the one who "rocks the boat," little progress is possible.

Fourth, it must be recognized that sound programs to eliminate *de facto* segregation are apt to be expensive. It is quite possible that in the South the elimination of a dual school system will result in substantial savings. Experience has indicated, however, that successful efforts to improve ethnic balance require extensive financial support. There are some school boards which have operated on the assumption that the only necessary ingredients are faith, hope, and a little re-tooling. This is just another case in which educators are asked to solve today's problems with yesterday's resources. The schools cannot do a reasonably good job in eliminating *de facto* segregation with bargain-basement budgets, nor can they atone for the misdeeds of society with conscience money consisting of a few pennies per pupil per day. Large funds will be necessary for a wide variety of purposes—improved services, teacher training, transportation, buildings, materials, and many others. Without such funds, even the best of integration plans may be useless in effecting change.

The fact is that such programs represent improved education and, like many other advances, may be costly. Quite obviously, whenever an important dimension is added to the structure of education, there is an added cost factor. A school site which facilitates integration may be more difficult to locate, thus requiring greater staff time and effort. It may also be more expensive to acquire and not quite so accessible to many students, thus requiring continuing expenditures for pupil transportation.

The costs of the Central Zoning Unit, of additional transportation, and of the greater complexity of site selection represent only one phase of the additional expense. The present purpose is not to discuss the concomitant services and adjustments necessary to make it possible for programs of improved ethnic distribution to be educationally successful. Nevertheless, it must be pointed out that budgetary extensions and administrative changes are often necessary adjuncts to the movement of pupils.

In New York City, programs to improve ethnic distribution are almost always accompanied by additional allotments to the schools affected. Many millions of dollars in additional funds are appropriated each year for extra supplies and for such compensatory services as more guidance counselors, reading specialists, school aides, and after-school study centers, as well as for reduced class size. This is true of the various plans described below as well as others.

Of course, the mere movement of children does not generally create the need for these services, but it does illuminate needs which already exist and it intensifies demands for the satisfaction of those educational needs. For example, retarded readers transferred into schools with high achievement levels have not changed academically because of the transfer. In the new setting, however, the need for assistance becomes more apparent and more pressing.

To many middle-class parents whose children are directly involved, either in the same classes or in the same school, the lower achievement levels of incoming pupils may appear to pose a threat of lowered quality. There is no objective evidence to support these fears, but their existence cannot be denied.

It is highly desirable that efforts to secure improved balance should be accompanied by improvements in education for all children. It is indisputable that movement toward school integration places new and difficult burdens upon teachers and administrators as well as upon children and parents. The schools at this time need the support of the entire community, from the economic point of view as well as the moral, political, religious, and social points of view.

Patterns of Response

The reaction of the school system of New York City to the Supreme Court decision of 1954 and to subsequent pressures was earlier and more intense than in other cities; but the city's pattern of response has become almost classic, in the sense that a model was established which has since been duplicated in other cities. Indeed, it appears possible to estimate the progress of a school system in its efforts to improve ethnic balance by noting its stage of development in terms of this model. The broad categories appear to be as follows:

1. *Charges of segregation, gerrymandering, inferior education, and inequality of treatment by various groups*

In New York City, the charges came early and from a most

influential source—Dr. Kenneth B. Clark, Associate Professor of Psychology at City College, whose work in social psychology had played an important part in the Supreme Court decision. Speaking at a symposium on June 21, 1954, only five weeks later, he charged that New York City was deficient in its treatment of minority-group children. He added, "Northern states are bound to put their own houses in order, if they are to obey the spirit of this decision— Northern public officials cannot afford to be either complacent or self-righteous with this issue."

2. *Appointment of a survey or investigating group*

The very next day after Clark's talk, the president of the Board of Education requested the Public Education Association to conduct "a full, impartial and objective inquiry into the status of the public school education of Negro and Puerto Rican children in New York City."[8] The Association, with the help of the New York University Research Center for Human Relations, issued a report[9] which substantially corroborated the allegations which had been made. Of particular importance here are its conclusions with reference to ethnic balance, as summarized in "Toward Greater Opportunity":

Of the city's 639 elementary schools, 445 (71%) enrolled either 90% or more Negro and Puerto Rican children, or 90% or more children of other ethnic origins. In general, principles in zoning school districts ignored possibilities both of separation and of integration of ethnic groups. It was not overall school policy to encourage integration through zoning.[10]

3. *Issuance of policy statement*

It is of course a far cry from policy to practice. If eloquent statements of board policy were alone sufficient to solve the problems of *de facto* segregation, then the solutions would have been found long ago in many cities. It is nonetheless true that a sound statement of policy supplies a direction and goal for concerted effort as well as a rallying cry for the friends of integration. It serves as an umbrella under which progress becomes possible and as a yardstick to measure the amount of progress. It can become a goad for a reluctant staff and a weapon in the hands of civil-rights groups. In short, a policy statement does not assure progress but certainly facilitates it.

A resolution of the New York City Board of Education on

December 23, 1954, only seven months after the Supreme Court decision, contained the following statements of principle:

. . . Modern psychological knowledge indicates clearly that segregated racially homogeneous schools damage the personality of minority group children. These schools decrease their motivation and thus their ability to learn. Public education in a racially homogeneous setting is socially unrealistic and blocks the attainment of the goals of democratic education, whether this segregation occurs by law or by fact . . . racially homogeneous schools are educationally undesirable. It is now the clearly reiterated policy and program of the Board of Education of the City of New York to devise and put into operation a plan which will prevent the further development of such schools and would integrate the existing ones as quickly as practicable.[11]

4. *Appointment of a group to make recommendations, usually including professional educators outside the school system or non-professionals, or both*

On December 23, 1954, the Board of Education directed the Superintendent of Schools to appoint a commission "to study and examine the racial composition of the schools within our city in order to determine whether the conditions therein conform to [proper] standards; and to report the facts with recommendations for such other or further action as may be necessary or desirable to approach more closely the racially integrated school in all localities . . ."[12] The thirty-seven members included twenty-three civic and educational leaders as well as members of the Board of Education and of the professional staff.

A review of the more than 100 separate recommendations of the Commission on Integration[13] indicates the extent of their influence on programs of education for disadvantaged pupils generally and for improved ethnic balance. There is hardly a single innovation of major consequence to minority-group pupils, and indeed for all pupils, which does not stem directly or indirectly from their recommendations.

5. *Collection of data with regard to ethnic imbalance and creation of a centralized zoning bureau*

The necessity for a yearly ethnic census has already been discussed, as well as the procedures followed in New York City. Quite obviously, basic data of this kind are a necessary prerequisite for action, and any community which refuses to take such a count is effectively foreclosing opportunity for change.

It is equally clear that in a large city the thrust toward zoning or other administrative arrangements for improved ethnic balance cannot be left to smaller local units or neighborhoods. A superordinate agency is necessary with extensive responsibilities and powers to effect change. In New York City, the nerve center of the effort to secure improved ethnic distribution of pupils is the Central Zoning Unit, headed by a director and acting as an arm of the assistant superintendent in charge of integration programs. This Unit, created in 1957, now has a staff of 20 and a budget of almost $175,000. Its major responsibilities are as follows:

—zone and rezone schools
—assist with site selection for new schools
—collect and analyze ethnic and demographic data
—maintain maps and charts
—administer programs to improve ethnic balance
—assist with pertinent evaluation of integration programs, busing, programs of public information, and the like.

6. *Specific activities and programs to promote ethnic balance*

By and large, there appears to be a direct relationship between a community's commitment to improved ethnic balance and its willingness to move pupils, particularly white pupils, if necessary to achieve this goal.

  a. The first efforts in this direction are apt to be administrative policies couched in general terms, such as inclusion of the factor of integration in site selection and in zoning.
  b. These are often followed by voluntary plans of the open-enrollment or building-utilization variety in which the entire burden of movement is placed upon minority-group pupils with more or less inconvenience to them and with more or less administrative difficulty as a bar to participation.
  c. Next may come voluntary plans in which white pupils will be permitted to travel farther.
  d. These may be followed by plans involving the mandatory movement of minority-group pupils, requiring them to travel farther.
  e. The greatest resistance appears to center about plans which require white pupils to move farther, to move out of their imme-

diate neighborhoods, or, finally, to move into a school in a minority-group area.

f. In a number of cases, changes in school organization are planned to facilitate integration.

g. Finally, innovative plans are prepared, such as the educational park, involving new educational concepts, requiring new administrative procedures, and emphasizing new community relationships.

The following section will deal with the specific activities and programs to promote ethnic balance. Again it must be remembered that this is only one part of a total integration effort, which includes broad programs to improve instructional excellence, human-relations aspects, compensatory services, as well as educational innovations.

SPECIFIC ACTIVITIES AND PROGRAMS

Site Selection

Since 1957 a cardinal consideration in the selection of a school site has been the effect it will have on the preservation or promotion of ethnic integration. This urgent need to advance integration is not, however, the only criterion. Distance, topographical features and safety considerations, transportation facilities, pupil-population density, and continuity of instruction must also be taken into account.

Between 1957 and 1965 it was the policy to place new schools in fringe areas so far as it was possible to do so, with the intention of drawing into the school an integrated student body. Unfortunately the fringe rarely remained stationary, and it was not unusual that a school built on a site calculated to produce fine ethnic distribution of pupils would open with a heavy preponderance of minority-group pupils, and would move more or less rapidly in the direction of *de facto* segregation.

Within the past year, acting upon recommendations of the Allen Committee,[14] the Board of Education has accepted somewhat different criteria for site selection, based upon the age and school level of the children. Schools for programs of early childhood and primary education, ranging from prekindergarten to grade 4 or possibly grade 5, will be built in the immediate community of the children to be served. Efforts will be continued even at this primary level to select sites which will serve the purposes of integration. However, higher priority will be given to the factor of distance, both for the convenience of very young children and for the active involvement of the parents in the educative process.

However, at or about the fifth grade there must be added to the primary program an extra ingredient of excellence—the sharing of learning experiences and life values among children of different races, nationalities, and economic statuses. Therefore, wherever possible, all new intermediate schools will be built in areas which can serve a cross section of the population without imposing undue hardship on individual pupils. This means that new intermediate schools should be placed where they can be reached both by minority- and majority-group students without burdensome travel. Another criterion is of course the reasonable assurance of an integrated student population, in the light of anticipated demographic changes, for a minimum number of years.

An example of the thrust of this thinking can be seen with reference to site selection for Intermediate Schools 32 Manhattan and 179 Bronx. Intermediate School 32 was originally planned as a junior high school to relieve overcrowding in the northwest portion of Harlem called Hamilton Grange. Since the public school population in the Hamilton Grange area is almost entirely Negro or Puerto Rican, it might be anticipated that the school would be *de facto* segregated if the site were selected within this area. On the other hand, Intermediate School 179 Bronx was originally planned as an elementary school to relieve overcrowding in the Riverdale area of the Bronx, with an anticipated pupil population largely middle-class white. Quite obviously, with the change from a 6–3–3 school system to a 4–4–4 organization, less elementary school space was needed while intermediate school sittings required expansion. At the same time, there was the urgent necessity of selecting a site to facilitate integration. Therefore, both intermediate schools are to be placed in the Marble Hill area, at the southernmost tip of the Bronx across the river from Manhattan, between the two communities. Pupils will travel north or south in order to reach these schools. Together with the new Kennedy High School, these two new intermediate schools will form an educational park.

Complete school integration is of course most possible at the high school level. To this end, all new high schools will be built as four-year comprehensive high schools, and those now under construction will be converted. They will be built at points available to mass transportation serving various parts of the city, with a view toward securing an integrated student body. An example of this is the new Kennedy High School, which has already been mentioned as part of the Marble Hill site educational park. Well placed with reference to mass transportation facilities, it is situated so as to draw pupils from different communities to form a well-balanced student population.

Zoning for Integration

Ever since 1957 integration has been a cardinal principle in the zoning of new schools and in the rezoning of existing schools. Between 1957 and the present, every one of the almost 1000 school zones in the city has been reexamined. This review is conducted on a continuing basis and each year dozens of changes are made, always with improvement for integration in mind. Impetus for change may come from the Central Zoning Unit, the District Superintendent, the Local School Board, a parents association, or community-minded individuals or groups. The District Superintendents and the Central Zoning Unit, who are charged with primary responsibility for the preparation of zoning plans, have repeatedly expressed their willingness to examine new and creative zoning plans to further integration, and each year they evaluate dozens of such proposals. The Office of Integration has a standing offer repeatedly made to all groups interested in improved ethnic distribution of pupils: if they can present reasonable and feasible proposals for zoning change, their ideas will be fully explored and the Central Zoning Unit will share freely its technical and staff resources in the evaluation.

In the plans for decentralization of the school system which became effective in September 1965, the Office of Integration, including the Human Relations Unit and the Central Zoning Unit, remained directly responsible to the Superintendent of Schools without any intervening authority. Indeed, the Superintendent of Schools has stated publicly on a number of occasions that the zoning of schools will continue to be a city-wide responsibility, and that he will retain direct and effective control in this area through the Assistant Superintendent for Integration.

Transportation of Pupils for Relief of Overcrowding and for Better Integration

In New York City, as in other large cities across the country, schools in the inner core attended largely by minority-group pupils tend to be overcrowded. At the same time, schools elsewhere in the city with largely white populations are underutilized. This is true despite the fact that in recent years most of the new school buildings were concentrated in such minority-group areas as Harlem and Bedford-Stuyvesant. For example, in 1964, 33% of the school buildings in the city had been built since 1950. Yet 61% of the Harlem buildings and 56% of the Bedford-Stuyvesant buildings had been constructed since 1950.

Thus, in recognition of the continued need for relief of overcrowding, a program of bus transportation to underutilized schools was begun in 1958. Since the overutilized schools were almost always in minority-group areas, and the underutilized schools were in white areas, the result was improved ethnic distribution for many pupils. The number who benefit from this movement of pupils is much greater than the number of pupils bused, since pupils in receiving schools also benefit from the change.

From the very beginning a number of basic principles were established which have since been used in other optional programs.

1. The movement of children was entirely voluntary.
2. Transportation was by contract bus.
3. The school to which the pupils were sent had no option of either assent or refusal.
4. Efforts were made to prepare the community and the faculty.
5. A careful record was kept of the resultant ethnic balance in each grade.
6. Within each grade pupils were distributed to classes in terms of ability and number of pupils. It was made clear to principals that the new pupils were to be thoroughly integrated within classes and in the life of the school.

Since 1958 approximately 55,000 elementary school pupils have been moved under this program. As already indicated, in almost every case integration of schools was improved while overcrowding was eliminated.

Originally there was considerable opposition in the receiving communities but this has tended to diminish with the passing of time. The chairman of the New York City Commission on Human Rights in a magazine article[15] quoted from a report of his Commission dealing with the transfer in 1959 of 400 Negro pupils from overcrowded schools in Brooklyn's Bedford-Stuyvesant area to the underpopulated schools in the predominantly white Glendale-Ridgewood area of Queens:

> Glendale was hostile, symbolized by some 800 persons attending a protest rally on June 4, 1959 . . . Alternate plans designed to keep the Bedford-Stuyvesant children out of Queens were designed by a local taxpayers' association . . . White supremacy groups began spreading "hate literature" . . . Ministers, seeking peaceful solutions, were pressured and, in some instances, threatened by their own congregation.

At the present time there appears to be no organized opposition to such changes. Indeed, a number of parent and civic groups in predominantly white residential areas have actively encouraged the movement of minority-group children into schools in their communities, and have engaged in dialogues with parents in minority-group areas to effect this movement.

Free Choice–Open Enrollment Plan

The Free Choice–Open Enrollment Plan, originally called the Open Enrollment Plan, was initiated on a pilot basis in September 1960. Since that time the total number of pupils transferred under this program has totaled 22,300—14,440 into elementary school grades and 7800 into the seventh grade, junior high school. This program has been widely imitated across the country, but no other has been so successful, largely because of the absence of one or more of the following features:

1. At the elementary level, bus transportation is supplied free of charge by contract bus.
2. Within each grade and class in the receiving schools, efforts are made to secure in each class an ethnically well-balanced situation.
3. Every effort has been made to present the program as a moral obligation of the Board of Education and a right of parents, as well as a method of improved education for all children.
4. Administrative problems for parents of children requesting transfers are reduced to a minimum.
5. Heads of schools involved undertake a wide variety of activities designed to ease the transition from one school to another.
6. Open-enrollment pupils continue with their new classmates to junior or senior high school, if they wish.

7. Additional services are supplied to the "receiving" schools. In September 1965, almost three million dollars was added to the elementary schools' budget for "receiving" schools, and further increases are planned for the school year 1966–1967.

Almost every city with a large proportion of minority-group pupils has some variation of the open-enrollment program, and their operation is too well known to require extended discussion. However, certain aspects are often confused or overlooked, and may require further explanation.

Among principals of "sending" schools, there is a general feeling that their most able pupils tend to leave the school. It seems clear that there is a positive correlation between the socio-economic status of a minority-group community and its desire to take advantage of optional enrollment plans.

On the other hand, principals of "receiving" schools often feel that the new pupils include a higher proportion of retarded readers and behavior problems than exists in the "sending" school. It seems entirely reasonable that parents of pupils who are having obvious difficulties in school will be more eager to seek a new environment for their children.

Thus the two viewpoints with reference to the nature of the pupils transferred are not mutually exclusive. By and large, those parents who transfer their children tend to be dissatisfied with the existing school situation. This dissatisfaction results from a variety of causes. Often the local school is seen as inadequate to provide the social mobility so much desired by the parents. In other cases the desire for change stems from the individual difficulties of the pupil. Generally, however, the group seeking transfers would appear to be in some respects atypical for the group at large.

In New York City, the option to transfer has been accepted more frequently by Negro pupils than by Puerto Rican pupils.

The principals in the "sending" schools often find themselves in an ambivalent situation. On the one hand, they must as leaders of the school extol the excellences of the institution. On the other hand, the open-enrollment program cannot escape the implication that the "sending" school is lacking in a vital element of prime importance to the educational process. How can a school leader urge pupils to leave a school while extolling its virtues? This is a fundamental contradiction which is extremely difficult to resolve.

The operation of the open-enrollment program in its early stages is apt to meet intense resistance from the receiving white community. The reaction of some parents to the program to eliminate overcrowding has already been described. In New York City, the open-enrollment program now meets with almost complete acceptance from the white community, with grudging tolerance from a good part of the Negro community, and largely with indifference from the Puerto Rican community. Mrs. Rosemary Gunning, the official spokesman for Parents and Taxpayers (P.A.T.), a group opposing various integration moves, observed:[16]

. . . the desire of those parents and others, who adhere to the belief that quality education requires the movement of their children to a school with a better admixture of races should be respected; that they be permitted to move them through voluntary open enrollment and free zoning in the broadest and freest sense possible and that free transportation be provided.

"Reverse" Open Enrollment

Between 1960 and 1963, the Free Choice–Open Enrollment program was operated as if the way to integration was a one-way street. Although technically any pupil in a "Y" (predominantly continental white in ethnic composition) school might apply for transfer to an "X" (predominantly Negro and Puerto Rican) school, in actual practice it never happened. Applications for transfer were distributed only to pupils in "X" elementary schools, and it was not considered at all possible that a parent might wish to transfer his child from a school with a high percentage of "Others" to a school predominantly Negro and Puerto Rican.

Yet a two-way approach was entirely in consonance with the Board of Education policy statement which had declared in 1954 that segregation, whether *de jure* or *de facto*, was harmful to white mainland children and to minority-group children alike. This idea had its greatest success in the borough of Brooklyn, where it resulted in the designation of a "receiving" school for white mainland children.

It is evident, of course, that the label "Reverse Open Enrollment" for this program is a misnomer. The word "reverse" is applicable only if one assumes that integration is one-way. This assumption is not valid, yet the name Reverse Open Enrollment has remained, at least partly as a testament to the surprise of the entire city that it should really have come to pass.

The original "receiving" school, P.S. 20 Brooklyn, is located near the fringe of a ghetto residential area and has a small number of "Other" pupils, numbering between 10% and 15% of the total school enrollment. A "campus" school for Long Island University, it already had many special services and more were added with the inception of this program.

At the present time there are 120 pupils from twenty predominantly white "sending" schools attending six "receiving" schools under this program. They include children in all elementary grades, from prekindergarten to grade 6. The parents generally feel, as one of them put it, that "segregation perpetuates in children the ignorance, fear, and bigotry which are the tragedy of our city. I am less afraid of children having to bus than learning to hate." Preliminary data appear to indicate that the program is successful and that both achievement and attendance levels of white pupils have been either maintained or improved.

Community Zoning Plan (Princeton Plan)

Of all the integration plans of the Board of Education, the community zoning plans, or "Princeton plans," as they were commonly known, or "school pairings," as they came to be known, evoked the greatest controversy. More than any single factor, they led to the polarization of positions during the 1963–1964 school year and to the white boycotts and sit-ins which accompanied the opening of schools in September 1964. Their legality has been tested in both state and federal courts, and upheld in every decision, including one by the Supreme Court of the United States refusing to review a favorable decision of a lower court.

A Princeton plan was first broached in New York City during the summer of 1963 by a joint committee of the Executive Boards of the Parents Associations of P.S. 149 Queens, predominantly white in pupil composition, and of P.S. 92, largely Negro. It was noted then that the two schools, although within five short blocks of each other, differed materially in ethnic composition. Under a community zoning plan, two schools which are near each other but different in pupil composition are given a common school zone. All children in this enlarged neighborhood attend some grades in one school and the remaining grades in the other. Each school has its own kindergarten.

A city-wide survey was made to determine which schools might be suitable for "school pairing." The basic criteria were:

—common boundary line, so that its removal would result in a single enlarged school zone

—school buildings close together (The distances between the buildings varied from .2 mile to .8 mile.)

—the farthest travel distance not excessive (Actually, the farthest travel distance of any pupil is about 1¼ miles.)

—travel time is not excessive (In actual practice the time is less than 30 minutes. Pupils in grades 3–6 are eligible for bus transportation beyond .7 mile rather than 1 mile as usual.)

—substantial difference in ethnic composition between the pairs of schools (This difference in percentage of "Others" varied between 61.3% and 86.6%. The resulting ethnic distribution was also considered.)

Table 5 indicates the important features of the schools which met the established criteria. It is important to relate the action taken in the community zoning plan to the usual criteria for zoning, which are Distance, Topography, Transportation, Utilization, Continuity of instruction, and Integration. All these factors were used. The only basic change was that the factor of integration received greater weight, while the factors of distance and continuity received somewhat less weight.

A number of additional services were given to the schools involved, in order to provide educational benefits to the children at the highest possible level. These included:

—average class size lower than usual, ranging from 24 to 27

—additional special services, such as reading specialists, guidance counselors, music teachers, school aides, books and supplies, supervisory and secretarial help, and the like

—building improvements

—priority in the supply of regularly appointed teachers.

These services now cost approximately $150,000 per year for each pair of schools, exclusive of building improvements.

The community zoning plan was instituted in September 1964 for the four pairs of schools noted above. In addition, a "partial" pairing

TABLE 5. SCHOOLS IN COMMUNITY ZONING PLAN

School	% Others	Pupil Population	New Grades	Distance Between Buildings (Miles)	No. of Pupils Bused Less Than 1 Mile	No. of Pupils Bused More Than 1 Mile
P-7-K	3.6	476	K, 5-6			
P-8-K	77.3	466	K, 1-4	.3	529	0
P-92-Q	0.4	497	K, 2			
P-149-Q	87.0	1057	K, 3-6	.2	29	0
P-111-Q	22.1	1040	K, 4-6			
P-112-Q	83.4	858	K, 3	.24	0	0
P-127-Q	6.0	754	K, 3-6			
P-148-Q	87.3	1201	K, 2	.8	124	0

was instituted at that time for P.S. 191 Manhattan and P.S. 199 Manhattan. Beginning in September 1964, all second-grade pupils in the two schools attended P.S. 191, a school which had in October 1963 about 5% "Other" children. All fourth-grade pupils attended P.S. 199, which in October 1963 had 66% "Other" pupils. In September 1965, P.S. 191 became a grade K–3 organization and P.S. 199 became a grade K, 1, 4–5 organization, while the sixth-grade pupils were transferred to junior high school. Thus in effect there are now five community zoning plans.

These pairings, the first of their kind in any large city in the country, are now being evaluated by the Bureau of Educational Research of the Board of Education, assisted by an outstanding group of university research experts. Until the evaluation is completed and interpreted, the present community zoning plans will be continued, but the number will not be increased. However, the evidence of objective observers appears to indicate that the schools are operating extremely well. Since the opening month, there has been very little loss, if any, of white pupils, and parents are generally enthusiastic about the changes which have taken place—sometimes even parents who were originally in opposition. Thus, the *New York World Telegram and Sun*, a newspaper which had not been in favor of "pairings," on November 7, 1964 published a headline reading, "Pairing Plan Is Paying Off." Leonard Buder, education reporter for the *New York Times*, made a rather extensive survey of the effects of "pairing" in the eight schools originally affected. His findings, reported on May 17, 1965, and subsequently in a magazine,[17] were generally favorable. He reported one woman as saying:

I had mixed feelings at first. Naturally, I didn't like the idea of my older daughter having to go to school by bus when this school is so close. But now I don't mind. She's in a smaller class and seems to be getting every advantage.

As the Allen Committee Report[18] has pointed out, the "pairing plan" has only limited applicability in New York City, and could not under any conditions be offered as a major solution to the problems of *de facto* segregation. It is, however, a useful device for all communities, and in smaller towns and suburbs might well represent a total solution.

The tremendous antagonisms engendered by the "pairing plans" have already been noted. Such proposals, since they involve the movement of white children into areas of minority-group concentration, may almost always be expected to create controversy. A Local School Board chairman, speaking just a month after the beginning of the "pairings," said:[19]

> Like any other TV viewer, like any other newspaper reader, I saw and read the ugly, hurled epithets, the raw hatred on the distorted faces, the repeated cheers for the Assembly candidate of an extremist political group, the deliberate vandalism of police equipment, the open and sometimes physical hostility toward the law, and the most shocking thing of all—the callous and willing exposure of 6-year-olds to this kind of frightening and dangerous scene.
>
> Are these the same mothers who were worried about the *safety* of their kids crossing Junction Boulevard? Are these the same fathers who were so concerned that their children might be a little late for *religious* instruction?

The discussions concerning the possible movement of large numbers of white children had some unanticipated and positive results. Alternatives less drastic in nature now appeared not only reasonable but highly desirable. Thus even those groups which had opposed open-enrollment programs and special services for disadvantaged pupils, either directly or indirectly, or who had been silent, have become among the most vociferous advocates of such programs.

Rogers and Swanson[20] have pointed to a number of factors which may influence the response of a community to the "pairing" idea—style of implementation of the plan by school officials; extent of compliance of field personnel; extent of integration in housing and in community-wide civic groups; and others. One of the most interesting hypotheses is that resistance in the white community may vary inversely with the social-class distance from the Negro community—the less the distance, the greater the resistance.

Changed Feeder Patterns for Junior High School

It has long been recognized that, since junior high schools include pupils from a wider geographic area than elementary schools, they can achieve ethnic balance more easily and more effectively. Between 1957 and 1963, zone lines of newly built junior high schools and of existing junior high schools were reexamined with a view to achieving maximum ethnic heterogeneity.

For example, in the zoning of new J.H.S. 275 Brooklyn, located in a "fringe" area, some pupils attending a preponderantly white school were zoned into this new school. The parents of some of the children affected complained bitterly. In addition to organizing boycotts and demonstrations, they instituted lawsuits. Indeed, the first case decided by the higher courts which gave school districts the right to take affirmative action to improve ethnic balance was this very one. The Supreme Court of the United States, refusing to hear the appeal, in effect sustained the decision of the lower court which upheld the right of New York City to zone affirmatively for integration.

However, lines which have been hardened by custom and hallowed by tradition cannot be easily changed, especially when some white children have to be moved into a school in which the majority of the students are Negro and Puerto Rican. Another complicating factor may be the existence of ethnic frontiers near the boundary lines between the districts of two district superintendents.

Early in the school year 1963–1964 all adjoining junior high schools where there was a marked difference in the ethnic composition of the student body were examined carefully. Specific criteria were established on the basis of which it might be possible to change elementary school feeder patterns. These were:

—common boundary lines or close proximity of feeding elementary schools
—school buildings relatively close together, certainly less than 2½ miles
—travel distance or time not too great
—substantial differences in ethnic composition of the junior high schools.

In September 1964, feeder-pattern changes were made for three groups of schools, and others have been made since. It is important to note here again, as in the case of the community zoning plans, that the six basic criteria for zoning are maintained. However, the factor of integration is receiving greater weight, while the factors of distance and transportation receive less weight.

The nature of these changes may be best explained by giving a concrete example. In 1963–1964, Junior High School 109 Queens in district 51 was a well-established school with a pupil population which had 94.9% "Other" pupils. In nearby district 50, Junior High School

192 was a new school which had only 28.5% "Other" pupils, despite the fact that it was only one mile away from Jr. H.S.109. Their elementary feeders and the changes are indicated in Table 6.

The changes were effective only for incoming seventh grade pupils, and therefore ethnic changes will be staged over a three-year period. By September 1965 the differences in ethnic composition between the two schools had decreased considerably. The percentage of "Other" pupils at Jr. H.S. 109-Q had dropped from 94.9 to 79.9; the percentage of "Other" pupils at Jr. H.S. 192-Q had increased from 28.5 to 37.0, with a further increase indicated for September 1966.

TABLE 6. JUNIOR HIGH SCHOOLS 109-Q and 192-Q, FEEDER-PATTERN CHANGES

Elementary School Feeders to Jr. H.S. 109-Q	
Before Change of Feeder Pattern	After Change of Feeder Pattern
P18Q, P33Q, P35Q, P135Q, P188Q	P18Q, P33Q, P118Q, P134Q (west of 198 St.), P135Q (east of Francis Lewis Blvd.), P188Q

Elementary School Feeders to Jr. H.S.192-Q	
Before Change of Feeder Pattern	After Change of Feeder Pattern
P34Q, P36Q, P118Q, P134Q, P136Q, P147Q	P34Q, P35Q, P36Q, P134Q (east of 198 St.), P135Q (west of Francis Lewis Blvd.), P136Q, P147Q

High School Organization

New York City has undoubtedly the most extensive and the most varied combination of high schools in the country or, for that matter, in the world. At the present time there are in the city 60 academic high schools and 29 vocational high schools, each one offering a wide variety of subjects and courses. The academic high schools are generally neighborhood schools, drawing their enrollment from pupils living in relatively close proximity to the schools (48); but there are also single-sex schools including only boys (3) or girls (5) and drawing their student bodies from one or more boroughs; or special schools requiring entrance examinations (3); or an examination school accepting only boys (1).

The 29 vocational high schools usually draw pupils from the entire city, and are either coeducational or for boys or for girls only. Twenty-three of them are multi-trade schools, while six are unit trade (Art and Design, Food and Maritime, Fashion Industries, Printing, Automotive, and Aviation). Some vocational high schools give entrance examinations while others have admission examinations only for certain courses. The total population of the senior high schools, as of October 1965, was 255,166—212,689 in academic high schools and 42,477 in vocational high schools.

Until February 1963, the neighborhood academic high schools were zoned in terms of geographic proximity, with the great majority of the students coming from the area surrounding each school and contiguous to it. Because of segregated housing patterns, many of the high schools tended to be ethnically unbalanced, particularly in the boroughs of Brooklyn and Queens, while others in the same boroughs located in fringe areas were tending to "tip" in the direction of larger numbers of minority-group students.

Actually, earlier policies of the Board of Education had helped to prevent the creation of *de facto* segregated high schools. For more than twenty years, with the support of community leaders in minority-group areas, no high schools had been built within these areas. For example, the last high school in the central Harlem area, Wadleigh, was closed many years ago, at a time when the student body had shrunk below 1000. Similarly, Girls High School in the Bedford-Stuyvesant area was closed in 1964, when its enrollment was approximately 850. The average academic high school in New York City has about 3500 students.

High School "Open Admissions"

Prior to the school year 1963–1964, a number of "variances" were issued giving special permission to some pupils to enter particular high schools in order to further integration. However, the number was small.

In February 1964, the Free Choice–Open Enrollment Plan was extended to the high schools, where it became known as the Open Admissions Plan. At the high school level, schools having 65% or more Negro or Puerto Rican enrollment were designated as "sending" schools. Those having a plant utilization of less than 115% of capacity and a favorable ethnic balance or a preponderance of "Other" students were designated as "receiving" high schools. At this time, eight schools qualified as "sending" schools and seventeen were designated as "receiving" schools. Of 13,200 students in grades 10 and 11 who were eligible, 410, or 3.1%, were actually transferred. However, it must be remembered that this first offer was made after the pupils had already entered a high school.

For September 1964, the plan applied to pupils at the point at which they were entering high school, either grade 9 or grade 10, and to those already in grade 9 in high schools with 65% or more Negro and Puerto Rican population. Of 7500 eligible pupils, 849, or 11.3%, were transferred to other schools.

In this same year, the movement of ninth-grade pupils from junior to senior high school began with the elimination of grade 9 from 10 junior high schools. Pupils were given a choice of 29 high schools, all of them with a considerably better ethnic balance than the junior high schools they were leaving. Under this "truncation" program as it was called, in September 1964, 4476 ninth-grade pupils were transferred from ethnically imbalanced junior high schools to better-balanced high schools.

In September 1965 the outlines of a new policy began to emerge. It was felt that each pupil ought to have, in addition to the special choices (vocational high school, single-sex school, special academic school), at least two choices of high school: the usual zoned high school, and any other high school in which there was space. Since there was not enough high school space available in September 1965 to extend the new system to all pupils, the option was given first to those leaving "X" junior high schools (e.g., junior high schools with 85% or more minority-group population) who had been zoned into schools with an unusually high percentage of minority-group pupils. Approximately 6000 eighth- and ninth-grade pupils in 26 junior high schools were permitted to apply for 26 high schools, with each pupil being given five choices. In the calculation of available space, utilization was estimated as high as 130% of capacity. Even under these conditions, the shortage of high school space was such that not all applicants could be accommodated in the schools of their choice. Of 25,000 pupils who were eligible, 4488, or 17.9%, applied for the offered schools, but only 3337 were actually assigned to the 26 high schools.

Change in High School Organization

As has already been indicated, the movement of ninth-grade pupils from junior high school to high school began in September 1964. During the school year 1964–1965, the Board of Education adopted the policy of the four-year comprehensive high school. As a result the movement of ninth graders accelerated in September 1965, with the truncation of 28 additional junior high schools, for a total of 38. Almost 19,000 ninth-grade pupils who would formerly have been in junior high schools were admitted to high schools in September 1965. As of that date, approximately 36,000 of 88,000 ninth-grade pupils, or 41%, were in high school.

A greatly expanded high school building program has been projected so that all ninth-grade pupils may be placed in high schools. However, for the next few years, very little additional high school space will be available, so that during this time the change will be extremely limited.

In the long run, the change to a 4–4–4 system will greatly enhance integration possibilities for a large number of pupils. For example, almost all of the ninth-grade pupils in high schools are in a better-integrated situation than that which prevails in the junior high schools from which they came. By the same token, the fifth- and sixth-grade pupils in the new middle schools will generally be in schools which are better-integrated than the ones from which they came.

The change from separate academic and vocational high schools to comprehensive high schools will also lead to greatly improved integration. As of January 1965 the percentage of Negro and Puerto Rican pupils in vocational high schools was 52.8, while in the academic high schools the percentage of minority-group pupils was only 27.1. There were, of course, wide variations within the individual schools. The combination of all courses under one roof will lead inevitably to increased possibilities for greater integration.

High School Zone Changes

Particularly during the last two years, increasing attention has been given to the possibilities of rezoning existing high schools so as to further integration. At the same time, the zoning of new high schools has created opportunities for natural rezoning in desired directions. The new high schools have had their boundaries carefully delineated in the effort to secure a more varied pupil population, and often it has been necessary to include both mandatory and optional features.

For example, two new high schools opened in Brooklyn during the last two years—Canarsie in 1964 and Franklin D. Roosevelt in 1965. Each is situated in an area whose population is almost entirely white. If zoned by traditional methods, both of these high schools would have had very small percentages of minority-group pupils, despite the fact that the Negro and Puerto Rican school population of Brooklyn is nearing 50%. However, as a result of rather unconventional zoning methods and the application of the Open Admissions Plan, the two schools are very well balanced ethnically.

Two other cases may be mentioned as illustrative of high school

TABLE 7. ETHNIC COMPOSITION OF TWO BROOKLYN HIGH SCHOOLS

	Canarsie High School		Franklin D. Roosevelt High School	
Ethnic Group	No. of Pupils	%	No. of Pupils	%
Puerto Rican	242	8.1	27	1.5
Negro	705	23.6	432	24.4
Others	2039	68.3	1309	74.1
Total	2986	100.0	1768	100.0

zoning problems and of the flexibility needed to make positive adjustments to changing situations.

When Wingate High School was opened during the 1954–1955 school year—indeed, it was the first high school opened in New York City after the 1954 Supreme Court decision—it opened as an excellent example of zoning to include the factor of integration. If the school had been zoned in the usual fashion, with the school in the approximate center of a geographic or population area, it would have been almost entirely white. However, the zoning boundaries were so located that the school included pupils far to the north, living in the southern portion of the Bedford-Stuyvesant area, while the southern boundary was only a few short blocks from the school. At that time, in 1954–1955, the ethnic composition of the school was about 80% white and 20% Negro.

The "ethnic frontier" to the north, however, began to move south. By 1962, the percentage of "Others" had dropped to 70.1; in 1963 to 58.4; in 1964 to 51.0. One junior high school, most of whose pupils were "Others," was added as a feeder to Wingate High School, but this resulted in only slight improvement. Therefore, an entire northern section of Wingate's zone was shifted to another school about five miles away, Grover Cleveland High School, in another borough. This was the first case in the history of New York City, and possibly in the history of any large-city school system, in which non-contiguous zoning, or "skip" zoning, was employed for high schools in order to improve integration. The pupils who had formerly attended Wingate, most of them Negro, had to pass at least one high school, Bushwick, in order to get to Cleveland High School. However, this latter school was better able to absorb the youngsters from the point of view of both ethnic balance and building utilization.

As a result of these changes, the entering tenth-grade pupils of Wingate were 56.3% "Others." By contrast, the previous year's group had been 39.1% "Others." In this case, too there was a lawsuit, *Silberfarb* v. *Board of Education.* Judge Cone, of the New York State Supreme Court, relying heavily on the precedents of previous cases won by the Board of Education, stated, "It is within the province of the Board to conclude that racial imbalance is harmful to education and to draw school zones in order to effectuate a better racial balance in the school system."

In much the same way, Andrew Jackson High School in the borough of Queens was probably saved for this year as an integrated high school. Through the application of the skip-zoning principle, a large group of youngsters, most of them Negro, were zoned northward to Francis Lewis High School in September 1965. At the same time, and as a result of the persistent requests of the Board of Education, the Transit Authority established a new bus route, Q77, in order to permit north-south transportation of pupils to facilitate integration. Again, this may well be the first time a franchised bus route has been established for this purpose.

Changes in High School Ethnic Composition

The impact of these various policies and practices may be seen particularly with reference to the high schools which formerly were almost entirely white.

TABLE 8. CHANGES IN ETHNIC COMPOSITION OF SELECTED ACADEMIC
HIGH SCHOOLS

	1963–1964			1965–1966		
School	% P.R.	% N.	% O.	% P.R.	% N.	% O.
Columbus	1.0	1.4	97.6	4.5	10.6	84.9
Madison	0.1	0.5	99.4	0.9	9.6	89.5
Fort Hamilton	1.7	2.6	95.7	5.1	9.1	85.8
Midwood	0.3	1.6	98.1	1.2	13.9	84.9
Tilden	0.8	2.2	97.0	5.6	13.1	81.3
Francis Lewis	0.3	1.3	98.4	1.2	12.6	86.2
Cleveland	0.4	2.1	97.5	2.1	15.3	82.6
Van Buren	0.4	2.7	96.9	0.4	10.3	89.3

Intermediate Schools

The junior high schools of the city tend to be better-balanced
ethnically than the elementary schools, although often the junior highs
reflect the same kind of ethnic homogeneity as the elementary schools.
It is clear, however, that upper-grade schools, because they cover
wider geographic areas and because older children are able to travel
longer distances, can more easily achieve better ethnic balance.

The transformation of grade 7-8-9 junior high schools to grade
6-7-8 schools, and probably eventually to grade 5-6-7-8 schools,
began in September 1964. As of September 1965, there were 38 junior
high schools which had lost their ninth grade. Approximately 18,500
ninth-grade pupils were sent to high school at that time, while 14,500
pupils were sent to the sixth grade of junior high or elementary schools
under the alternate assignment plan. It is estimated that the movement
to the three-year or four-year middle schools will be substantially
completed by 1972–1973 as additional new building is completed. So
far as possible new intermediate schools will be located in order to
result in an integrated student body.

Special Plans of Assistant Superintendents

A great many assistant superintendents in the field or at headquarters have devised special plans to improve ethnic balance in
specific schools while securing other educational advances for all the
children. It is not possible to note all such plans within the limits of
this chapter, but a brief description is included of three representative

plans which took effect in September 1964 or 1965 and whose effect is continuing.

Assistant Superintendent Douglas, District 19

One of the elementary schools in the district, P.S. 260 Brooklyn, is fed entirely by children from a low-cost housing project. Between 1960 and 1963, the percentage of "Others" dropped rather steadily.

The objective of the assistant superintendent's plan was to establish classes for pupils talented in music and/or art in P.S. 260, making it a district school for talent classes. Thus the school was able to draw from all parts of the area and to some extent overcome the effect of segregated housing. The plan is a voluntary one, and the parents may accept or reject the invitation to the talented child. Pupils are brought to the school by contract bus.

The plan was begun in September 1964 in grade 4, when two special classes were organized, one in art and one in music. In 1965, the original group advanced to grade 5, and a new group was admitted. In this second year, community enthusiasm was so great that more applications were submitted than could be accepted. Between 60 and 65 pupils have been accepted each year. Applications were open to all the schools of the district, and slightly more than half the pupils admitted are "Others."

Special services added to the school included teachers of art and of music. A teacher of foreign languages was also added, since the pupils involved were programmed for either French or Spanish. Other special services were added in order to create as fine a teaching-learning situation as possible.

Assistant Superintendent Scalea, District 2

During the 1963–1964 school year, P.S. 6 Manhattan had a very large school district and was operating at 110% of capacity. It had 1171 pupils, of whom 94.6% were white, and was surrounded by other schools which were underutilized. It should be mentioned that P.S. 6 had acquired an excellent reputation over the years—so much so that it was not uncommon for renting agents to advertise apartments including the words "in the zone of P.S. 6."

In September 1964, the school zone was made smaller, and 275 pupils living on the periphery of the former zone were sent to surrounding schools. In the great majority of cases these new schools were closer to the children transferred than P.S. 6. Nevertheless, a number of parents sued the Board of Education, claiming that the zone change was illegal. At the same time that this zone change took place, approximately 160 pupils, mostly Negro and Puerto Rican, were transferred into P.S. 6 on a voluntary basis. The parents who sued claimed that the rezoning had taken place "solely to provide vacancies at the school for Negro and Puerto Rican children" and was thus a violation of both the state and federal constitutions.

State Supreme Court Justice Lupiano upheld the action of the Board of Education, and his ruling was subsequently affirmed by the Appellate Division and by the Court of Appeals, the highest court in the state. A portion of Justice Lupiano's decision read as follows:

It is within the province of the Board to conclude that racial imbalance is harmful to education, and to draw school zones in order to effectuate a better racial balance in the school system. While we agree with the dissent that no constitutional or statutory mandate directs the Board to promote integration, there is equally no prohibition against the Board's attempt to achieve integration. The Board is free to act in this sphere untrammeled by the courts. Certainly in the area of educational value judgments, the courts should not attempt to substitute their views for those of the Board if there is some reasonable basis for the Board's conclusion.

The change in the ethnic composition of P.S. 6 is indicated in Table 9.

TABLE 9. ETHNIC COMPOSITION: P.S. 6 MANHATTAN

Year	Puerto Rican		Negro		Others		Total
	No.	%	No.	%	No.	%	
1963	15	1.3	60	5.1	1096	93.6	1171
1964	35	3.6	122	12.5	816	83.9	973
1965	21	2.0	167	18.0	630	80.0	818

Special Academic High Schools

Three of the four special academic high schools—the Bronx High School of Science, Stuyvesant High School, and Brooklyn Technical High School—have had unusually low percentages of minority-group pupils. Pupils for these schools are selected largely on the basis of an entrance examination heavily weighted in terms of language and mathematics.

It was recognized that there were undoubtedly some applicants with excellent potential who had not passed the entrance examination for these special schools. Therefore, in the tests given for admission in September 1965, the entire records of those who were below the cutoff point were carefully examined. When in the judgment of the junior high school principals and counselors an individual seemed to possess abilities sufficient to warrant a trial in the special high schools, and when objective test scores were not too far below the admission norms, the pupils were given conditional acceptances. These pupils were required to attend special classes in summer high school, usually in mathematics and English. Subsequently they were accepted as regular students. Under this plan, approximately 50 students were accepted into each of the high schools noted above. The majority—but by no means all—were Negro and Puerto Rican.

Of the 155 pupils who were eligible for the summer session, 141 actually began attendance and all but one remained for the entire session. Of the remaining 140, 121 were admitted to the special high schools. Of the 121 pupils admitted, 117 completed the first term at the high school. Of this number, 79, or more than two-thirds, passed all their major subjects, while the great majority of the others failed only one subject.

In view of the apparent success of this project, it is intended to increase the number selected for each school from 50 to 100, to a total of 300 for the three special schools.

Educational Parks

An educational park[21] has been defined as the clustering of educational facilities in a campus-like setting, utilizing centrally organized common facilities and drawing its student population from the whole community. An educational park, because of the large number of pupils it might include and the wider zoned area, certainly might be a powerful aid in facilitating integration.

The Board of Education has embarked upon the creation of two urban educational parks—one in the Marble Hill area, already described, and the other in Co-op City, a huge housing development in the northeastern section of the Bronx. This latter park will include two intermediate schools as well as a high school, all of them to be fully

integrated. A planning grant has been made by the United States
Office of Education under Title III of the Elementary and Secondary
Education Act. Preliminary work has already been done in connection
with joint use of such facilities as kitchen, cafeteria, heating, and
recreation.

It must be understood that these educational parks represent
experimental ventures. There is at present no policy of having educational parks to replace intermediate or high schools. It may be that if
the projected parks prove successful the concept will be accepted as
a basis for policy, but such a determination must await the test of
experience. To date there has not been established a single urban
educational park, particularly with integration as the focus, so that the
two which are planned represent pioneer ventures.

SCHOOLS AND SOCIETY

Schools and Change

It is most unfortunate that the evils of segregated and inferior
education for minority-group children in the schools of the North and
West have been most often exposed by civil-libertarians, sociologists,
and social psychologists rather than by the gatekeepers of the educational establishment. As has already been indicated, the 1955 report of
the Public Education Association,[22] following upon the charges of
Clark, indicated clearly that in 1954 New York City was deficient in its
treatment of minority-group children.

Yet there is no reason to believe that the New York City Board of
Education was any more delinquent in this respect than boards of other
great cities. In fact, there is ample evidence to indicate that on the
whole it was less negligent than most, if not all of them.[23] For example,
the Public Education Association found that New York City schools
with heavy concentrations of minority-group children generally received more services than other schools. This is the only such case
existing in 1954 which has come to light. In other cities, the reverse
was often true.

It is equally unfortunate that changes in the educational patterns
of minority-group children have often seemed to result more from
political and social pressures than from the convictions of school
boards and administrators. Thus Goldaber[24] has developed the interesting hypothesis that Boards of Education are likely to take action on

problems affecting the Negro when the magnitude of protest is greater than the magnitude of the problem. This knowledge, together with the indurated conservatism of the educational hierarchy of the great cities, has tended to foster the belief among civil-rights groups that important changes result from displays of power rather than from programs of persuasion.

This distrust of educational leadership is heightened by the tendency of superintendents to deal with the present in terms of the past, and to compare the Negro, for example, with immigrant groups of other years. School administrators often assume rather naively that the same methods and procedures which succeeded with the German, the Irishman, and the Jew will bring the Negro into the mainstream of American society. As Dodson[25] has stated,

Superintendents tend to program from the experience they had with other minority groups. They indicate the fact that these groups never complained when a school was segregated if the community housing was also segregated and the school ethnic composition reflected that of the community.

It is also clear that for the foreseeable future, as Stewart[26] has pointed out, the big-city school system is likely to be the "whipping boy" in the efforts of minority groups to better themselves. The school today is the most important distributor of future status and rewards.[27] It is entirely understandable that parents should attribute to the schools almost sole responsibility for the failures of society.

The schools represent of course only one segment of a much larger societal structure, and educational decisions may be governed as much by political and social considerations as by educational goals. Thus, for example, the Board of Education of New York City has stated that segregated education is harmful to all children, white as well as Negro. Children are encouraged to transfer to other schools where greater integration is possible even when travel time may be as much as one hour each way. Every year thousands of pupils volunteer at the urging of the Board of Education for this improved program of education. These pupils are often those who are furthest behind in their school work and for whom extensive travel imposes the greatest burden.

Yet solutions have not been advanced which will impose the burden of travel upon those who are better able to bear it. The reasons are not only educational, but social, political, and economic as well. The existence of options in the form of non-public schools is also an important consideration. As the Allen Committee Report[28] has stated,

> It should be obvious . . . that integration is impossible without white pupils. No plan can be acceptable, therefore, which increases the movement of white pupils out of the public schools. Neither is it acceptable, however, unless it contributes to desegregation.

Administrative and Logistical Problems

The problem of eliminating *de facto* segregation from the schools of New York City, and of other great cities, is probably one of the most complex of our times. Practices which may give promise of representative total solutions for smaller communities are often of limited impact in the cities. As Decter[29] has said, "When it comes to a problem of the New York City school system, proposing is a far simpler activity than disposing."

For example, in July of 1962, the National Association for the Advancement of Colored People (NAACP) published a booklet[30] which outlined several plans for desegregation: zoning; Princeton plan; school reorganization; changed feeder patterns; and site selection. As explained above, every one of these methods has been explored fully in New York City, but the problems of *de facto* segregation remain.

As Dentler[31] said recently,

> While the suburb of Englewood . . . eliminates a single segregated school, neighboring New York City will continue to be burdened with hundreds of highly segregated public schools. . . . There are technical solutions to minority school segregation in the great cities, but they are few in number and generally drastic in effect. . . .

Other Generalizations

A number of broad principles with respect to programs of improved ethnic balance have been specifically mentioned in an early section of this chapter and others have been noted in passing. Additional important generalizations include the following:

1. It is important to assure a firm financial basis for future moves. Thus it is only recently that New York State assumed 90 percent of

the cost of transporting children to school more than a mile and a half within the city. Without such a provision, changes in the direction of improved ethnic balance might not only be financially prohibitive, but would also provoke greater opposition from economy-minded segments of the community.

2. Efforts to improve ethnic balance must be presented so as to assure better-quality education for all children. The negative arguments stressing the harm to children, particularly to Negro children, of the existing pattern are hardly persuasive with white parents who are reasonably well satisfied with the schools. In this connection, Riessman[32] says,

> We have already implied that integration strategy suffers because it attempts to win white parents to integration by citing the negative effects of segregation on the Negro. This is a logical and deeply moral argument, but psychologically, it is not only ineffective with most white resisters, but actually may boomerang when these same white parents begin to anticipate the products of segregation retarding their own children in the new integrated situations.

3. In view of the constantly shifting ethnic character of the populations of great cities, long-range plans involving urban planners and social scientists, as well as educators, are of vital importance. A single high-rise complex can destroy the most carefully planned integration program. By the same token, the time factor involved in the results of change assumes a greater importance. The probable gain must be balanced against the probable loss, and it hardly pays to wage a major battle for a change of very limited duration.

4. The manner of implementation of changes designed to improve ethnic balance is of prime importance. The preparation of communities, the training of staff, and the education of children will in the largest measure determine success or failure. The most important single factor is the principal. No new program can possibly be successful without adequate leadership on the local level. In many cases, changes in administrative personnel prior to innovations are highly desirable.

5. It is much easier to embark upon bold ventures with a new facility than with an old one. A new building can be zoned more freely, administered more imaginatively, and organized more creatively, while attempts to carry on a similar undertaking in an existing structure might be doomed to defeat.

6. In the same way a changed organizational pattern provides new opportunities to deal creatively with problems of desegregation. It is necessary in the process of reorganization to create new relationships among children as well as teachers. This is one of the reasons why New York City has decided to change to a four-year high school, and to move toward a four-year middle school.

7. All things being equal, improved ethnic distribution is more possible when there are fewer grades in a given building, and when buildings are as large as possible. The combination of a small building and a K–8 grade organization makes the neighborhood-school pattern almost inevitable. As buildings become larger, or as a number of buildings are placed in close juxtaposition, the school zone becomes more inclusive. This result also follows from a reduction in the pupil population within a building.

SUMMARY

Gauging the impact of the entire program for ethnic balance upon the 1,076,000 pupils in the New York City school system is extremely difficult. For example, the actual number of pupils who were transferred in September 1965 either to improve ethnic balance, or to eliminate overcrowding while improving ethnic balance, or to move to a school organization which will foster integration, was probably about 50,000. However, in terms of impact, it seems likely that more than half of the total school population was directly affected, either through actual movement or as a result of direct contact with those who changed. Although the children moved were most often Negro or Puerto Rican, the greatest number of pupils involved in the results were white.

During the four years from 1960–1961 to 1964–1965, the number of mid-range (integrated) schools—that is, those neither in the "X" nor "Y"* category—increased. This occurred despite an increase of minority-group population from 37.1% of the total to 45.5%, and in the face of an extension and consolidation of minority-group residential areas. This increase in mid-range schools resulted largely from the explicit policies of the Board of Education as described above.

---

* "X" = predominantly Negro and Puerto Rican in ethnic composition. "Y" = predominantly white in ethnic composition.

In 1960–1961, the first year for which statistics of this kind are available, 337 of 782 schools were mid-range in ethnic composition. In 1964–1965, the last year for which data are available, 387 of 811 schools were mid-range. This represented an increase of 50 schools which were better-integrated, and a percentage increase from 43.1% to 47.7% of all schools. At the same time, the total number of pupils in mid-range schools increased by 72,079—from 417,308 to 489,386. It is true, of course, that the number of "X" schools has also increased— from 118 in 1960–1961 to 187 in 1964–1965.

The necessity to improve ethnic distribution of pupils has confronted New York City and other great cities with the most complicated educational problem of our time. In essence, they are trying to correct a condition which resides in the total fabric of society and has its roots in residential segregation, social discrimination, and economic inequality. There are those who hurl at the school system the term "social engineering" as if it were an ugly epithet.

The schools cannot possibly do the job alone. But the fact that they cannot be completely successful in this area does not mean that they should do nothing. Indeed, they have a responsibility to do as much as they can. On the one hand, there are those who counsel the maintenance of the status quo, with complete reliance upon self-contained systems of neighborhood schools at all educational levels through high schools. On the other hand, there are those who are so eager for change that they advocate unsound and impractical courses of action, regardless of the desires of parents, the probable impact upon communities, and even the consequences for the children.

Sheldon and Glazer[33] have summed up the efforts of New York City programs as follows:

> The various devices employed under the general rubric of zoning and school reorganization policies have not had a great numerical impact on *de facto* segregated schooling. This is due more, however, to the combined forces of the changing ethnic composition of the city schools and segregated residential patterns than to Board programs and policies that ardently attempt to promote integration and stem the creeping segregation inherent in both the demographic and ecological patterns of growth and succession.

part V

Some Lessons
for Policymakers

13

THE POLITICS
OF EDUCATION

FREDERICK M. WIRT

In this summary chapter, the case studies are considered as an application of the decision-making process outlined in the opening chapter. Values generally held, whether by members of special groups or by elected and appointed officials, help to explain the social interaction that is depicted. An important concept is now introduced, that "opinion closure" follows the taking of a decision and conflict is thereby depressed.

Under the cover of seeming complexity, a number of principles are seen to be operating. The neighborhood-school concept while acclaimed by mothers genuinely fearful of dangerous journeys by children to distant schools, is also acclaimed by those who are prejudiced against either race or class. Indiscriminate mixing of children with varying potentials for education is feared as a threat to standards by many teachers, and this fear, coupled with sympathy for the less capable child, prevents these teachers from taking a firm stand in favor of desegregation or even compensatory education. A third principle is the tendency to refer a difficult problem, such as school segregation, to a

larger political unit, thereby increasing the number of viable alternatives as well as the extent of the deliberation prior to the making of a
choice. Discussion of this principle leads to the prediction that school
districts embracing "urbs" as well as suburbs will increasingly be suggested.*

A number of arrangements calculated to reduce the extent of
racial segregation in the schools are listed. But even in desegregated
schools ability grouping tends to separate the children on a social-class
basis and this, because of the Negro's history of cultural deprivation,
usually means a race basis as well.

The search for excellence in education will continue to guide
deliberations about desegregation. A final principle, unsaid but fully
implied, is that the greater the deliberation prior to making the choice,
the more the long-range consequences of various alternatives are considered, the better the choices that will be made.

....

The opening chapter raised for consideration the essential elements of the public policy-making process. Policy was viewed as the
outcome of the interplay of broad cultural values and specific group
values pursued within a legal framework and pressed upon public
officials.

This chapter seeks to determine how this model applies to the
policy of ending northern *de facto* school segregation. Such consideration should serve two purposes, namely, fitting education policy making into a more general context and suggesting some clues about the
course of desegregation policy in the future.

One of the first impressions from reading these cases is the remarkable variety as well as continuity which they exhibit. There is
variety in the sizes of school systems, the time required to solve the
problem, the number of citizens who became involved, and the way in
which the authors view their cases. Englewood and Teaneck are
reported by a newspaperman fascinated by the cut and thrust of
interest groups. New York City is viewed by a professional educational
administrator whose focus is not upon persons but upon the astound-

---

* Theodore L. Reller, *Problems of Public Education in the San Francisco Bay
Area,* Institute of Governmental Studies, University of California, Berkeley, California, 1963.

ing weight of numbers; all the other areas studied in this book could be combined and forgotten in one corner of the vast empire of that city. Size brings with it not merely an arithmetic addition in school functions, but a geometrical increase, so that totally new problems are involved and new solutions must be sought. A Berkeley junior high school is seen through the eyes of teachers who candidly view the concerns of the professional teacher caught up in the midst of a great social change.

San Bernardino and Riverside provide an opportunity to compare adjoining communities and their differences in facing the challenge. The problems of the great cities find their echoes in the small towns. In Manhasset on the East Coast, and in Sausalito–Mill Valley on the West Coast, we find many of the issues, actors, and solutions reported on in the large cities.

Such variety has been purposely offered in this book because of the variety it reflects in the larger society. These are the ways Americans have sought to deal with an emerging problem. These ways do not conform easily to a single pattern, yet there are some patterns.

For if there is a variety, there is also some similarity in these cases. The greatest similarity lies in the way in which a problem emerges (affecting interests differently), remedies are proposed to satisfy those claiming injury (resulting in proposals that adversely affect others), resort is had to the mechanisms of formal government (boards, councils, or courts), those officially responsible for solutions frantically seek one which will minimize complex grievances, and in the end there is some resolution of the conflict. If these cases are read at one sitting, one senses that each is echoing the previous one and that, while the names of the actors and agencies may change, their problems, roles, and actions are the same. In the day-to-day grappling with the ever present "now," those involved in one place have little time to reflect on the relationship between their situation and that somewhere else. In the hope of providing some opportunity for reflection and generalization, the following comparative analysis is offered.

CONFLICTS OVER GENERAL VALUES

Innumerable surveys have demonstrated that most Americans are attached to general democratic values, but differ sharply on specific interpretations. Popular sovereignty is enshrined as the cornerstone of democracy; majority rule translates that popular sovereignty into law; but minorities have certain rights protected against the state and even the majority. Through time, education free and open to all has come to be regarded as a necessary ingredient of the democratic system. Prejudice and bigotry are condemned as incompatible with an individualism which emphasizes the importance of a person, regardless of his race, religion, or creed. Throughout these cases one can see the contenders enunciating such democratic values, but one also can see them interpreting these values so as to support their specific interests.

Thus proponents of ending *de facto* segregation who can muster voting support, as in Berkeley and Teaneck, argue the legitimacy of majority decisions and applaud the will of the people. But when electoral processes produce candidates or referenda unfavorable to their interest, that legitimacy and will are criticized as unfair and restrictive; as the Englewood councilman said under the latter conditions, "The hope of little people, it seems, will always be with the courts and state agencies. They work well but exceedingly slow." On the other side, those who resist efforts to eliminate *de facto* segregation have equally equivocal notions about popular sovereignty and majority will. Repeatedly we see such resisters of reform turning to the courts to challenge unfavorable electoral decisions, when they are not applauding favorable electoral outcomes.

Further, we see conflicting interpretations of the meaning of minority rights. A white majority resisting proposals for reform seems to believe that it should define the extent of a minority's rights. But for that minority, such a definition meant *no* rights; hence the minority's recourse to other agencies for help. Thus majority and minority each felt that it should define the meaning of minority rights, each relying upon different instruments for such a definition as the circumstances dictated. Yet each side probably would contend that it supports the democratic creed concerning minority rights. Given the lack of consensus on specific interpretations, rights came to be determined by the application of political power to different decision-making centers in the governmental system.

Such a condition is an invitation to a continuing fight, and yet what might be permanent turmoil is reduced by another consideration. Note that throughout the cases after the struggle had been resolved those most opposed to reform learned to live with it. In Berkeley, Manhasset, Teaneck, or New York City, the reasons for this post-decision reduction of conflict might vary—desires for an improved quality of education, indifference, a sense of inevitability—or simply finding that the once-feared parade of imagined horrors did not exist. This "opinion closure" depresses conflict, thus contributing to the stability of the political system. For if every dispute were to be made permanent, like the blood feuds of Appalachia, the resulting instability could shatter the total system.

The heat of this controversy should not blind us to the historical fact that a somewhat similar fight occurred in rural America in this century over the question of school consolidation. Many of the sub-themes of that earlier fight also appear in the previous pages—reluctance of parents to have their children come into physical contact with the children of other townships or to be bused to a central school because of the physical danger, the travel time involved, the fears of educational quality being diluted, and so on. Yet that rural conflict has been mostly settled today. In most areas where it occurred the consolidated school is the norm, while the old one-room schoolhouses are merely memories, of interest only to the very old.

The American creed's commitments to free and open education and to an individualism unattended by prejudice also became variously interpreted in these cases. On the educational theme, note that no one in these cities argues against open education. Those resisting reform seem to have consciously understood the bleakness of that ground on which to stand. Instead, they offered the alternative of compensatory education, with its often-stated assumption that the quality of minority education was inferior as a consequence of segregated schools. On the other side, those urging reform defined educational quality as something beyond mere compensation, without denying the need for that. For the Negroes, open education meant also racial mixing in school in order to expose their children to those values and outlooks unavailable in the segregated situation; that there is something to their hope seems amply demonstrated in Alan Wilson's article. Contrasting with the foregoing disagreements, note that both reformers and resisters agreed on the need for the best education, not only for their children but for the sake of a better society. Such agreement may account for some signs in schools which have become desegregated that the change is working out better than the resisters feared.

Possibly underlying the conflict over the meaning of open education is another conflict, that over the emphasis upon individualism and the reality of prejudices. The white reformers reported on here seem surprisingly free of bigotry, but it would be most unrealistic to believe that racial prejudice was absent. Prejudice and the fears it occasions may be seen at least by inference—the decrease in number and size of fringe areas in New York City, the Berkeley teachers' fears of violence before desegregation, the assumptions underlying many of the quotations in the Manhasset survey, and, above all, the ever present assertion that if neighborhood schools made compensatory efforts, separate education could be equal education. The neighborhood school thesis seems to tie together the contradictions, on the one hand, between the democratic values of universal education and individualism, and, on the other hand, between individualism and prejudice. Neighborhood schools enable one to support the best education possible for others in their neighborhoods while protecting one's own children from interracial contact and the poorer education which such contact is supposed to bring. Further, supporting neighborhood schools enables one to talk about the values of individualism and education without raising the question of prejudice. Thus a white mother in Englewood said, "I'm not anti anything, except, perhaps, anti-school bus. If these children from Lincoln lived in this area, they would have the right to be here and would be welcomed." It may well be that she was not consciously prejudiced, but from the nonwhite viewpoint neighborhood-school and compensation plans seemed evidence not merely of discrimination but of open bias. Sensitized to an environment where prejudice is on every side, the minority groups viewed opposition to their proposals for any reason as evidence of covert prejudice—although as we saw in the Englewood case, Negroes themselves may divide on strategies.

The tendency to view all opponents of rezoning as racially prejudiced seems unjustified; after all, when farmers earlier opposed busing to a consolidated school for fear of danger to their children and for dislike of the travel time, no racial prejudice was involved. Many observers of the American scene have noted our child-oriented culture's sensitivity to protecting the young from dangers real and imaginary. For many white Americans, expressions of concern for the children may have a component not of racial prejudice but of class prejudice. Elsewhere, upper-middle-class parents have shown no enthusiasm for placing their children in schools with large numbers of children from working-class or immigrant origins. But opponents in

public controversies are not known for their sensitivity to the subtle-
ties of motivations of those on the other side, and this policy area
seems to be no exception.

In this policy controversy as in others, Americans are wont to
ascribe lofty motives and enlist prestigious cultural values to their
proposals. Such actions may seem hypocritical to some, but more
likely they arise out of the very nature of our broad cultural values.
After all, these high aims by their very generality permit, and indeed
encourage, a variety of meanings. When one man's freedom interferes
with another's, both will necessarily justify their reactions under the
broad rubric of liberty, and both will be correct. When one man's
freedom results in unequal treatment or differential acquisition of
rewards for others, this outcome reflects the inherent conflict between
the democratic values of liberty and equality. These competing claims
to freedom and equality most often work themselves out in some kind
of compromise in which neither party gets all that he wants. Such a
resolution does not always work for all groups or all issues, it is true, as
the Negroes have well known over the last century. But the political
and governmental mechanisms of our system operate on this impulse
to compromise, in which nobody gets everything, nobody gets nothing, but everybody gets something. The mechanism of compromise
will next be sketched in as another component of the policy-making
process.

INTEREST-GROUP ACTIVITIES

Americans are surrounded by a clamoring host of special groups
offering an extraordinary opportunity for expressing their interests and
values. This complex of interest groups is the obvious way by which
the citizen can have his interests represented and his values fostered as
democratic theory requires. Such is not the case in all societies. As the
Banfields have shown, two equally small towns, one in southern Italy
and the other in the United States, demonstrate one striking difference. In the American town the local newspaper is filled with stories
of group meetings, petitions, social gatherings, elections, protests—all
reflecting the manifold interests of even the smallest constituency. But
in southern Italy no such interest- or pressure-group activity is detectable.[1] When grievances are felt in our culture, we turn almost automatically to association for redress of grievances and protection of inter-

ests. Such is obviously the case in the controversy over eliminating *de facto* segregation in northern schools. In the welter of groups concerned, it is possible to distinguish certain patterns in their compositions, resources, and strategies.

We begin with the reformers, those initiating the move to eliminate *de facto* segregation. Negro groups are most prominent, notably the National Association for the Advancement of Colored People, the Congress of Racial Equality, and the Urban League. In only one case (Englewood) is there any evidence of division among the Negro groups. There, when the board of education suggested a central sixth-grade school as a first step toward integration, the NAACP and CORE saw this as tokenism while the Urban League found it acceptable; later the boycott of schools was acceptable to some Negroes but not to others. But, with little exception, the Negro groups in these cases spoke with a remarkably unanimous voice on the complaints and solutions before them.

The Negro groups did not stand alone, of course. Their cohorts included ministerial associations, some parent-teacher organizations, branches of national liberal groups (for instance, in Sacramento, the American Civil Liberties Union and the National Council of Jewish Women), and numerous *ad hoc* citizens committees. These citizens committees, as in other public controversies, were designed to provide nonpartisan sponsorship by prestigious community leaders, as in Sacramento and Berkeley. Another form of *ad hoc* citizens committee is that appointed by administrative agencies to establish the facts in a case, as in Manhasset and Sausalito. Such committees invariably supported the reformers with findings of segregation, although never finding it purposely fostered by education officials.

On the other side, those resisting the ending of *de facto* segregation by opposing busing or rezoning proposals show little similarity. Taxpayer groups are found in some places (as in Berkeley), but not in every case. There is no national group to counter the NAACP and CORE in this matter; the efforts of neighborhood-school associations to form a regional organization out of efforts in Teaneck and Englewood came to nothing after one meeting. What similarity we find among the resisters is in their enthusiastic endorsement of the neighborhood-school concept. Only one outright hate group appears in these chronicles, and that was in only one section of the New York City schools. White-supremacy groups, so often present in the South, seem to have played little part in the North on this issue.

There is a third group whose members in some locales appear on one side and elsewhere on the other. That is the municipal press, which in Berkeley opposed integration, in Riverside supported it, in San Bernardino was silent, and in Sacramento was equivocal. The position of the press, as Hickerson concludes from his San Bernardino–Riverside studies, may well be subordinated to the viewpoint of a prevailing community power structure. In Riverside, where that structure was an active reform element, the newspaper reflected it through editorials and news coverage; but in San Bernardino this medium was silent just as the local power structure was "almost totally silent concerning the need for desegregation."

While it seems a reasonable proposition that public policy can be affected by the local power structure, the proposition assumes that a local power structure exists. Research studies indicate that a unified elite dominated by business leaders exists in some places, but that elsewhere no one group dominates decision making, power being shared among many groups.[2] Because the authors of the case reports were not concerned with the role of the power structure, the editors can only conclude that where such a structure exists, it can influence the outcome. But sometimes no such structure exists because power is split—as in New York City.

Another group not always found on the same side is the corps of professional teachers. In Manhasset, teachers seem to have taken the lead in initiating complaints against *de facto* segregation and advertising its disadvantages. But in Berkeley, resisters to reform came in part from a retired-teachers association and some university professors. Galbraith reports among his teaching colleagues there an "unhappiness [which] was not an expression of racial prejudice, but of self-interest. After all, the comfortable middle-class atmosphere of the school they knew would be disrupted, and they would be forced to deal with problems that they would rather not face." What is most noteworthy, however, about the role of the teachers in this controversy is that their voices are not often recorded. One explanation may be the often alleged timidity of public school teachers confronting issues over which their community is sharply and bitterly divided. Possibly their silence results also from a real uncertainty about the effects of educational integration upon the quality of instruction; since there is no conclusive body of evidence on this question, teachers could not appeal to it as experts seeking to provide a rational basis for public policy. Uncertain of their expertise, apprehensive over how proposed changes might affect their own work, highly dependent for positions and promotion upon a board often divided on the question, and influenced by a tradition that teachers are to be non-political, the professional teachers wrote little of the record in these cases.[3]

If these were the groups involved, what can be said of their resources? By resources are meant the pool of money, skills, time, and energy available to influence the outcome. These groups had differential access to resources, so that here as elsewhere in social life some were "more equal" than others. No one resource, including money, is sovereign. The cohesion and morale of one group may overcome the superior financial resources available to its opponents. Circumstances can affect what resources may be used or the conditions of their use; in some cases, spending money can be the "kiss of death" in deciding the outcome.

Surprisingly little money seemed to have been involved in these cases. Of course, there were financial considerations operating in the background, for, as the authors point out, whether the remedy for inferior minority education is compensatory education or elimination of *de facto* segregation, considerable sums of money are needed. Consequently, for those taxpayers to whom any increase in taxes is objectionable, a financial stake may guide their feelings.

Both sides had access to publicity, both that generated within their own organization by meetings and circulars and that transmitted through the formal media of communication. These media have become a not-so-silent partner in the civil-rights controversy. Their orientation usually is to the sensational, which means emphasis on conflict; this has shaped the publicity programs of civil-rights groups, who have sought the public eye in sensational ways in order to publicize their grievances and mobilize support for remedies. Both sides in this controversy might be thought to have equal access to these media, but there is some indication that such is not the case. The condemnation of practices regarded as immoral by Negroes and their partisans carries an emotional charge which the opponents of school integration in the North have been hard put to match. A corollary resource of research findings has been of great utility to the reformers. The facts of housing segregation which produces educational segregation are too overwhelming for the supporters of neighborhood schools to match. Many social scientists have contributed to the pool of research on the reality of segregation effects, a reality which the other side finds difficult to match with the potential future danger to children who must use a bus. The advantage to one side becomes even greater when, as in Englewood, a group can bring in a Congressional committee chairman, national civil-rights leaders, and leading entertainers to back its cause—even when the constitutional grounds for a threatened investigation by that Congressman were very weak. For the media of communication, particularly television, this is headline material, and it helps draw in nationwide support for those who are marching or sitting.

Other resources are available in the skills and status of the competing leaderships. Note the special advantage to the reform leaders of having contact with national organizations which can provide moral, financial, and publicity support. This means that such leadership moves in an environment where the members share a universe of discourse about facts, arguments, and access to government which are not available to the opposing leadership; the latter must rely upon local *ad hoc* groups who often prepare their cases from scratch. An effective leadership can draw from this universe of discourse another asset, namely, skill in communication, whether with supporting leadership echelons, government, or the press. A related factor of some potency is the status of the reform leaders. When high-status members in the community are drawn into the leadership of groups allied with the NAACP and CORE, or into fact-finding committees appointed by local school boards, those resisting reform are disadvantaged. When high-status leaders tend also to be skilled in communication about community affairs, status then tends to reinforce and be reinforced by the leadership skills.

Some mention should be made of the resource of mere numbers, particularly in a democracy where public policy ostensibly reflects the will of a majority. Such majorities do not always support *de facto* segregation, as was seen in Berkeley, Manhasset, and Teaneck. But in other cases the majority seems reluctant to reform; elsewhere on the national scene, we see majorities opposed to other desegregation reforms. The reader gets the feeling that if decisions were made by simply counting heads, *de facto* segregation would be supported more often than it would be rejected.

In the present cases the effect of numbers is unclear. The reformers most often had full support from their racial groups. But, in Manhasset, Negro leaders admitted that before the challenge to the system "only fifteen or twenty percent of the [Negro] people wished for a change in the segregated pattern." And, in New York, Landers reports that, even after the adoption of an open-enrollment program to reduce racial concentrations, this program "now meets with almost complete acceptance from the white community, with grudging tolerance from a good part of the Negro community, and largely with indifference from the Puerto Rican community." Yet leadership, if it is to be effective, must mobilize a maximum number on its side, if for no other reason than to demonstrate to politically sensitive officials that here is an ideal whose time has now come and that failure to support it might bring retribution. The leadership's program is further complicated by the fact that members once mobilized may not always remain that way; the occasional school boycott reported here shows initial support fading relatively quickly.

On the other side, for those resisting reform, many of the same problems existed of mobilizing and retaining support. But this side did have one advantage, for often it could bring the issue to the electorate in the hope of majority support for the status quo. Yet the results here are mixed, for in Berkeley, Manhasset, Teaneck, and Sausalito, efforts to use the electorate to overthrow reform tickets were not successful. One gets the sense that the opponents of reform never mobilized all the potential support which lay in the electorate. This impression is supported by the number of referenda and election results in the North in recent years opposing efforts at elimination of segregation in housing and education. Certainly efforts to combine school districts, especially efforts to consolidate city and suburban schools in a metropolitan area (a possible solution to increasing intracity segregation), may bring to the surface a latent hostility.

In resources of time and energy, the sides seem about equal. Housewives on both sides seem prepared to spend considerable amounts of time and energy in attending meetings, picketing, and organizing details of the campaign. If the number of Negro mothers prepared to go to the streets in Englewood seemed impressively large, one merely need go next door to Teaneck, where an equally large number of white mothers spent time and energy on the opposite side. In any policy controversy, we cannot really know how much of these dual resources are employed. And indeed, if such a measure were possible, it is uncertain what its weight might be in the outcome. If the active, dedicated minority always overcame an apathetic majority, we would long ago have abolished death penalties in this country. Where there are two highly active and opposed interest groups seeking to secure the majority's will, possibly all one can say about the time and energy of the two is that they tend to cancel one another out, but that without these contending forces the nature of the struggle would have been different.

If the resources of these interest groups were similar, a great contrast can be drawn between their strategies. The reformers attempted to avoid appeals to the electorate; even though they sometimes won at the polls, the electoral resort was always thrust upon them by the resisters, who hoped to arouse the majority to see the rightness of their cause. Reformers tended to rely on local or state boards of education or the courts, and like the resisters escalated to higher levels of decision making when defeated at lower levels. The reformers started with the local board of education; the decision here determined the strategy of both sides. If the board supported the reformers, as in Berkeley, the resisters would appeal to a higher state educational agency or the courts, or both. However, if the reformers were unsuccessful with the local board of education, they were the ones who appealed to the higher authority, while the resisters proclaimed the rightness of the decisions arrived at below.

Alternative strategies existed also on the matter of the issues to be emphasized. Both sides argued the need for improved educational opportunities for the Negro, but differed sharply on the means to that general good end. Reformers, while agreeing with the need for compensatory education, were dissatisfied to let the issue lie there, unlike the resisters. The reformers moved either initially or very quickly in a second step to challenge *de facto* segregation. Whether focusing on educational quality or the physical segregation itself, this group emphasized the injury to both Negro and white child from existing policies. Meanwhile, the opponents of reform seemed to have adopted compensatory education as their one solution to the problem. It is instructive that the Negro groups did not assert that physical proximity of their children to the white children would in itself overcome the results of past segregation; for them, it is always both integration and compensation which they seek. But for the opponents of reform the integration efforts were alleged to raise more problems than they settled. Busing was fraught with dangers for the very young; lengthy bus rides unnecessarily cut into the time of the child when he already

had a school close by; and the mixing of students of vastly different
training would lower the educational attainment of the white child.

In some cases, compromises appear between these sharply diverse
solutions. Whereas in San Bernardino the neighborhood-school concept had the standard meaning of sending children only to the school
in their neighborhood, in nearby Riverside this term meant busing
children from a given block to the same school, thereby retaining in
part the imbalances. Another compromise is use of the "multitrack"
system of placement within the same grade. Ostensibly created to
group children of similar educational abilities in order for them to
learn together, it may well have the effect of separating the races
because of differences in educational preparation stemming from previous *de facto* segregation. In Berkeley, Negro groups have begun to
criticize tracking on the ground that it maintains in-school segregation
behind the facade of all-school integration.

Another difference in strategy appeared in the resort to mass
activities of a direct kind. The reformers seemed far more willing to
engage in mass direct action such as marches, demonstrations, boycotts, and sit-ins. This was most evident in Englewood, where there
were sit-ins in the city hall, at the governor's office, at board of
education meetings, and in schools; large crowds assembled for
speeches by Adam Clayton Powell and James Farmer; children's boycotts of schools alleged to be segregated, and adult boycotts of merchants; picketing of schools; attempts to register Negro children in
white schools; and a great number of rallies and marches. Mass direct
action has been noted in such large cities as New York, Boston,
Chicago, and Milwaukee, as well as in such small cities as New
Rochelle, New York, and some reported in this book. Very little mass
direct action appears on the part of resisters, aside from picketing and
a boycott by white mothers in Teaneck against what the school board
had done—occurring about the same time, ironically enough, as Negro
mothers in next-door Englewood were boycotting their schools because of what the board had *not* done.

In this differential use of such action there are clearly different
values reflected. Outside of New York City and possibly Sacramento,
the towns here analyzed are predominantly white and middle-class,
often upper-middle-class. The political life-style of this class has not
traditionally included use of mass direct action, possibly because other

methods of achieving political ends are available to it. But in the Negro segments of northern cities, the political life-style has in the last decade been greatly influenced by the success of the direct mass-action techniques used in the South to overcome its widely publicized discrimination. Application of these techniques, born in the turmoil of the hot streets of Birmingham and Selma, to the sedate and well-kept suburban residences of the North seemed a likely move.

After all, such mass direct action serves a number of purposes. It brings dramatically to the attention of public officials complaints which no longer can be passed off as merely those of a few malcontents, and thus helps put such issues on the agenda for decisions which can, in one way or another, modify the objectionable status quo. Mass direct action also has other functions. It provides the members of the protesting groups a sense of identification with others who share their feelings, an outlet for frustrations which arise from the sense that no one is listening to them, and, if the movement is successful, an enhanced sense of importance as individuals—supporting that individualism which the democratic creed proclaims. For those who lead direct action, it can help justify their *raison d'être* by uniting membership in the direction desired by the leaders, and if successful, it enhances the standing of the leader in the eyes of his followers and group decision makers. Thus mass direct action has a far more complicated set of functions than may be realized by the general public which, often unfamiliar with the techniques, becomes exasperated because these are unfamiliar—and just a little bit unmannerly to boot.

In adopting this strategy the reformers enlisted resources which their opponents seldom would choose. For the opponents, appeal to the electorate was the traditional strategy for resolving conflicts—and far more mannerly. Thus the resisters in Englewood and elsewhere insisted upon adherence both to due process of law and to order—by which they meant the orderly method of doing things as they were done in the past. For the Negroes, the standard process was not sufficient. It had led to the educational segregation which they regarded as deplorable, and it had left them unheard and the conditions unchanged.

To summarize, there is some system in the seeming confusion of interest-group activities. There is a line-up of groups opposing and supporting reform of *de facto* segregation. These groups strive to realize specific values which are always translated in terms of the general cultural values of the democratic system. Both groups possess certain resources, which are differentially employed. The strategies open to each side are shaped both by available resources and by differential access to various decision-making centers. These factors cannot be neatly weighed and evaluated, for there are contingencies involved. Contingency plays a role in creating uncertainties, as was seen in the case of Sacramento or Riverside, in which a school burning was the event leading ultimately to the modification, if not elimination, of *de facto* segregation. There is no evidence reported that anybody started these fires in order to set in motion the ensuing chains of events. Rather the fires seem to be instances of those unexpected crises which occur in the course of a community's life and have unexpected consequences in rearranging the structure of public policy. As the Thalidomide controversy of 1962 resulted in the drastic reshaping of laws regulating the manufacture of drugs, as the earthquake of 1906 effected the redevelopment of San Francisco, and as the mass bombing of England in World War II accelerated town and country planning, so it is that unplanned events can restructure the distribution of public rewards implicit in public policies. This recognition of contingency cautions us against overconfidence in planning, although plan we must if we seek to avoid being mere victims of events.

Under conditions where some uncertainty may exist, analysis of available strategies and resources cannot offer one complete confidence in his predictions, but some things seem rather constant. Whatever the strategies employed, changes in *de facto* segregation seem to have come about only after pressure by those complaining of the segregation. All disadvantaged ethnic groups do not always cooperate: in San Bernardino–Riverside, the Negroes and Mexican-Americans did not cooperate, and in New York City the Puerto Ricans were relatively indifferent to integration efforts. But in no case reported here did the change come *before* the Negroes organized to seek it. This may be nothing more than a demonstration of the old principle of social life that only the squeaky wheel gets oiled. But just because it is a truism its validity in real life is not thereby weakened. One finding is clear—if the minority ethnic group disadvantaged by school segregation does not act to do something about its grievance, nothing much gets done.

THE FRAMEWORK OF GOVERNMENT

This interplay of interest groups takes place within the formal structure for governing education. As in all such group activities, the main thrust is to secure and promote a particular value by getting it embedded in law. In brief, both sides wanted the government to do or not do something, in this case eliminate or continue *de facto* segregation.

Most laymen have a picture in their heads of the operation of government which encompasses such elements as passing laws, adjudicating disputes, and administering public policies. These are what we may call the *manifest* functions of government, those carried out by all governments, whether democratic or authoritarian. Yet the formal structure and process of government are accompanied by what we may term *latent* functions, which are not immediately obvious and not always consciously intended by those involved in them. It is generally recognized that the primary function of government is the regulation of conflicting interests. Government may also serve to unify its different constituencies by socializing them to accept a proper way of acting—such as obedience to the law and patriotism.

Such governing, however, does not operate in any automatic fashion, because there is always a certain amount of discretion about how the governing mechanism may operate. One area of discretion arises from the differing motivations of the officials who operate the mechanism, a consideration to be examined in the next section. But discretion may arise also from the fact that the constitutions which governmental mechanisms reflect are not always specific in their dictates. Thus, in our Constitution, the grants of power to Congress to regulate commerce among the several states has created throughout our history a conflict over exactly what was meant by "commerce" and exactly who may be regulated and in what fashion. Discretion arises not only from the ambiguity of the Constitution but also from the fact that constitutional dictates may distinguish between what governing officials *must* do and *may* do. Positive authorizations as well as taboos are a different form of constitutional dictate from those creating permissive limits within which officials may operate. Moreover, constitutional dictates may sometimes conflict. Thus the dictate to provide a fair trial may conflict with the dictate not to abridge freedom of the press, an issue squarely joined when a defendant claims that excessive publicity prevents his getting an unbiased jury. Someone must decide, that is, exercise discretion, among competing authorizations and taboos.

Some of these considerations have application to the cases in this book. The Supreme Court of the United States, as chief interpreter of our Constitution, had after 1954 decreed that school segregation explicitly posited on racial grounds was forbidden. But the Court had not yet settled the corollary question of whether school segregation resulting from *de facto* housing segregation was equally forbidden. Hence it makes a great deal of difference to local educational policy whether state superior courts have decided against such segregation or have been silent on the matter. Note that in California, after a decision by that state's supreme court, measures to eliminate *de facto* segregation were constitutional and indeed to be encouraged. But no such dictate to local education bodies existed in New Jersey at the time of the Englewood–Teaneck controversy. In California, proponents of reform were encouraged in their efforts to eliminate segregation because they could justifiably claim a positive authorization for their cause. But in New Jersey, where such authorization was in doubt because not yet authenticated, the cause of reform was restrained.

For example, look at the situation in Sacramento, where both state-court decisions and state statutes differed from those in Englewood and Teaneck. The Sacramento school-district criteria for setting school boundaries were sixfold, including the factor of ethnic balance. In such a case it becomes very important in the policy outcome to determine which of the criteria has priority, for if the ethnic factor can be devalued by local officials out of preference for other criteria, the school board can operate within permissive limits and produce a policy sustaining *de facto* segregation with the authority of law. But when state courts and statutes emphasize the priority of ethnic balance, then the local board no longer has such permissive limits available to it. Nor does the matter get settled there, for the question arises: Does the ethnic-factor priority apply only in creating new school boundaries or does it apply to existing boundaries as well? The Sacramento school district, operating within assumed permissive limits, applied it only to new boundaries, and it was against this decision that reformers secured a court decision extending the ethnic-balance criterion to existing boundaries.

This is why, as Alexis de Tocqueville noted over a century ago, in our system all political questions eventually become judicial ones. Because positive authorizations from the Constitution or higher bodies cannot always be specific enough to cover every eventuality, interest groups seek the support of government to link positive authorization to a discretionary action which they desire; but, if successful, they must face a challenge in the courts by disaffected parties. Thus the formal structure of the Constitution gives us only the broad outline of the dynamic process of governing. It also affects interest-group strategy, as was seen earlier, since a group's choice of remedy depends upon estimates of which part of the structure is likely to aid it.

A special consideration in the structure of our government is the factor of federalism, which operated repeatedly in these cases. In Sacramento, the first solution to the burned-school issue proposed by the board moved the superintendent to confer with the State Department of Education and its special section dealing with potential discrimination. In this conference, state and local officials explored their responsibilities under the state law and court decisions, and although there were no specific dictates handed down by the higher agency, it was clear in what followed that the existence of the state law must have influenced the local board's deliberations. In Sausalito, when its board sought state help, it obtained a report on the alleged segregation, which defined racial imbalance while absolving the board of intentional discrimination. This same report noted the necessity of help from the county, state, and federal governments, a recognition that in the federal system cooperation is increasingly necessary for solving some of a community's more pressing problems. In the New Jersey cases, reformers opposing the local board appealed both to the governor and to the State Education Commission to redress their grievances. Note the care with which higher state agencies treated the sensitivity of local boards in these conflicts. They never condemned the local boards for a prevalent school segregation, accepting at face value the boards' claims that such conditions resulted from existing housing segregation. But the higher agencies always insisted that the segregation must be changed, even while mollifying local feelings.

Little is said in these cases about the role of the national government, though it is clear that the role has been growing. The Supreme Court decision of 1954 has laid the groundwork for all of the cases reviewed here. The Court's later refusal to overturn desegregation

decisions by state and local education agencies is in keeping with its
explicit statement in the 1954 decision that separation could not be
equal. Until very recently, however, the national government had but
a minimal contact with local education, unlike the governments in
most nations today. It is likely that recent education laws of the Great
Society program will have effect upon local education, although its
exact direction seems unclear at this point. A question which remains
unanswered is the degree to which *de facto* segregated schools may
receive federal funds under these new laws. In the first few years of
their administration, there have been some efforts to refuse funds to
such schools; but when that was attempted against the school system
of Chicago, the city's political leadership seemed to have had enough
influence in Washington to get the order countermanded. What will
happen in future challenges is unclear, but political pressures on both
sides will be tremendous. If the past record of federalism in roads and
social welfare is any guide, the provision of federal funds to implement education programs at the state and local level will carry an
increasing number of restrictions upon local discretion. Thus *de facto*
segregation may be more thoroughly attacked than it has been in the
past.

In the absence of national control a variety of policies has arisen
at the local level over *de facto* segregation. Note not merely the
variety of programs which emerged in New York City to handle that
educational Goliath, but also the contrast between that city and neighboring Manhasset. Policies appropriate for the city, such as the educational park, are meaningless in the small town where needs and
resources are something else. The Princeton plan of pairing schools
may work in the big city, where there are enough schools to create a
satisfactory number of pairs, but not in a Berkeley or a Riverside,
where the number of schools is small yet more than two. Variety exists
also in such minor matters as the titles, composition, selection, and
tenure of the educational boards. Local variety is a function not
merely of federalism, which encourages decentralized policy making,
but also of the heterogeneity of the American people, whose different
backgrounds produce different structures and policies.

A final consideration of the legal framework of government is
seen in the check and balance mechanisms which appear in every
case. Decisions of a local board are countered by decisions of higher
education agencies, courts, or the electorate. The situation in Engle-

wood exemplifies this notion of partitioning power. There the school board's budget is overseen by a Board of School Estimate on which the mayor and two councilmen have a majority. As a consequence, school board efforts to innovate were frustrated by a council and mayor seemingly responsive to another constituency; certainly the results of the mayor's opinion survey and of the subsequent referendum seemed to support him. Things can sometimes get quite complicated. In Berkeley, reformers fought a recall election with a court challenge. Although the courts decided against their claim, the decision delayed the election until the reform supporters were back in full force from vacation and thus defeated the recall. In Teaneck, opponents of reform simultaneously attacked in the courts and in a school board election, although to no avail.

All of these considerations point up the curious ambivalence of Americans toward governmental powers. As surveys have demonstrated repeatedly, Americans think very highly of their form of democracy but very poorly of the politicians who operate that system. Too, while decrying power exercised at one level, they seek it themselves at another level. The national government is regarded by many as the embodiment of evil when it seeks to operate upon some matter thought to be of local concern only. But those who believe this, will often praise Washington for its operation in another local concern. Or they will support government at the local level because it is "closer," even though this can mean that it may more restrict one's personal affairs. One explanation of this ambivalence lies in Americans' heightened notion of self-interest. In baldest terms, what we may see here is the working out of the belief that whatever *interferes* with one's interests is *bad*, whether it is local or national power, while whatever *supports* one's interests is *good*, no matter at what level of government. It may be too severe to judge such belief as hypocritical. After all, our democratic system does place great, if not prime, emphasis upon the value of individualism.

Possibly all of our governmental principles and mechanisms spring from the notion of the importance of the individual and of promoting his welfare. What happens, of course, is that people divide on the question of what constitutes personal welfare, interests thus come into conflict, and government necessarily is invoked, as our system permits, to regulate this conflict. Necessarily in the outcome some are disadvantaged while others are not, and the losers seek recourse in court or at the polls while condemning the unreasonableness of the government which hurt them. It seems to us that those who condemn in blanket terms this search for self-interest are perhaps unconsciously condemning also the system of government which fosters such self-realization. The formal government of our democratic system, in far more ways than are contemplated by the layman, does reflect the basic impulses of a widely varied population. As such, it necessarily is embroiled in the conflict among competing claims of self-interest, which means it is involved in politics. This politics may be messy, disorderly, and sometimes irrational, but as noted earlier, we Americans have never been noted for the orderliness of our philosophy, our lives, our manners, or our interests. Why then should we expect from the government what does not lie in the constituency?

THE ROLE OF PUBLIC OFFICIALS

All of the preceding factors impinge upon the public officials whose duty is to make decisions. It is necessary to analyze the official separately from the legal framework, for he is not a phonograph who automatically reproduces the law. When, as the case often is, that law is ambiguous or delegates discretion in administering it, what the official does is a function of his values, his perception of his role, and pressures upon him.

The important point here is that the same authority may be applied differently with a resulting difference in policies. Most instructive on this point are the findings in the San Bernardino–Riverside case. In these adjoining communities, both boards of education and superintendents moved with a pace and achieved results which were obviously different. While in both cases change occurred only after pressure from the Negro communities, the San Bernardino board reluctantly appointed an advisory committee to examine Negro charges of discrimination, and even in this move had to be prodded by the State Department of Education. In Riverside, the board reaction, while hardly prompt, was more adaptive than its neighbor's. In the former, the superintendent actively led the resisters, while in the latter the superintendent led the reformers. Even the superintendents' staffs differed, reflecting the prevailing attitudes of their superiors and boards. Note, too, that different policies emerged from these different stances. Thus in these two cities, where the same state constitution, state-supreme-court directive, and later, state law operated with ostensibly equal force, different official attitudes produced different policies.

Differences arise even within a single community when the membership of the board or the superintendency changes hand. In Berkeley, when the issue first arose in early 1958, officials were termed by the author as "reluctant" and staff members "cautious." By mid-1958, with a new superintendent, while the board was still reluctant to accept recommendations of a citizens' committee and its finding of discrimination, the new superintendent backed the report with "persistent recommendation" and had already undertaken programs of compensatory education "despite the more than passive resistance of too many staff members." When in mid-1962 the board was forced to turn to charges of *de facto* segregation in the schools, the superintendent and the board supported all but one of a series of recommendations for eliminating such discrimination. The author of this case study clearly states that this superintendent's report was "most responsible for Berkeley's pioneering role in finding solutions to interracial problems." His successor did more than merely continue that support, for he has in recent years led in the movement to eliminate *de facto* segregation in the elementary schools. In Sausalito is visible a similar pattern of an early board and superintendent moving slowly to meet charges of discrimination, followed by a later set of officials who met Negro demands much more fully.

We should be clear on the matrix of claims within which officials must operate and which help account for differential policy responses. Interest groups, authorizations by higher authority, personal values, and role expectations create four major sets of claims with which they must deal, and whose content and intensity vary with time and place. The same interest group varies in size, resources, and program from place to place. For example, the results obviously will differ among communities, depending upon whether the ethnic group or the taxpayers' association is well or poorly mobilized, financed, and led. Different mixes of interest groups create different pressures upon the public officials. Further, we have seen how the positive authorization which operates upon these officials varies from state to state within the union, depending upon each state's constitution, statutes, and court decisions. The role expectations of these officials are not always the same either. One board of education member may perceive his role to represent taxpayer groups, who are more concerned with an economical budget than with improving educational quality; another may operate from the reverse perception. While obviously not all the details were provided in the preceding cases, it does seem as though in some places the board member's expectation was that the superintendent would exercise a policy-innovation role, while elsewhere the board seemed to expect itself to be the source of innovation.

Finally, as if the preceding considerations did not complicate things enough, the varying values of these officials contributed possibly the most to producing different results. Thus, does the official believe that disadvantaged ethnic groups should have their grievances redressed even if this puts new and special burdens upon the existing educational system, or does he believe that these grievances should not be settled in such a fashion as to threaten the existing order? Is a popular representative on a board placed there to represent the dominant or majority will of the community, or is he to decide in light of all the facts available to him what is best, regardless of what the majority wishes? Should a superintendent respond to the dominant viewpoint of the community which hires him, even though it means supporting policies which are professionally and even personally objectionable, or should he respond to a professional directive, hoping that the community will in time come around to seeing things his way? Different men with the same authority give different answers to such questions and so provide different solutions to problems before them.

While we may analytically separate and evaluate each of these four sets of claims which focus upon the public official, enough has been offered here to suggest that they are not very amenable to quantification and hence to any kind of precise predictions. But some inferences do seem reasonable, even though general. If the claim of positive authorization upon the official is specific and demanding, with little option or discretion, other claims upon him will be subordinated. When the law tells him that he *must* desegregate a specific school, he cannot tell other groups or himself that he can do otherwise, if he wishes to remain in the office. As Jack Peltason has demonstrated in his study of the role of federal judges in enforcement of the Supreme Court order against segregated schools in the South, when a district judge was specific in his demands, the school officials complied, using the judge as a scapegoat to explain the compliance to the local community.[4] When one of the judges temporized or otherwise contributed to obstruction on the question, then local boards were free to avoid compliance. Given the widespread tendencies of northern courts to uphold plans eliminating *de facto* segregation, educational officials can generally expect positive authorization if they exercise leadership in changing segregation, despite the challenges of disaffected interest groups.

However, if the positive authorizations are not specific, and the permissive limits of policy making are thereby widened, the other claims upon an official become more important. In this case, the increasing pressure of ethnic groups to reduce educational imbalances become more important in determining policy outcomes. Note our earlier emphasis upon the finding that reform took place only *after* ethnic groups' pressure to secure it. This is so not merely because of the weight of their numbers, but because the prevailing judicial opinion, which is supportive of integration, operates as a shotgun behind the door to induce public officials to redress imbalance. This occurs even when the local educational officials are reluctant to do so. Among the factors influencing desegregation in such cases, the contribution of officials' values may be of minor significance.

If the law permits discretion, if the interest groups are of equal force and their claims of equal validity, then under these conditions there is a correspondingly greater freedom for the play of the personal values of officials. We would normally expect in such cases that the policy outcomes would be more varied. We need to know, therefore, a great deal more than we do now about the role expectations and value preferences of educational officials at the community level. If they were free to make choices in this matter, would most superintendents and boards of education prefer to integrate or to retain the physical segregation—or to compromise with some form of compensatory education? What are their role perceptions? Are there important differences in values and perceptions between the elective and the appointed educators? At this point, all we can say is that we know little systematically about this matter, and that some kinds of differences probably exist. For students of the politics of education this is a field of inquiry which should rate high on the agenda of future research.

EDUCATIONAL DESEGREGATION POLICY OUTCOMES

A distinction must be drawn between organizational and substantive policies. Organizational policies involve location of authority. When authority on the question of *de facto* segregation is decentralized, great variety occurs in substantive policies, those involving decisions about what is to be done. When organizational authority is more centralized, in state constitutions, statutes, or court decisions, then substantive policies are more uniform. If there is more likelihood of changing school segregation in the latter case, as there seems to be, it becomes very important for both reformers and resisters to determine where authority lies. Reformers then will seek organizational policy changes which escalate authority to higher levels, while resisters will strive to de-escalate it.

The case of rural-school consolidation is illustrative. Before educators could improve the quality of rural education (substantive policy), they found it imperative to change the location of the decision centers (organizational policy). This meant achieving a state statute or constitutional amendment moving authority to the county and away from the township. The organizational policy change at the state level created an organizational policy change at the county and local level —all necessary before major substantive policy change was possible.

An examination of the substantive policy outcomes in the present cases shows that complete desegregation occurred only in Manhasset. Elsewhere, the desegregation was partial, affecting one or at most a few schools, utilizing a variety of schemes. Further, complete or partial desegregation was linked everywhere with compensatory education. Clearly, a fourth policy outcome would be that in which no desegregation occurs at all.

The focus here is not upon the specific contents of these policies and their rationales, but rather upon the diversity of the American system which is represented in these various answers to a social problem. Here we see reflected the proposition advanced in the first chapter, that the American people lack a uniform doctrine about most public problems. Definition and awareness of any problem vary, as do the consequent alternatives offered for solution. While this undoctrinaire quality may arise out of distinctive cultural traits in our history, one need not get too mystical in explaining it. After all, we are a people of varying resources, preferences, and needs, and as we gather together in our cities, each city yields a different "mix" of resources, preferences, and needs, which in turn gives rise to varying answers to public problems.

Clearly, *needs* vary widely. A community's needs, in education or elsewhere, are very much a function of size. Comparison of New York City and Manhasset is illustrative of this point. In Manhasset, with 17,000 population, the problem arose over only one school. But in New York City, where the student population alone was over one million, the problem involved scores of schools. Note, too, that an increase in population produces a similar increase in the alternative policy solutions. Landers makes clear that for New York City there is no one plan which will solve the problem, but that a battery of solutions is necessary. New York City *needs* are great, as are the array of administrative arrangements for eliminating *de facto* segregation. Even so, however, as late as the fall of 1965, only about 50,000 ghetto school children in New York had transferred under various programs, although more than one half the students were involved either through transfer or through contact with transferees.

Difference in *preferences* also affect the diversity of policy outcomes. Clearly, the larger the population, the larger the number of preferred solutions. But variety of preferences does not exist merely in the largest cities; even in the smallest place cited (Marin City), there were different views on the program of limited merger with Sausalito. There is not even agreement within the segregated group. Different preferences also arise among public officials from the matrix of forces described earlier. All of these preference variations stem from different life-styles, which affect definitions of problems and available resources for solving problems. Yet a homogeneous life-style such as that found in Manhasset does not yield a single preference set. Even persons similarly placed in the social order differ among themselves as to what should be done.

Finally, to understand the existence and diversity of policies, one should comprehend that even where there may be an agreement on needs and preferences, the *resources* available may vary and so affect the policy outcome. As Landers notes, a school-pairing system may work in a large city with a large pool of potential receiving and sending schools but be totally inapplicable in a smaller place where the pool is sharply reduced or nonexistent. Similarly, where large sums of money are needed for desegregation, not all communities have financial resources available for it. Cities vary widely in available financial resources, depending upon residential valuation, the presence of taxable industries, and the use of an income tax. As a consequence, communities of similar preferences may have different resources and hence different policies, as they may when resources are similar and preferences are different.

This intermixture of needs, preferences, and resources across the sweep of American communities seems to account more for the variety of public policy than does the more remote explanation of historical factors. As an example of the slipperiness of historical explanations in the policy area, and as an illustration of Americans' undoctrinaire approach to policies, one might examine the ostensibly widespread belief in the superiority of local control of government. This belief has long been regarded as a general characteristic of Americans and an aspect of the constitutional principle of federalism, with its long and continuing influence upon our government. It can be argued, however, that the situation is not quite so clear-cut.[5]

In a number of policy areas, Americans have been perfectly willing to surrender exclusive local control over a given matter to higher governmental authorities. In roads, social welfare, and agriculture, a transfer of power over policy has taken place. In all three areas, at the beginning of the republic, matters were handled privately and certainly locally. For some time, roads were maintained by individuals, each taking care of that stretch which went by his place. Social welfare was primarily private or church welfare; dependents and defectives were handled by the family involved or by church charity. Agriculture was a matter for a farmer and nature, with the private market an invisible but real partner in the operation. Yet through time private effort yielded to community, township, and county regulation and taxes, then to state participation, and in our time to a full-scale federal participation through grant-in-aid expenditures. Private social welfare yielded to local and state public authorities, and after the 1930's to massive federal intervention when localities and states were overwhelmed by the demands for help and when the electorate seemed to endorse heartily somebody's doing something. In the farm marketplace, state and national governments now participate through acreage controls, commodity quotas, and price supports. The point here is not to evaluate all this as good or bad. The point is to demonstrate a long-run tendency by Americans to throw away the supposedly sacred doctrine of local control when the circumstances seem incompatible with the doctrine.

Such a trend is detectable in the field of education, although certainly local control is far more extensive in this area than in the three discussed above. Yet even without the current federal involvement in education, local control, in the sense of community control, is far removed from the earliest days of the republic. The massive movement of the nineteenth century for free public education brought in its wake extensive state control. The state government is now a powerful partner of local communities in setting educational policies, with local control remaining but operating within the discretionary standards set by state policies. The time is long past when an itinerant schoolmaster, paid in food, lodging, and possibly a small fee by local families, could satisfy local needs for education.

Thus the diversity of educational policy outcomes in the American system also stems from Americans' changing interpretation of an ostensibly inflexible and sacred doctrine of local control. Communities differ in how much or how little outside control they will sustain, as has been seen in these cases. But in every case, whether in California or in New Jersey, local insistence upon segregation yielded ultimately to the legal requirements imposed by government at the state level. It may be too sweeping to assert that without decisions by superior bodies none of the communities here studied would have moved toward desegregation, but there is a clear sense that far less would have been accomplished had we existed under a system of truly local control in education.

SPECULATION ON FUTURE POLICY DIRECTIONS

The local-control doctrine may be even further diluted by current changes in the population structure of the great metropolises. In 1910, 73 percent of Negroes lived in rural areas, but a half century later 73 percent lived in urban centers. The increasing urban concentration of American Negroes is beginning to render meaningless efforts at eliminating school segregation within the cities proper. Galbraith, in commenting upon the Berkeley situation, pinpointed the problem: "local control makes local solutions to ending racial segregation difficult if not impossible. . . . The problem of integration and segregation is more than a local community problem; it is a regional and state problem." With a gigantic school district in the core city and a host of smaller districts in the surrounding suburbs, it is becoming increasingly difficult to find enough nonwhite children inside the city to eliminate segregation. Such elimination would logically require treating this multiplicity of districts in a metropolis as a combined, single super-district, within which the pupil-transfer programs could operate.[6]

The explosive potential of increasingly fostering ghetto schools under present conditions has been attested to by James B. Conant, but an equally explosive potential abides in the logical solution of a super-district. The attractiveness of the concept of the neighborhood school, the latent fears and hostility of the white suburbanites toward the nonwhite, and the ever-present resentment of any government policy which restricts us—all operate to make the logical solution an invitation to the greatest fight over education which this nation has known. It seems unlikely that this struggle can be avoided, because there are census estimates that the concentration of nonwhites inside the cities will continue to rise in decades to come and because ethnic leaders are, if anything, increasing their demands to eliminate educational restrictions. Thus there is a need as never before in the history of American education for those interested in the continuing improvement of the quality of education to apply all possible reason, understanding, and skill in order to reduce the conflict to manageable levels and to shape the nature of the final outcome.

Whether the conflict takes place within a city, a metropolitan area, a state, or a region, the authors hope that this book has produced some suggestions about how a critical policy problem arises, develops, and is resolved. This chapter has suggested some conclusions, a few of which should be highlighted. The general cultural values of the American system offer no specific guidelines for the specific situation, for these values are subject to differing interpretations and to conflicting impulses. The nonwhites' impulse to equality of treatment runs counter to other Americans' impulse to have freedom of association with those they regard as their own kind. One man's definition of freedom of association as limited to his kind counters another man's definition as freedom to associate with other kinds. Yet we can hope that underlying such conflict of value is a standard of decency of treatment of all people, a standard to which humane, intelligent, and reasonable men and women may rally. The responsibility to lead those who are uncertain and to soothe those who are hostile and fearful is the greatest domestic responsibility facing our civic leadership. If the responsibility is denied or avoided, the consequences for social disharmony and damage to the best in the American tradition are evident.

For those seeking reform, it is clear from these cases and from our history that social change does not come without a precipitating agent. In bluntest terms, the elimination of *de facto* segregation seems to come only when the segregated start to do something about it. Group action is one of the critical keys of social change, and awareness of the importance of that key can only serve to embolden aggrieved groups to seek further remedies in action. This awareness indicates no lessening of the potential conflicts mentioned above. Parents of ghetto school children can look to the history of other disadvantaged minority groups in America's past to read the lesson there that advantages are secured and enjoyed only as the result of cohesive, persistent effort. Social analysts are correct in observing that no other minority has had the Negroes' special disadvantages of slavery and color to overcome. But awareness of these liabilities, seen as unjust to those experiencing them, may serve not only to increase frustration but also to invigorate efforts "to secure the blessings of liberty to ourselves and our posterity."

Another critical key in this situation is the thrust of state or federal law, reflected in statute or court decision, in facilitating or blocking social change. This chapter has emphasized how such positive authorization, with all of the legitimacy and power which it implies, is crucial in eliminating *de facto* segregation when that condition has been challenged. It is crucial because it limits the discretion of educational officials in avoiding reform, it provides an opportunity for a resolution arrived at after thorough debate and evaluation by all involved (thus avoiding the stamp of arbitrariness), and it serves as a guide to the law and order which most Americans regard highly. Local officials facing an unhappy majority opposing reform can find within the law's arch a protection against the storm, and reenforcement for doing what most of them may want to do anyhow.

Finally, in the matter of the rationale justifying the elimination of *de facto* segregation, the authors find much merit in Landers' suggestion that the strongest argument lies in explaining the benefit to white, as well as to Negro, children in sharing their educational experiences.

The existence of *de facto* segregation is overwhelmingly clear, as is its effect upon nonwhite children. But more needs to be known and transmitted about its effects upon the segregated white children. For one reason, such information is needed because white parents find it difficult to empathize with the conditions facing children not of their color or life-style. This difficulty is understandable because their children, or those close to their place in life, are the only children they know. Further, it is hard to involve ourselves in the lives of the less fortunate; the emotional costs fend us off. But if it could be made clearer to the white parent that the continuance of *de facto* segregation reduces the excellence of the education which his own children receive, such a finding is one he may be able to perceive and understand. Edwards, and others in this volume, have noted that excellence in education means more than exposure to books, that it encompasses exposure to all aspects of the world in which the child will spend his years. Failure to have contact with the varieties of American life, particularly in the early formative years, means that his education is incomplete, his preparation for life insufficient, and the consequences for his future role as a citizen most serious.

Possibly amid the swirl of battle chronicled in the pages of this book many have lost sight of the fact that it is the *child* who should be our main concern, the child to be educated fully to participate in a meaningful existence. Antagonists are not without concern for their children in this dispute, of course, but too often one senses greater concern for the adults' values, wishes, and fears. He who cries "Never" to another who shouts "Now" may be more wrapped up in the adult world than in that of the child. If so, the chances for resolving the conflict are reduced—which means that the chances for improved education are also reduced.

For those whose attitudes are completely set against school integration, leaders armed with facts are needed to calm their worst fears. For those whose attitudes are attuned only to immediate change, leaders armed with facts are needed to teach the difference between the possible and the desirable. For those uncertain of where the right lies, leaders are needed to raise that banner of decent treatment of all people which is our best heritage for our children. These are great demands upon leadership. They are also great for the layman. But to realize a standard of decency for our children, these demands must be met.

Like all who teach, we live with hope.

NOTES

CHAPTER 1

[1] For a clearly drawn model and analysis of decision making on education in four suburbs of New York, see Warner Bloomberg, Jr., Morris Sunshine, with Thomas J. Fararo, *Suburban Power Structures and Public Education: A Study of Values, Influence, and Tax Effort* (Syracuse: Syracuse University Press, 1963). Their bibliography at pp. 171–174 is a useful introductory guide to the literature on the politics of education.

[2] *Ibid.,* p. 10.

[3] For some of the ambivalence on the equality question, see John H. Schaar, "Some Ways of Thinking About Equality," *Journal of Politics,* November, 1964, 867–895; Robert E. Lane, "The Fear of Equality," *American Political Science Review,* March, 1959, 35–51. For a systematic analysis of Americans' verbal behavior which shows this ambivalence, see Herbert McClosky, "Consensus and Ideology in American Politics," *Ibid.,* June, 1964, 361–382, or James W. Prothro and Charles M. Grigg, "Fundamental Principles of Democracy: Bases of Agreement and Disagreement," *Journal of Politics,* May, 1960, 276–294.

[4] Bloomberg and Sunshine, *loc. cit.*

[5] For a fine systematic study of the relationship between ambition and decisions, see Joseph A. Schlesinger, *Ambition and Politics: Politi-*

cal Careers in the United States (Chicago: Rand McNally, 1966). John F. Kennedy's *Profiles in Courage* is a classic analysis of this phenomenon.

[6] For a particularly well integrated study of how these various sets of claims operate on public actors, see James D. Barber, *Power in Committees: An Experiment in the Governmental Process* (Chicago: Rand McNally, 1966).

[7] The literature on this process is very extensive. For a good, recent overview, see Daniel J. Elazar, *American Federalism: A View from the State* (New York: Crowell, 1966), or Aaron Wildavsky (ed.), *American Federalism in Perspective* (Boston: Little, Brown, 1967), *passim.*

CHAPTER 2

[1] James S. Coleman *et al., Equality of Educational Opportunity* (Washington, D.C.: National Center for Educational Statistics, U.S. Government Printing Office, 1966), p. 218.

[2] *Ibid.,* p. 219.

[3] *Ibid.,* p. 218.

[4] Mrs. Marian Fox Graves, Director, "A Six Year Evaluation of the White Plains Racial Balance Plan," presented to the public by Superintendent of Schools Carroll F. Johnson, October 16, 1967. For an excellent summary, see Leonard Buder, "Good Marks for Integration," *New York Times,* Sunday, October 23, 1967, p. E-9.

[5] Coleman *et al., op. cit.,* p. 40.

[6] *Ibid.,* p. 22.

[7] Alan B. Wilson, *Educational Consequences of Segregation in a California Community* (Berkeley: Survey Research Center, University of California, 1966, mimeographed), p. 41.

[8] H. L. Shapiro, "Revised Version of UNESCO Statement on Race," *American Journal of Physical Anthropology,* New Series, 10 (1952), 362–368.

[9] Gunnar Myrdal, *An American Dilemma: The Negro Problem and Modern Democracy* (New York: Harper and Row, 1962).

[10] Louis E. Lomax, *The Negro Revolt* (New York: New American Library, 1963).

[11] James B. Conant, *The American High School Today* (New York: McGraw-Hill Book Co., 1959).

[12] August B. Hollingshead, *Elmtown's Youth, the Impact of Social*

Classes on Adolescents (New York: Wiley, 1949), p. 173, and Morris Krugman, "The Culturally Deprived Child in School," *NEA Journal*, L (April, 1961), 23–24.

[13] T. Bentley Edwards, *Cultural Patterns of Differentiated Youth* (Berkeley, Calif.: University of California, 1965, mimeographed). (Evaluation Report of HEW Grant No. 63228, under the direction of Joseph D. Lohman.)

[14] Fred T. Wilhelms and Dorothy Westby-Gibson, "Grouping: Research Offers Leads," *Educational Leadership*, XVIII (April, 1961), 410–413.

[15] Nathaniel Hickerson, "Comparisons Between Negro and Non-Negro Students in Participation in the Formal and Informal Activities of a California High School" (unpublished Ed.D. dissertation, University of California, Berkeley, 1963).

[16] California (State) Liaison Committee of the Regents of the University of California and the State Board of Education, *California (State) Master Plan Survey of Higher Education*, A master plan for higher education in California, 1960–1975, prepared (by the Master Plan Survey Team) for the Liaison Committee of the State Board of Education and the Regents of the University of California (Sacramento, Calif.: California State Department of Education, 1960).

[17] J. P. Guilford, "A Revised Structure of Intellect Studies of Aptitude of High-level Personnel" (Reports from the Psychological Laboratory, University of Southern California, April, 1957); Jacob W. Getzels and Philip W. Jackson, *Creativity and Intelligence: Explorations with Gifted Students* (New York: Wiley, 1962); Michael A. Wallach and Nathan Kogan, *Modes of Thinking in Young Children: A Study of the Creativity-Intelligence Distinction* (New York: Holt, Rinehart and Winston, 1965); and E. Paul Torrance, *Education and the Creative Potential* (Minneapolis: University of Minnesota Press, 1963).

[18] J. W. Atkinson, *Motives in Fantasy, Action, and Society: A Method of Assessment and Study* (Princeton, N.J.: Van Nostrand, 1958), and T. Bentley Edwards and Alan B. Wilson, "Attitudes Toward the Study of School Subjects," *Educational Theory*, VIII (October, 1958), 275–283, 285.

[19] Ralph H. Turner, "Sponsored and Contest Mobility and the School System," *American Sociological Review*, XXV (December, 1960), 855–867; XXVI (June, 1961), 455–456.

[20] Talcott Parsons, "School Class as a Social System: Some of Its

Functions in American Society," *Harvard Educational Review*, XXIX (Fall, 1959), 297–318.

[21] Bernadine Schmidt, "Changes in Personal, Social, and Intellectual Behavior of Children Originally Classified as Feebleminded," *Psychological Monographs*, LX (1946); William B. Featherstone, *Teaching the Slow Learner* (Revised; New York: Bureau of Publications, Teachers College, Columbia University, 1951); Elsie H. Martens, *Curriculum Adjustments for the Mentally Retarded* (Washington, D.C.: Office of Education, 1950); and H. Fuller and J. Davis, "Reaching the Low Performer," *Educational Executives Overview*, II (September, 1961), 54–55.

[22] For years, Monmouth College in Illinois was noted as an undergraduate source of M.A.'s and Ph.D.'s in chemistry largely as a result of the single-minded efforts of Professor S. W. Haldeman, who in 1952 received an award for his teaching from the American Chemical Society. Also see Maria Montessori, *The Montessori Method*, translated from the Italian by Anne E. George (New York: Schocken Books, 1964), and Alexander S. Neill, *Summerhill: A Radical Approach to Child Rearing* (New York: Hart Publishing Company, 1960).

[23] T. Bentley Edwards, "Teacher Attitudes and Cultural Differentiation," *The Journal of Experimental Education*, XXXV, 2 (Winter, 1966), 80–92.

[24] James Cass, "What Happened at Berkeley," *Saturday Review* (January 16, 1965), pp. 47–48, 66–69.

[25] Alan B. Wilson, "Social Stratification and Academic Achievement," *Education in Depressed Areas*, edited by A. Harry Passow (New York: Bureau of Publications, Teachers College, Columbia University, 1963), and Ralph H. Turner, *The Social Context of Ambition* (San Francisco: Chandler Publishing Company, 1964).

[26] T. Bentley Edwards and Alan B. Wilson, *Attitudes as Related to Success in School*, Abstract (Moravia, New York: Chronicle Guidance Publications, Inc., 1963).

[27] For example, Johntz in Berkeley (William F. Johntz, "Mathematics and the Culturally Disadvantaged," in *The Disadvantaged Learner*, edited by Staten W. Webster [San Francisco: Chandler Publishing Company, 1966], pp. 573–581).

[28] Michael D. Young, *The Rise of the Meritocracy, 1870–2033: An Essay on Education and Equality* (London: Thames and Hudson, 1961, © 1958).

[29] Commission on School Integration, "Public School Segregation

and Integration in the North," A Special Issue of *The Journal of Intergroup Relations*, National Association of Intergroup Relations Officials (November, 1963), pp. 48–53.

[30] *Ibid.*, pp. 51–52.

[31] NET (National Educational Television), "Marked for Failure," *America's Crisis*, Kinescope Film.

[32] Private data supplied by William Weichert, Personnel Officer, Oakland City Schools.

[33] Research Council of the Great Cities Program for School Improvement, *Promising Practices from the Projects for the Culturally Deprived* (Chicago: April, 1964).

[34] J. Cecil Parker, T. Bentley Edwards, and William H. Stegeman, *Curriculum in America* (New York: Crowell, 1962), Chapter 15.

[35] Staten W. Webster, "The Influence of Interracial Contact on Social Acceptance in a Newly Integrated School," *Journal of Educational Psychology*, LII (December, 1961), 292–296.

[36] Basil Bernstein, "Social Class and Linguistic Development," *Education, Economy, and Society*, edited by A. H. Halsey, Jean Floud, and C. Arnold Anderson (New York: Free Press of Glencoe, 1961), pp. 288–310; Bernstein, "Some Sociological Determinants of Perception," *British Journal of Sociology*, IX (June, 1958), 159–174; Bernstein, "A Public Language," *British Journal of Sociology*, X (December, 1958), 311–323; Patricia Sexton, *Education and Income* (New York: The Viking Press, 1961), pp. 262–263; and Walter D. Loban, *The Language of Elementary School Children* (Champaign, Ill.: National Council of Teachers of English, 1963), pp. 51–52, 64–65, 81–89.

[37] Bernstein, "A Public Language," *op. cit.*; Loban, "A Sustained Program of Language Learning," *Language Programs for the Disadvantaged*, Report of the NCTE Task Force on Teaching English to the Disadvantaged, edited by Richard Corbin and Muriel Crosby (Washington, D.C.: National Council of Teachers of English, 1965), pp. 221–231.

[38] This point has been emphasized by a number of authors including Sexton, Conant, and Lomax in works that have already been cited; see Frederick Harbison and Charles A. Myers, *Education, Manpower, and Economic Growth: Strategies of Human Resource Development* (New York: McGraw-Hill Book Co., 1964), p. v.

[39] John I. Goodlad, *School Curriculum Reform* (New York: Fund for the Advancement of Education, March, 1964), pp. 9–12.

[40] *Ibid.*, p. 49.

[41] James Ridgeway, "Computer-tutor," *The New Republic*, CLIV, 23 (June 4, 1966), 19–22.

[42] B. F. Skinner, "Teaching Machines," *Science*, CXXVIII, No. 3330 (October 24, 1958).

[43] Sidney L. Pressey, "A Simple Apparatus Which Gives Tests and Scores—and Teaches," *School and Society*, XXIII (1926), 373–376.

[44] Norman A. Crowder, *The Concept of Automatic Tutoring*, Training Analysis and Development Directorate, Headquarters, Technical Training Air Force, Gulfport, Mississippi.

[45] Patrick Suppes and D. N. Hanson, "Accelerated Program in Elementary School Mathematics—The First Year," *Psychology in the Schools*, II (1965), 195–203.

CHAPTER 3

[1] Herbert H. Hyman and Paul B. Sheatsley, "Attitudes Toward Desegregation," *Scientific American*, CCXI (July, 1964), 16–23.

[2] Stanley Elam, "What Have We *Done* Lately?" editorial in *Phi Delta Kappan*, XLV (May, 1964), 361.

[3] Meyer Weinberg, "Civil Rights and School Men," *Phi Delta Kappan*, XLV (May, 1964), 371–376.

[4] *Brown* v. *Board of Education*, 347 U.S. 483.

[5] Alameda County, Planning Commission, *Estimate of Berkeley, California's 1964 Population* (Alameda County: November, 1964).

[6] Berkeley Unified School District, *Estimated Enrollment of Negro Pupils, K-12, Berkeley Public Schools, 1939–40, 1945–46, 1947–48, 1955–56, 1958–59, 1960–61* (Berkeley, Calif.: Berkeley Unified School District, February 20, 1961, mimeographed). 2 pp.

[7] Berkeley Unified School District, *Estimated Enrollment of Negro Pupils, K-12, Berkeley Public Schools, 1963–64* (Berkeley, Calif.: Berkeley Unified School District, February, 1964, mimeographed). 1 p.

[8] *San Francisco Examiner*, August 9–12, 1964, Stewart Toy's "Portrait of a City."

[9] C. H. Wennerberg, "Developing Policy and Program in Intergroup Education in an Interracial Community," *California Elementary Administrator*, XXVI (February, 1963).

[10] *Ibid.*, pp. 4–5.

[11] Minutes, October 27, 1959, Berkeley Unified School District,

Board of Education, Berkeley, California. Hereinafter cited as "Minutes, B. of E.," with date.

[12] Berkeley Unified School District, Board of Education, Advisory Committee of Citizens, *Interracial Problems and Their Effect on Education in the Public Schools of Berkeley, California* (Berkeley, Calif.: Berkeley Unified School District, October 19, 1959), pp. 18–19.

[13] *Ibid.,* pp. 3–5, 6–17.

[14] Minutes, B. of E., January–May, 1959.

[15] *Ibid.*

[16] Berkeley Unified School District, Office of the Superintendent, *Notes on Implementation of the Staats Committee Report* (Berkeley, Calif.: Berkeley Unified School District, February 21, 1961, mimeographed). 7 pp.

[17] Berkeley Unified School District, *Improving Racial Relations in the Berkeley Unified School District* (Berkeley, Calif.: Berkeley Unified School District, March 20, 1962, mimeographed). 6 pp.

[18] Berkeley Unified School District, *Continuing Implementation of Staats Committee Report in 1962–63 and 1963–64* (Berkeley, Calif.: Berkeley Unified School District, June 28, 1963, mimeographed). 10 pp.

[19] Congress of Racial Equality, Berkeley Chapter, *Presentation to the Berkeley Board of Education on De Facto Segregation* (Berkeley, Calif.: Congress of Racial Equality, May 1, 1962, mimeographed). 7 pp.

[20] Minutes, B. of E., May 1, 1962.

[21] Minutes, B. of E., September 19, 1962, "Resolution on De Facto Segregation."

[22] Berkeley Unified School District, Board of Education, Citizens Committee, *De Facto Segregation in the Berkeley Public Schools* (Berkeley, Calif.: Berkeley Unified School District, November 19, 1963; mimeographed), 109 pp.

[23] *Berkeley Daily Gazette,* January 22, 1964.

[24] *Berkeley Daily Gazette,* December 20, 1963, Dr. Wallace R. Matson, "The Liberal Case Against the Hadsell Report."

[25] See Minutes, B. of E., November 3, 1963.

[26] Minutes, B. of E., January 22, 1964.

[27] *Berkeley Daily Gazette,* January 22, 23, 31, 1964.

[28] *Ibid.*

[29] Minutes, B. of E., February 4, 1964.

[30] Memorandum from Milton Loney to all certificated staff, February 11, 1964.

[31] Berkeley Unified School District, Office of the Superintendent, *Superintendent's Report on Staff Reaction to Citizens De Facto Segregation Study Committee Report* (Berkeley, Calif.: Berkeley Unified School District, March 3, 1964, mimeographed). 15 pp.

[32] Berkeley Unified School District, Office of the Superintendent, *Desegregation of the Berkeley Public Schools: Its Feasibility and Implementation—The Superintendent's Report of a Task Group Study* (Berkeley, Calif.: Berkeley Unified School District, May, 1964), 25 pp.

[33] Berkeley Unified School District, *Appendices to Desegregation of the Berkeley Public Schools: Its Feasibility and Implementation—The Superintendent's Report of a Task Group Study* (Berkeley, Calif.: Berkeley Unified School District, May, 1964), 112 pp.

[34] Minutes, B. of E., May 19, 1964.

[35] *Berkeley Daily Gazette*, May 20, 1964.

[36] *San Francisco Chronicle*, May 19, 1964, editorial.

[37] Minutes, B. of E., May 19, 1964.

[38] *San Francisco Examiner*, May 20, 1964.

[39] *Oakland Tribune*, May 20, 1964.

[40] *Berkeley Daily Gazette*, May 21, May 23, June 3, 1964, editorials.

[41] *San Francisco Chronicle*, May 20, 1964, James Benet, "Berkeley School Integration Plan."

[42] *Berkeley Daily Gazette*, January to May 1964, "Ramsey Plan Poll."

[43] *Berkeley Daily Gazette*, May 1–30, 1964, "Open Forum Comments on Ramsey Plan."

[44] *California Voice*, June 5, 1964.

[45] *The Berkeley Post*, September 19, 1964.

[46] *Berkeley Daily Gazette*, June 3, 1964, advertisement.

[47] *Oakland Tribune*, June 5 and 10, 1964.

[48] *Berkeley Daily Gazette*, June 4, 6, 9, and 10, 1964.

[49] *Berkeley Daily Gazette*, June 4, 1964, editorial.

[50] *Berkeley Daily Gazette*, June 1, 1964, "Voice of the People."

[51] *San Francisco Chronicle*, May 29, 1964, Don Wegars, "Berkeley Backs Integration Report."

[52] *Berkeley Daily Gazette*, June 10, August 19 and 21, 1964.

[53] *San Francisco Chronicle*, August 19, 1964.

[54] *San Francisco Examiner,* August 19, 1964.

[55] *Oakland Tribune,* August 19, 1964.

[56] Minutes, B. of E., July 1 and 15, 1964.

[57] *Berkeley Daily Gazette,* August 23, September 1, 3, 8, 11, and 14, 1964.

[58] *Oakland Tribune,* September 10, 1964.

[59] *Berkeley Daily Gazette,* September 1 to October 6, 1964.

[60] *Berkeley Daily Gazette,* September 24 to October 5, 1964, advertisements.

[61] Berkeley Friends of Better Schools, *Better Schools* (Berkeley, Calif.: Berkeley Friends of Better Schools, September, 1964), 4 pp.

[62] Minutes, B. of E., September 1, 1964.

[63] Memorandum to the Board of Education from Neil V. Sullivan, September 1, 1964, "Goals and Objective."

[64] *Oakland Tribune,* September 2, 1964.

[65] *San Francisco Examiner,* September 3 and 16, 1964.

[66] *Berkeley Daily Gazette,* September 2 and 16, 1964.

[67] *San Francisco Chronicle,* September 2, 1964.

[68] *San Francisco Chronicle,* October 7, 1964.

[69] *Berkeley Daily Gazette,* October 7, 1964, editorial.

[70] *San Francisco Examiner,* October 7, 1964.

[71] *Oakland Tribune,* October 7, 1964.

[72] *San Francisco Chronicle,* October 8, 1964, James Benet, "Peace Comes to Berkeley."

CHAPTER 4

[1] For the elementary-school distribution, see Berkeley Unified School District, *De Facto Segregation in the Berkeley Public Schools, Report of a Citizens Committee* (Berkeley, Calif.: Berkeley Unified School District, November 19, 1963, mimeographed), p. 62 *et seq.*

[2] Advisory Committee, *Interracial Problems and Their Effect on Education in the Public Schools of Berkeley, California* (Berkeley, Calif.: Berkeley Unified School District, October 19, 1959). This was known as the "Staats Report," so-called after its chairman, Judge R. Staats.

[3] *De Facto Segregation in the Berkeley Public Schools, op. cit.* in note 1.

[4] Berkeley Unified School District, *Desegregation of the Berkeley*

Public Schools: Its Feasibility and Implementation—The Superintendent's Report of a Task Group Study (to the) Board of Education (Berkeley, Calif.: Berkeley Unified School District, May, 1964, mimeographed). 25 pp. C. H. Wennerberg, Superintendent, Elementary recommendations: pp. 15–17.

[5] The adopted plan, called the "Ramsey Plan" is given in detail in *Desegregation of the Berkeley Public Schools: Its Feasibility and Implementation, op. cit.,* pp. 13–14.

[6] *Ibid.,* p. 14. There were recommendations made for in-service training in the Staats report (p. 20).

[7] *Ibid.,* p. 19, contains the guidelines for the achievement groups. The honors classes were formed as a result of recommendations from an interim committee of school department heads and administrators.

[8] There is some confirmation in Patricia Cayo Sexton's *Education and Income* (New York: The Viking Press, 1964).

[9] Richard Madden and Thorsten Carlson, *Success in Spelling: Workbook Edition, Grade 7* (Sacramento, Calif.: California State Department of Education, 1959).

CHAPTER 6

[1] Minutes of the Board of Education of the Sacramento City Unified School District, August 19, 1963, p. 1, inserted agenda item No. 3731, cited by Edward B. Fort, "A Case Study of the Struggle to Secure an Administrative Plan for Eliminating De Facto Segregation in the Junior High Schools of Sacramento, California" (unpublished doctoral dissertation, University of California, Berkeley, California, 1964). These minutes are hereinafter cited as "School Board Minutes," with date and other pertinent details. The dissertation is cited hereinafter as "Fort."

[2] *De facto* segregation, as used in this chapter, may be defined as "that condition which results from the concentration of a homogeneous racial group in a particular area served by a neighborhood school." (See Wilson C. Riles, "School Board Approaches to De Facto Segregation," *California Elementary Administrator,* 26:13, February, 1963.) Because this study is particularly concerned with this condition as it relates to the Negro, Kaplan's definition is also referred to, that is: "racial imbalance (*de facto* segregation) in the schools which occurs when the number of Negroes in a compact Negro area becomes so great that drawing school zone boundaries on a geographical basis

causes the great majority of Negro children to attend schools which are overwhelmingly Negro in population." (See John Kaplan, "Segregation Litigation and the Schools—Part I: The New Rochelle Experience," *Northwestern University Law Review*, 18:1, March–April, 1965.) The condition is manifest when the ethnic composition of the student population in a particular school differs significantly from the ethnic composition of the population in the total school district.

[3] Willard Goss, Memorandum: "Insurance Values for Replacement of Stanford Junior High School Fire Loss," Sacramento City Unified School District, August 19, 1963, cited by Superintendent Lawson, School Board Minutes, August 19, 1963.

[4] U.S. Bureau of the Census, *U.S. Census Population: 1950, Volume 1, Census Tract Statistics*, Table P-1, Report PEC (1) 129 (Washington, D.C.: U.S. Government Printing Office, 1950), pp. 15–25, cited by Leonard Cain, "Housing Discrimination in Metropolitan Sacramento" (unpublished research monograph, Sacramento Committee for Fair Housing, Sacramento, November, 1961), p. 2.

[5] Oak Park Analysis: Census tract 18 from 6.3 percent Negro in 1950 (422 persons) to 17.0 percent Negro in 1960 (1094 persons); tract 27 from 3.0 percent Negro in 1950 (194 persons) to 20.8 percent Negro in 1960 (902 persons), that is, a 17.8 net increase percentage; tract 28 from 6.8 percent Negro in 1950 (260 persons) to a massive 42.7 percent Negro (1712 persons) for 1960 (35.9 percent gain).

[6] Cain, *op. cit.* in note 4, cited by Fort, based on U.S. Bureau of the Census, *U.S. Census Population: 1960, Volume 1, Census Tract Statistics*, Table H-3, Report PHC (1) 129 (Washington, D.C.: U.S. Government Printing Office, 1960), p. 82.

[7] Sacramento Citizens Advisory Committee on Equal Educational Opportunity, *Equal Educational Opportunity in the Sacramento City Unified School District* (Sacramento: Board of Education Publication, May, 1965), p. 6.

[8] Interview with Dr. Donald E. Hall, Assistant Superintendent, Planning and Research, Sacramento City Unified School District, October, 1963, citing Research Report No. 14, Series 1958–59, "Protection of Classroom and Other School Facility Needs for the Five Year Period, Fall, 1959–Fall, 1964," p. 2.

[9] Sacramento Citizens Advisory Committee for Equal Educational Opportunity, *op. cit.* in note 7, p. 6.

[10] Research Report No. 3, Series 1963–64, "Preliminary Report on the Ethnic Composition of Pupil Population of the Sacramento City

Unified School District," September 25, 1963, Sacramento City Unified School District, Planning and Research Services Office, pp. 6–8.

[11] *Sacramento Bee*, November 8, 1961, p. A4.

[12] Dr. Lawson and Dr. Hall, administrators at the time of the inception of the crisis, are still (1967 school year) with the District in their then capacities.

[13] Sacramento Citizens Advisory Committee for Equal Educational Opportunity, *op. cit.*, pp. 6–7.

[14] Research Report No. 20, Series 1949–50, "A Study of Senior High School Attendance Boundary Lines in Sacramento," April 12, 1950, Sacramento City Unified School District, Office of Assistant Superintendent, Planning and Research, p. 2.

[15] F. Melvyn Lawson, Administrative Bulletin No. 73—"Policy on Factors to be Considered in Establishing School Attendance Boundaries," Sacramento City Unified School District, Sacramento, California, February 25, 1963.

[16] School Board Minutes, February 18, 1963.

[17] Sacramento Citizens Advisory Committee for Equal Educational Opportunity, *op. cit.*, p. 7.

[18] *Ibid.*, p. 10.

[19] U.S. Bureau of the Census, *op. cit.*, as cited by Cain (note 4, preceding), p. 2.

[20] Interview with Dr. Donald Hall, Assistant Superintendent for Planning and Research, Sacramento City Unified School District, March 6, 1964, cited by Fort, p. 151. Note: District boundary records indicate that the jagged lines between Stanford Junior High and Peter Lassen occurred as a result of distance and building-utilization factors. Lassen students temporarily transferred to Stanford were returned to Lassen after the completion of Will C. Wood Junior High in 1961. These lines do not represent racial gerrymandering as some community participants may have privately inferred. Dr. Hall reiterated the unsoundness of such a contention, publicly, September 3, 1963.

[21] Based on the analysis of questionnaire data secured from a random-sample distribution to half of the Stanford student body. Randomizing procedures followed were similar to those advocated by C. Selltiz, M. Jahoda, M. Deutsch, and S. W. Cook in *Research Methods in Social Relations* (New York: Holt, Rinehart and Winston, 1959), p. 521.

[22] Superintendent Lawson's recommendation had *not* stipulated where the new school, when built, would be located. He did, however, indicate that two years would be a reasonable time for reconstruction. Peter Lassen had been selected, according to Assistant Superintendent Hall, because of distance and availability of space (corroborated in interview with Dr. Lawson, March 6, 1964).

[23] The idea of immediate student dispersal to the surrounding schools (predominately Caucasian) was to become a focal point for pressure groups arguing for integration of the Stanford student body into the surrounding junior high schools.

[24] The Lassen parent-speakers, at this point, were basically seeking their "fair share" of the Stanford load. They were willing to accept 100 or 200 students. Other schools, they contended, should do the same. They opposed double sessions. Dr. Hall suggested that dispersal would mean as much as one and one half hours of bus travel per day for some Stanford students. Taped proceedings of the meeting of the Board of Education of Sacramento City Unified School District, August 19, 1963. These taped proceedings are hereinafter cited as "School Board Tapes," with date and other pertinent details. Cited by Fort, p. 167.

[25] Interview with Mr. Ralph Tyler, member of the Education Committee of the Congress of Racial Equality, February 8, 1964. Mr. Tyler's views were later corroborated by Reverend Cyrus Keller, initiator of the lawsuit against the school district. Also by records of the Fair Housing Committee (August 1963) and CORE. Also by the *Sacramento Bee*, August 21, 1963, p. C2. Mr. Tyler, as well as others later, maintained that a return to Stanford in portable classrooms would, despite Dr. Lawson's assurances to the contrary, be followed by reconstruction of that school on the *same* site.

[26] Research Report No. 2, Series 1963–64, "Revised Junior High School Attendance Boundaries," November 4, 1963, Sacramento City Unified School District, Planning and Research Services Office, p. 1. This report summarized the plan adopted August 19, 1963.

[27] *Sacramento Bee*, August 20, 1963, p. B1. Mrs. Cushman strongly disagreed with the earlier contention that the matter of emergency housing should be handled apart from any discussion of *de facto* segregation. (Interview, February 2, 1964; Fall, 1963.)

[28] School Board Tapes, August 19, 1963.

[29] Leonard Finder, "Racial Issue Threatens Community Har-

mony," *The Sacramento Union*, Sacramento, December 19, 1962. This quotation is taken from Article 1 in a series of fifteen written by the editor on the subject "De Facto Segregation in Sacramento."

[30] School Board Minutes, September 3, 1963.

[31] Letter from Cyrus S. Keller, president, Sacramento Chapter of the NAACP, to Mrs. L. Blucher, president, Sacramento Board of Education, August 21, 1963.

[32] Letter from Albert S. Rodda, Nineteenth Senatorial District, to F. M. Lawson, Superintendent, August 30, 1963.

[33] *Jackson* v. *Pasadena City School District*, 59 A.C. Cal. Sup. Ct. 907 (June, 1963), cited by Albert S. Rodda, *op. cit.*

[34] *Sacramento Bee*, August 22, 1963. Editorial, p. F12. The *Bee's* position at this juncture was similar to that presented by Board Member Schwartz on August 19.

[35] *The Sacramento Union*, August 25, 1963. Editorial.

[36] Interview with Wilson Riles, State Department of Education Consultant, January 6, 1964. Verified by Dr. F. M. Lawson, Superintendent, March 6, 1964.

[37] School Board Tapes, September 3, 1963.

[38] Letter from Reverend David McCulloch, Chairman of the Social Relations and Action Commission, Sacramento Council of Churches, and Reverend Glen Holman, Executive Director of the Commission, to Dr. F. Melvyn Lawson, Superintendent of Schools, September 16, 1963.

[39] School Board Tapes, September 16, 1963.

[40] Interviews with two members active in the Council, November, 1963, and February 15, 1964. The Council sent a letter, dated October 10, 1963, to the Board, indicating its membership, goals, and hopes.

[41] Letter from Mel Spear, Chairman, Committee on Civil Rights and Inter-Group Relations, Sacramento Chapter of the National Association of Social Workers, to Mrs. L. Blucher, President of the Sacramento City Board of Education, September 30, 1963.

[42] School Board Tapes, September 30, 1963.

[43] *Keller* v. *Sacramento City Unified School District*, No. 146525, Sup. Ct., Sac. County, September 30, 1963.

[44] Fort, p. 241.

[45] *Branch* v. *Board of Education of Town of Hempstead*, 204 F. Supp. 150 (D.N.Y., 1962), cited by the Court in *Keller* v. *Sacramento City Unified School District, cit. supra.*

[46] *Jackson* v. *Pasadena City School District, cit. supra*, cited in *Keller* v. *Sacramento City Unified School District, cit. supra*.

[47] Interview with Dr. Donald Hall, Assistant Superintendent, Sacramento City Unified School District, March 6, 1964.

[48] School Board Minutes, October 16, 1963. Alternate Plan No. 2 is referred to as the Einstein plan and also as the Desegregation plan and the Redistricting plan. These two alternate proposals were cited by the superintendent in reference to the document "Possible Plans for Elimination of Racial Imbalance," Item No. 63–475, pp. 3–4, cited by Fort, pp. 270–273.

[49] School Board Tapes, October 14, 1963.

[50] Research Report No. 2, Series 1963–64, "Revised Junior High School Attendance Boundaries," November 4, 1963, Planning and Research Services Office, Sacramento City Unified School District. In order to effect the proper boundary changes without precipitating overcrowded conditions in some of the schools, Dr. Hall indicated that the Einstein plan would involve some shifting of students away from Lassen and Carson schools to nearby junior high schools.

[51] Research Report No. 2, Series 1963–64, *op. cit.*, pp. 6–7.

[52] *Sacramento Bee*, October 17, 1963, p. D1.

[53] School Board Tapes, October 16, 1963.

[54] Citizens Advisory Committee on Equal Educational Opportunity, *Equal Educational Opportunity in the Sacramento City Unified School District* (Sacramento: Board of Education Publication, May, 1965).

[55] *Ibid.*, pp. 24–25. Based on comprehensive interviews of certificated personnel.

[56] Citizen Advisory Committee Report, *op. cit.*, pp. 35–41.

[57] "Report of Progress of the Junior High School Redistricting Implementation Committee" (Special Services Office, Sacramento City Unified School District, March 11, 1964), p. 1.

CHAPTER 8

[1] G. R. McConnell, *Financial and Practical Applications: Interdistrict Attendance, Annexation, Unionization of Mill Valley and Sausalito School Districts* (Mill Valley, Calif.: Mill Valley School District, September 18, 1964), p. 36.

[2] *Loc. cit.*

[3] *Loc. cit.*

[4] *Ibid.,* p. 31.

[5] *Ibid.,* p. 29.

[6] 59 A.C. Cal. Sup. Ct. 907 (June, 1963).

[7] Citizens Advisory Committee, *Educational Needs of the Sausalito School District* (Sausalito, Calif.: June 25, 1965), Appendix E.

[8] Wilson Riles, *Report to the Board of Trustees, Sausalito School District, on Ethnic Problems in the Sausalito School District* (Sacramento, Calif.: Commission on Equal Opportunities in Education, State Department of Education, July 29, 1964), p. 4.

[9] *Ibid.,* p. 3.

[10] *Ibid.,* pp. 11–12.

[11] Bernard Berelson and G. A. Steiner, *Human Behavior: An Inventory of Scientific Findings* (New York: Harcourt, Brace and World, 1964).

[12] Riles, *op. cit.,* pp. 13–14.

[13] Citizens Advisory Committee, *op. cit.,* Appendix B.

[14] *Ibid.,* Appendix C.

[15] Citizens Advisory Committee, *op. cit.,* p. 19.

[16] *Ibid.,* p. 20.

[17] McConnell, *op. cit.,* p. 2.

[18] *Loc. cit.*

[19] *Ibid.,* p. 3.

CHAPTER 9

[1] See, e.g., H. H. Hyman, "The Value Systems of Different Classes: a Social Psychological Contribution to the Analysis of Stratification," R. Bendix and S. M. Lipset, editors, *Class, Status and Power,* Glencoe, Ill.: Free Press, 1953, pp. 426–442; J. A. Kahl, "Educational and Occupational Aspirations of 'Common Man' Boys," *Harvard Educational Review,* 23 (Summer, 1953), pp. 186–203; W. H. Sewell, A. O. Haller, and M. A. Straus, "Social Status and Educational and Occupational Aspiration," *American Sociological Review,* 22 (February, 1957), pp. 67–73.

[2] See especially, S. M. Lipset and R. Bendix, *Social Mobility and Industrial Society,* Berkeley: University of California Press, 1959, Chapter 9.

[3] See, e.g., R. K. Merton, *Social Theory and Social Structure,* Glencoe, Ill.: Free Press, 1957, Chapters 8 and 9; E. Katz and P. F.

Lazarsfeld, *Personal Influence,* Glencoe, Ill.: Free Press, 1955, *passim.*

[4] R. W. Berenda, *The Influence of the Group on the Judgment of Peers,* New York: King's Crown, 1950; the technique is presented in S. E. Asch, *Social Psychology,* New York: Prentice-Hall, 1952, pp. 450–501.

[5] T. H. Newcomb, "Attitude Development as a Function of Reference Groups: the Bennington Study," in E. E. Maccoby, T. H. Newcomb, and E. L. Hartley, editors, *Readings in Social Psychology,* New York: Henry Holt, 1958, pp. 265–275. Several studies are summarized by P. E. Jacob, *Changing Values in College,* New Haven: Hazen Foundation, 1957.

[6] Hyman, *op. cit.,* pp. 441–442.

[7] The schools were selected purposively from those accessible which had been stratified on the basis of census data. Confidence in the findings depends upon their internal consistency and their congruence with the body of parallel research and relevant theory. Ultimately, the generalizability of the study must depend upon replication with other populations rather than statistical inference to a population of schools which, necessarily, would also be arbitrarily limited by their accessibility.

[8] The census data use different classifications, based upon a wider population (not limited to the parents of high school boys), and were gathered at an earlier date than the sample data. The concordance of ranks rather than the correlation of actual percentages is all that is pertinent, in any event, to confirm the appropriateness of the ordering and grouping of schools.

[9] The grouping of schools on the basis of occupational and educational dimensions of stratification, and the subsequent pooling of a predominantly Catholic with a predominantly Negro school as working-class schools might be unjustified if religion and race were independently associated with the dependent variable, i.e., educational aspirations. Altogether, 58 percent of the Protestants and only 47 percent of the Catholics in the sample aspire to go to college. But within educational and occupational strata the difference between Protestants and Catholics is small and unsystematic, while within each religious group the differences between occupational and educational strata are large. For example, among the children of professionals with at least some college education, 87 percent of both Protestants and Catholics wish to go to college; among the children of manual workers

who are high school graduates, 44 percent of the Protestants and 46 percent of the Catholics so wish; 34 percent of the Protestants and 28 percent of the Catholics whose fathers are manual workers who have not finished high school, want to go to college.

Similarly, the overall differences in educational aspirations between Negroes and Whites are "explained" by the predominantly working-class and low educational status of the Negroes.

[10] Educational aspirations were inferred from the following question:

> After I graduate from high school (and, if necessary, serve in the military forces)—
> 1. ....I plan to get a job right away
> 2. ....I plan to be a housewife
> 3. ....I plan to go to a technical or trade school
> 4. ....I plan to go to a junior college
> 5. ....I plan to go first to a junior college, and then to a four-year college or university
> 6. ....I plan to go directly to a four-year college or university
> 7. ....I have other plans
>
> . . . .
>
> (What are they?)

Responses 5 and 6 were considered as indicating an aspiration to go to college. Since there are several free junior colleges in the area which are open to all high school graduates regardless of past scholarship, poor students can and often do use them as a means of remedying their academic deficiencies. Any student who *wants* to go to college can *plan* to do so, unless, of course, he does not believe he is capable of improving and, therefore, has no intention of trying. A student might value higher education without aspiring to attain a higher education. However, differences in school achievement do not account for the differences between schools in aspirations. (See Tables 11 and 12.)

[11] The largest irregularities—the sons of merchants at the group C schools, and the sons of semi- and un-skilled manual workers at the group A schools—are based upon very few cases.

[12] Hyman, *op. cit.*, pp. 431–432.

[13] Percentages are shown in Table 9 for each classification where

there are ten or more cases in two school groups on which to base a comparison. The empty cells and categories not shown have fewer than ten cases.

[14] The number of cases on which these percentages are based reflects the fact, shown in Table 10, that far fewer students do receive "A's" at the group C schools.

[15] Note that the aspirations of the students who receive high grades at the group B schools resemble those of the students of the group A schools, while those who get low grades have aspirations similar to those students at the group C schools. This suggests the possibility of two dominant norms in the intermediate schools providing alternative normative references.

[16] This relationship disappears among those with IQ's below 89 —that is, those for whom collegiate aspirations are unrealistic.

[17] This requires no apology—the step from data to a theoretical proposition is always inferential. One does not *see* a cause.

[18] Lipset and Bendix, *Social Mobility . . . , op. cit.*, pp. 220–224.

[19] *Ibid.*, p. 203.

[20] Katz and Lazarsfeld, *op. cit.*, p. 52.

[21] Richard Centers, "Children of the New Deal: Social Stratification and Adolescent Attitudes," in *Class, Status and Power, op. cit.*, pp. 359–370; S. M. Lipset *et al.*, "The Psychology of Voting: An Analysis of Political Behavior," in G. Lindzey, editor, *Handbook of Social Psychology*, Cambridge: Addison-Wesley, Vol. II, pp. 1124–1175.

CHAPTER 10

[1] "Court Decision, January 24, 1964: 12 Minors v. Manhasset Board of Education—Zavatt." *Blocker v. Board of Education*, 226 F. Supp. 208 (1964).

[2] *Bell v. School City of Gary, Indiana*, 213 F. Supp. 819 at 831 (1963). The lower court had found that there was "no support for the plaintiff's position that the defendant has an affirmative duty to balance the races of the various schools under its jurisdiction, regardless of the residence of students involved." The Supreme Court decision was a year later—it took that length of time to appeal—in May, 1964.

[3] Unless otherwise noted, the quotations included are taken directly from respondent comments.

[4] *Contract Document Submitted to the Youth Services Committee,*

Health and Welfare Council of Nassau County from the Community Service Center, Inc., Manhasset–Great Neck, New York; section II, p. 5.

[5] Carol McNeary, "From Rags to Enrichment," *North Shore Community*, January, 1965.

[6] *Contract Document, op. cit.*

[7] *Ibid.*

[8] Mrs. William November, "The President's Report on the Year 1963," *Contract Document, op. cit.*, VIII-C, p. 1.

[9] Excerpts from pamphlet called "Town of North Hempstead": "In public housing North Hempstead was the first town to establish a housing authority in the State of New York. This occurred in 1946. The Town Board appoints the five-member authority, one of whom is the chairman, to five-year terms. The North Hempstead Housing Authority by law is required to plan for and provide low-cost public housing for low-income families. In addition to providing clean, airy, comfortable living quarters through the Housing Authority, the Town has a continuing program of eliminating substandard dwellings and demolishing shacks, preventing the creation of slums."

CHAPTER 12

[1] Alex Rosen, "Social Change and Professional Responsibility," *Pathways* (Bureau of Child Guidance, Board of Education of New York City), June, 1965, Vol. 7, No. 4.

[2] Public Education Association, *The Status of the Public School Education of Negro and Puerto Rican Children in New York City.* New York: The Association, 1955.

[3] Source: *U.S. Department of Commerce, Bureau of the Census, 1960 Census of Population.*

[4] *Desegregating the Public Schools of New York City.* A Report Prepared by the State Education Commissioner's Advisory Committee on Human Relations and Community Tensions, May 12, 1964.

[5] *Public School Segregation and Integration in the North.* Commission on School Integration of the National Association of Intergroup Relations Officials. New York: November 1963.

[6] Stanley H. Lowell, *Equality In Our Time.* New York: N.Y. City Commission on Human Rights, 1963.

[7] Oscar Handlin, "Is Integration the Answer?" *The Atlantic Monthly,* June 1964.

[8] New York City Board of Education, *Toward Greater Opportunity*. New York: June 1960.

[9] Public Education Association, *op. cit.*, pp. 13–18.

[10] *Op. cit.*, p. 3.

[11] Resolution of the New York City Board of Education, December 23, 1954.

[12] *Ibid.*

[13] New York City Board of Education, *Toward the Integration of Our Schools: Final Report of the Commission on Integration.* New York: 1958.

[14] *Op. cit.*

[15] Stanley H. Lowell, "Can New York City Integrate Its Public Schools?" *American Unity*, January–February 1961.

[16] Rosemary R. Gunning, "The P.A.T. Viewpoint," *Integrated Education*, August–November 1965.

[17] Leonard Buder, "School Pairing in New York City," *Integrated Education*, August–November 1965.

[18] *Op. cit.*

[19] Speech of Mr. Robert Pigott, Chairman of Local School Board 45–46, October 8, 1964.

[20] David Rogers and Bert Swanson, "White Citizen Response to the Same Integration Plan: Comparisons of Local School Districts in a Northern City," *Sociological Inquiry*, Winter, 1965.

[21] New York City Board of Education, *The Educational Park in New York City: Concept for Discussion.* April, 1965.

[22] *Op. cit.*

[23] See Patricia Sexton, *Education and Income.* New York: The Viking Press, 1961.

[24] Irving Goldaber, "The Negro Protest Against the New York City Board of Education," *Journal of Intergroup Relations*, Vol. IV, No. 4, Autumn, 1965.

[25] Dan Dodson, "The School and the Civil Rights Revolution," *Integrated Education*, August–November 1965.

[26] Charles E. Stewart, "Racial Issues Confronting Large City School Administrators," *Urban Education*, Vol. I, No. 4, 1965.

[27] See Charles E. Silberman, *Crisis in Black and White.* New York: Random House, 1964. Also Eleanor B. Sheldon and Raymond A. Glazer, *Pupils and Schools in New York City: A Fact Book.* New York: Russell Sage Foundation, 1965.

[28] *Op. cit.*

[29] Midge Decter, "The Negro and the New York Schools," *Commentary*, September 1964.

[30] *The Jim Crow School—North and West*. New York: NAACP, 20 West 40 Street.

[31] Robert A. Dentler, "Barriers to Northern School Desegregation," *Daedalus: Journal of the American Academy of Arts and Sciences*, Winter 1966.

[32] Frank Riessman, "Integration: The Key to Quality Education for All," in *A Symposium on School Integration* (East Lansing: Michigan State University, 1964).

[33] *Op. cit.*

CHAPTER 13

[1] Edward C. Banfield and Laura F. Banfield, *The Moral Basis of a Backward Society* (Glencoe, Ill.: The Free Press, 1958).

[2] For a survey of the research, see Willis D. Hawley and Frederick M. Wirt (eds.), *The Search for Community Power* (Englewood Cliffs, N.J.: Prentice-Hall, 1968).

[3] See Harmon Ziegler, *The Political Life of American Teachers* (Englewood Cliffs, N.J.: Prentice-Hall, 1967); Stephen K. Bailey *et al.*, *Schoolmen in Politics* (Syracuse, N.Y.: Syracuse University Press, 1962).

[4] Jack Peltason, *Fifty-Eight Lonely Men: Southern Federal Judges and School Desegregation* (New York: Harcourt, Brace and World, 1961).

[5] For a brief review of the operational meaning of the closeness of local government, see Morton Grodzins, "Centralization and Decentralization in the American Federal System," in Robert A. Goldwin (ed.), *A Nation of States* (Chicago: Rand McNally, 1961), pp. 1–23.

[6] In mid-1967, when a federal district court overthrew Washington, D.C.'s education system on grounds that its *de facto* segregation was unconstitutional, the judge suggested exploring merger with schools in adjoining Maryland and Virginia suburbs. This is the first move in the direction of the super-district. A recent study along these lines for the San Francisco Bay area is being made by the former superintendent, Harold Spears.